Palestine between Politics and Terror

THE SCHUSTERMAN SERIES IN ISRAEL STUDIES

EDITORS
S. Ilan Troen / Jehuda Reinharz / Sylvia Fuks Fried

The Schusterman Series in Israel Studies publishes original scholarship of exceptional significance on the history of Zionism and the State of Israel. It draws on disciplines across the academy, from anthropology, sociology, political science, and international relations to the arts, history, and literature. It seeks to further an understanding of Israel within the context of the modern Middle East and the modern Jewish experience. There is special interest in developing publications that enrich the university curriculum and enlighten the public at large. The series is published under the auspices of the Schusterman Center for Israel Studies at Brandeis University.

For a complete list of books in this series, please see www.upne.com

Motti Golani
  Palestine between Politics and Terror, 1945–1947
Ilana Szobel
  A Poetics of Trauma: The Work of Dahlia Ravikovitch
Anita Shapira
  Israel: A History
Orit Rozin
  The Rise of the Individual in 1950s Israel: A Challenge to Collectivism
Boaz Neumann
  Land and Desire in Early Zionism
Anat Helman
  Young Tel Aviv: A Tale of Two Cities
Nili Scharf Gold
  Yehuda Amichai: The Making of Israel's National Poet
Itamar Rabinovich and Jehuda Reinharz, editors
  Israel in the Middle East: Documents and Readings on Society, Politics, and Foreign Relations, Pre-1948 to the Present

PALESTINE BETWEEN POLITICS AND TERROR,

1945–1947

Motti Golani

BRANDEIS UNIVERSITY PRESS

Waltham, Massachusetts

BRANDEIS UNIVERSITY PRESS

An imprint of University Press of New England

www.upne.com

© 2013 Brandeis University

All rights reserved

Manufactured in the United States of America

Designed by Richard Hendel

Typeset in Arnhem and Clio by Integrated Publishing Solutions

University Press of New England is a member of the
Green Press Initiative. The paper used in this book meets
their minimum requirement for recycled paper.

For permission to reproduce any of the material in this
book, contact Permissions, University Press of New England,
One Court Street, Suite 250, Lebanon NH 03766; or
visit www.upne.com

Library of Congress Cataloging-in-Publication Data
Golani, Motti.
Palestine between politics and terror, 1945–1947 / Motti Golani.
    pages; cm. — (The Schusterman series in Israel studies)
Includes bibliographical references and index.
ISBN 978-1-61168-387-5 (cloth : alk. paper) —
ISBN 978-1-61168-450-6 (pbk. : alk. paper) —
ISBN 978-1-61168-388-2 (ebook)
1. Palestine—History—1929–1948. 2. Palestine—Politics and
government—1917–1948. 3. Great Britain—Politics and govern-
ment—1936–1945. 4. Jews—Palestine—Politics and government
—20th century. 5. Mandates—Palestine. 6. Terrorism—Palestine.
7. Jewish-Arab relations—History—1917–1948. 8. Palestine—
History—Partition, 1947. I. Title
DS126.4 G65   2013
956.9405—dc23   2012035765

5 4 3 2 1

Contents

Preface

    On July 22, 1948, the Royal Institute of International Affairs at Chatham House, in London, held an evening in honor of the last British High Commissioner in Palestine, General Sir Alan Gordon Cunningham. A few dozen members of the institute turned up for the event, along with interested members of the public, most of them Jews. Tea and cookies were served. At exactly 8 p.m., the chairman made his opening remarks. The former high commissioner spoke about his perception of his term of office and added some personal impressions. A few questions from the audience, to which Cunningham replied in brief, and the evening was over. From that day until his death, thirty-five years later, Cunningham never spoke in public again about his period in Palestine. His name was rarely mentioned in the press. The last high commissioner in Palestine seemed to fade away, like an old soldier, after that summer evening in St. James's Square in the center of London. Other memories too—of the drama that accompanied his appointment, the tumultuous events that marked his tenure in Jerusalem, and its abrupt end—seemed to recede with him, at least for a time.

    Lieutenant General Cunningham's appointment, at the beginning of November 1945, as high commissioner of Palestine and Transjordan and commander-in-chief of the British forces there, came as a surprise. No one had prepared him for the post. He was a veteran army officer whose future lay behind him. His rich military career bore no direct connection with Palestine. Moreover, he had no experience in managing civilian systems or in dealing with diplomatic and political issues of the sort the new appointment would entail. A few days earlier, Field Marshal Lord John Vereker, 6th Viscount Gort, who had been high commissioner for only a year, had announced that he was stepping down due to failing health. Two days after Gort landed in London, his successor was declared—a case of unusual alacrity by the British governmental bureaucracy.

    Ironically, it was on the eve of the new high commissioner's arrival in Palestine that the fate of the Mandate was, to all intents and purposes, decided. It is difficult to pinpoint the exact moment of irreversibility after which, as is apparent in retrospect, the contemporary actors could no longer alter the historical process or its pace and, above all, its direction. Probably, there is no such moment. However, it is possible to identify the historical framework within which those who decided the fate of the British Mandate for Palestine functioned and its influence on them. Thus, in late 1945, against the background of the end of the Second World War and the onset of the Cold War, the status of the Great Powers—whether on the decline (Britain and France) or surging forward (the United States and the Soviet Union)—as they intersected with U.S.-British relations, particularly as they applied to the Palestine question, brought about a situation in which the fate of the Mandate was effectively decided by late 1945.

The historic event that made it possible to discern clearly the thrust of history—from today's perspective, but also, in large measure, in real time—encompassed the appointment, activity, and failure of the Anglo-American Committee of Inquiry in the period between November 1945 and May 1946. As it happened, the committee's work coincided with Cunningham's initial period in Palestine—the British government announced the committee's establishment on November 13, 1945, a few days after his appointment. That congruency of events would mark his term of office indelibly.

Alan Cunningham's years of service in Jerusalem were a period of intense hostility between Britain and the Zionist movement and the Yishuv, the Jewish community in Palestine. That, at least, is how the Jewish side saw it. The last high commissioner came from a society that had paid a high price in order to vanquish Nazi Germany. His roots lay in the British Army and civil administration, the self-perceived saviors of the world and, above all, of the Jews, from the Nazi scourge. Although the British discourse was tinged with a not-always-conscious antisemitism, there was also understanding for the plight of the Jewish refugees. Even the revilers of Zionism within the British administration justified their approach with the argument that Jewish Agency policy was detrimental to the Jewish interest after the Holocaust. Some British officials, Cunningham among them, thought it was detrimental to the Zionist cause itself.

Neither the sagacity shown by the British government and the Mandatory regime in Palestine, nor their diplomatic, political, and military effectiveness, nor even the moral aspect of their behavior can be said to have been unequivocal. From his vantage point in Jerusalem, Cunningham watched as his government endeavored to engineer a political solution to the Palestine question for the benefit of the two adversaries—the Jews and the Arabs—against the sprawling backdrop of the empire's crumbling and, more immediately, the friction mounting between the government and the Yishuv.

This book covers the period from Cunningham's arrival in Jerusalem, on November 21, 1945, until his return to the city, at the end of September 1947, following a visit to Britain during which the government decided definitively on withdrawal from Palestine. His tenure as high commissioner did not end immediately. But what remained of it—less than eight months, as it turned out, from October 1947 until mid-May 1948—was characterized not so much by a more or less successful effort to govern, like the six high commissioners before him. Its hallmark was, rather, an almost desperate effort to allow Britain to leave Palestine with a semblance of honor and with minimal casualties and material damage, amid an escalating Jewish-Arab civil war. To put it another way: for the first two years after his arrival, from November 1945 until October 1947, Cunningham dealt with the "chronic" problems of Mandatory Palestine. Beginning with the period of the British military regime (1917–1920), and more strikingly since the arrival of the first high commissioner, Sir Herbert Samuel, the focus of all the high commissioners was on Palestine's political future. The absence of a concrete solution, acceptable to both Jews and Arabs, fomented sporadic confrontations between the two national groups and between each group and the British, if the British were perceived as favoring the other group. The persistent tension between the political effort and the desire to maintain tranquility and security resulted in many policy wrangles, not to say internecine disputes, between London and its emissaries in Jerusalem and among the ministries involved—mainly the Colonial Office, the War Office, and the Foreign Office. Caught in the middle, the high commissioner came under fire from all sides: from the Jews, the Arabs, and from those who questioned his analysis of the unfolding situation in Palestine or disagreed with the way he or the British government chose to address the problems in Palestine.

Naturally, the situation faced by Sir Herbert Samuel or by Field Marshal Lord Herbert Plumer in the 1920s was very different from what Sir John Chancellor encountered in the transition from the 1920s to the 1930s and the conditions under which General Sir Arthur Wauchope operated in the late 1930s. Each period possessed its own distinctive characteristics. This was certainly so in regard to the tenures of Sir Harold MacMichael and Field Marshal Gort, the high commissioners during the Second World War.

At the same time, it is crucial to bear in mind that all the high commissioners in Palestine functioned in the shadow of the dismantlement of the British Empire after the First World War. In addition, all of them were at loggerheads with the Zionist movement over British versus Zionist interests and whether the two could ever meet, and all faced growing Palestine Arab discontent. Basically, and certainly at the local level, all the high commissioners encountered a situation spawned by these seemingly intractable problems. Wauchope, for example, had to deal with a revolt by the Palestine Arabs; Cunningham, with an insurgency mounted by the Jews. Although the two uprisings contained marked differences, a comparison is unavoidable.

The watershed can be dated to the beginning of October 1947. From then on, the high commissioner was responsible for taking apart the British infrastructure in the country amid a war. It was a situation unprecedented in the history of the Mandate. This book is about Cunningham's methods of coping with problems that were typical of the Mandate era as such and were a product of British rule in Palestine. But it is also about how he dealt with a very particular and extraordinarily dramatic period: the end of the Second World War—and of the Holocaust—and its diplomatic, political, and military consequences. A separate book will cover the riveting period of the evacuation from Palestine.

In the period covered by this book, Cunningham's tenure as high commissioner was shaped by three basic elements. First was the dire political and economic plight of Britain and the British Empire following the Second World War and its impact on the developments in Palestine, throughout the empire, in Britain itself, and in the international arena, where the empire's status had declined sharply. Second, there was the understandable sense of helplessness felt by the Jewish community in Palestine after the Holocaust and its consequent inability to sustain a political process without a foreseeable time frame for the establishment of a state. The Yishuv and its leadership were unquestionably the dynamic element in Palestine in the waning part of the Mandate period, and particularly after the British suppression of the Arab Revolt (1936–1939). The Arabs tended to react to Jewish moves rather than take independent initiatives. The result was that the Jews "hijacked" Cunningham's agenda. This situation engendered a Jewish uprising—accompanied by terrorism—aimed at forcing Britain to revise its policy immediately. The third element was the singular biography of High Commissioner Cunningham himself.

Accordingly, Cunningham's tenure as high commissioner is examined through the prism of these three elements, which occupied most of his time in his headquarters at Government House in Jerusalem. His biography until 1945 is recounted briefly in the service of the primary purpose: to further an understanding of his performance as high commissioner. From late in 1941, Cunningham was engaged in a struggle for his reputation after being replaced mid-campaign as commander of the Eighth Army in the Western Desert, in Libya. That struggle for personal rehabilitation was much on his mind during his term as high commissioner and undoubtedly affected his perception of the unfolding events in Palestine. As such, it influenced the decisions he made—and those he did not make. About a month before the end of the British Mandate, at the peak of the internal British argument on how and exactly when to leave Palestine, Cunningham wrote to the colonial secretary, Arthur Creech-Jones, that he was unable to express his opinion freely because of "an unpleasant episode in my own personal history."[1]

The two other elements of the historical situation each involve substantial sections of the story. The first, under the part heading "A Political Process as Though There Is No Terrorism, November 1945–December 1946," describes the high commissioner's efforts to further the idea of partition as the desirable solution, in his view, for Palestine. The second, "To Fight Terrorism as Though There Is No Political Process, July 1946–August 1947," narrates his struggle against Jewish violence and terrorism. There is nothing arbitrary about the decision to separate Cunningham's efforts to press the political issue from his attempts to cope with Jewish violence. He himself was determined to set policy in terms of that differentiation. How successful this approach was is a major theme of this book.

A critical motif in this connection is Cunningham's complex relationship with British institutions other than the Colonial Office (for which he was emissary) that were instrumental in shaping British policy in Palestine and the Middle East, particularly the War Office (incorporating the army) and the Foreign Office. The disputes that arose between these entities were not always substantive in character and were often tainted by residues of the past. In Cunningham's case, what was at stake was the "right memory," namely, the rehabilitation of his war-tarnished reputation. Some, mainly in the army, missed no opportunity to dredge up the Western Desert episode almost as an "unconventional weapon," certainly an irrelevant one, in connection with the disagreements over Palestine policy. In my reading, Cunningham's agreement to take up the post in Palestine with only a few days' advance notice and no preparation, his behavior there, and the decisions he made cannot be understood without reference to his past and the deep psychic scars it left. Did he not grasp fully the nature of the arena he was entering? Almost certainly he did not know how his tenure as high commissioner would end. He harbored opinions of his own, certainly, even as the situation increasingly lurched out of his—and Britain's—control. He was an actor in a time of high drama.

The narrative and analysis of Cunningham's tenure as high commissioner in Jerusalem, which was without a doubt the pinnacle of his professional life, shed new light on the waning period of the British Mandate in Palestine. This book takes the British perspective as its point of departure, not the Jewish or the Arab viewpoint. Our view of the events in Palestine in this fraught time is through the high commissioner's window in Government House, a mansion perched atop the Hill of Evil Counsel, in southeast Jerusalem. As such, the story related in these pages juxtaposes biography with British imperial/colonial history, specifically the case of Palestine. My underlying assumption is that the subjective understanding of events by the senior official of the Mandatory administration in its final years is of surpassing importance. I have not counterpoised Cunningham's approaches with other approaches espoused by the British authorities or by the Jews or the Arabs. I have dwelled on such approaches only when they seem to have helped shape the high commissioner's outlook.

As for terminology: it presents problems of language, time, and subjective perception. A cardinal case in point is the very name of the country in which these events took place. The British called it Palestine, and for the English-language version of this book I have used that name. However, the Jews, certainly at this late stage of the Mandate period, referred to it almost exclusively as Eretz Yisrael (Land of Israel), whereas for the Palestine Arabs it was Filastin. The Jewish community in Palestine is called the Yishuv (more fully, *hayishuv hame'urgan*, the organized Yishuv), the name used by the politically organized Jewish community in Palestine from the 1920s until 1948. The overwhelming majority of the Jews in the country, across the political spectrum, belonged to that community. Indeed, this was the chief source of the Yishuv's strength. Nothing comparable existed on the Arab side. For the small Jewish underground groups that engaged in terrorism, Etzel and Lehi, I use the term *breakaways* (*porshim*), as they were dubbed at the time, for having broken away from the organized Yishuv's voluntary authority. They are also referred to, in certain contexts, as the Irgun and the Stern group or Stern gang, respectively—as they were called by the British. It is important to bear in mind that these groups, though small, posed a challenge both to the Yishuv and to the British, both of which suffered as a result of their violence. At the same time, a considerable disparity exists between the groups' actual historical role and the place they occupy in the contemporary memory in Israel and elsewhere, especially among those who are not well informed about the historical reality. The British used the term *Jewish terror* mostly in reference to the breakaways. One can argue about the motivation, but not about the type of operation. In the Hebrew version, I occasionally make use of the present-day term *pigua*, translated as "terrorist attack."

The contemporaries referred to a "political solution," which I sometimes supplement with the notion of a "political process." The term *administration* refers to the Mandatory government; the term *government* to the governmental apparatus in London. The *army* is the British Army. Because the land forces were part of the War Office, the term *army* is sometimes used for the ministry to which it belonged. Cunningham and his staff used the terms *Jews*, *Zionists*, and *Yishuv* interchangeably. Yishuv was generally used in a positive context. Use of *the Arabs* might refer to Arab states, but more usually refers to the Palestine Arabs. I have refrained from using short forms of people's names or pet names, unless they were in regular use or appear in a quotation.

The military historian Correlli Barnett was the first to interview Cunningham extensively, in the second half of the 1950s. Their conversations revolved around the 1941 episode in the Western Desert, when Cunningham was relieved of his post as commander-in-chief of the Eighth Army. Barnett informed me that he could not locate the drafts of the interviews. Accordingly, I resorted to the sections from the interviews that appear in his book *The Desert Generals* (1960). In 1958, Cunningham was interviewed by the Israeli mass-circulation newspaper *Yedioth Ahronoth* on the occasion of the tenth anniversary of the end of the Mandate and Israel's establishment. He also spoke in later years with the Israeli historian Gabriel Cohen. The Palestine question was central here, but the conversations were not published and the drafts have been lost. In 1972, the Israeli newspaper *Ma'ariv* published a "conversation" between former Lehi member Geula Cohen and the former high commissioner. To the best of my knowledge, the historian and politician Nicholas Bethell was the last to interview him, in the fall of 1975.

Alan Cunningham did not keep a diary and did not publish an autobiography. Some of his personal papers were lost during the hasty departure from Palestine by the British, but also because until the end of the 1940s Cunningham had no permanent home. He eventually deposited his

Palestine papers in the collection of private archives held by the Middle East Centre of St. Antony's College at Oxford University. This important archive also houses the papers of other senior officials who worked with Cunningham in Palestine.

Before the end of the Second World War, Cunningham transferred the papers that remained in his possession from the war period to his friend and patron Field Marshal Viscount Alanbrooke, the chief of the Imperial General Staff at the time. Alanbrooke, in turn, deposited them with the National Army Museum, in London's Chelsea quarter. Years later, Cunningham also gave this museum his subsequent correspondence, from the 1950s until the 1970s. Additional correspondence, which includes his personal exchange of letters with the colonial secretaries with whom he worked, is deposited in the Colonial Office section at the National Archives in Kew, London. That archive also houses the correspondence of the Foreign Office and the War Office and their Middle East branches with the high commissioner, and their internal correspondence on matters relevant to Cunningham's tenure in Palestine. The National Archives also possess essential material from the Office of the Prime Minister. Material of a more general character relating to government decisions about Palestine can be found in the cabinet files of the National Archives. I found important primary material concerning Cunningham's relations as high commissioner with the headquarters of the Middle East Land Forces in the Liddell Hart Centre for Military Archives at King's College, London. The personal archive of Colonial Secretary Arthur Creech-Jones, who worked with Cunningham, first as deputy minister and from October 1946 on as minister, is housed in the library of Rhodes House, in Oxford. The same library also houses testimonies of contemporaries, among them the army commander-in-chief in Palestine from February 1947 until the end of the Mandate, Lieutenant General Gordon MacMillan. The Royal Institute of International Affairs at Chatham House made available to me the original transcript of Cunningham's summing-up talk at the institute in July 1948, and of the discussion that followed.

The high commissioner signed all the cables that were sent from the Palestine administration to London and elsewhere. However, he did not write them all. The same principle applies to the colonial secretary. I have indicated cases of saliently personal letters.

This book is the product of many years of research, involving a fascinating voyage into a British way of life that was foreign to me when I first set out. I familiarized myself with it by reading contemporaneous documents and diaries, supplemented by an abundance of research material and other literature on the subject. The bibliography generally reflects only the sources on which I drew directly. They were amplified by visits to Britain and conversations and correspondence with people who lived and worked in what is now Israel during the endgame of the Mandate, under the guidance of the high commissioner. Special thanks to Sir John Swire, who was Cunningham's assistant and stayed in touch with him for a time after the final withdrawal from Palestine; and to Mr. Assad Azar, from the Galilee village of Rama, Israel, who was employed in Government House from 1938 until 1948, for making available valuable photographs and documents.

It is of some consequence that in this research project I was, ultimately, a host as well as a guest. I wrote about the years in Palestine of a British general of Scottish extraction in a country whose landscapes and customs I have been familiar with since birth. It was necessary, so it turns out, to overcome many prejudices, both here and there, on this time-tunnel journey.

Everyone who immerses himself in research knows the sometimes urgent need for a sympathetic listener who understands why you are not sleeping at night. Everyone who wishes to turn over every stone of an intriguing subject is beholden to the crucial professional assistance of archivists. Every researcher knows that, as the saying goes, "Without material sustenance, there is no spiritual fulfillment." Space limitations make it impossible for me to mention everyone who helped me during the years of research. I remember them all and am grateful to them. Nevertheless, I will mention a few who were especially meaningful for this project.

Thanks to the Middle East Centre at St. Antony's College and to the Oxford Centre for Hebrew and Jewish Studies at Yarnton for their support in spirit and matter, and for providing a congenial work atmosphere. Debbie Usher, a superb professional, guided me through the sometimes dense trails of the archive at the Middle East Centre, where she is the director. Prof. Avi Shlaim made it possible for me to photocopy the archive's entire Cunningham collection. He and Dr. Eugene Rogan, the director of the MEC at the time, gave me endless support. I am grateful to all these individuals.

I was fortunate to have the ear and the good advice of teachers and colleagues: Dr. Mordechai Bar-On, Prof. Yoav Gelber, Dr. Meir Hazan, Prof. Michael Cohen, Prof. Roger Louis, Prof. Rory Miller, Prof. Ron Zweig, and Prof. Anita Shapira. This book would not have seen the light of day without my students and research assistants, Gal Oron and Hagit Krik. Bracha Zimmerman lent a hand in organizing the wealth of primary material—an immeasurably important task. My thanks to all of these individuals, though I alone am responsible for the final text.

It is my pleasure once more to thank the book's translator, Ralph Mandel, with whom I have worked for many years. His help has long since transcended the realm of translation. My heartfelt gratitude goes also to Sylvia Fuks Fried, the director of publications of the Schusterman Center for Israel Studies at Brandeis University, and to Dr. Phyllis Deutsch, editor in chief, University Press of New England, and the staff at the publishing house, for pronouncing this book worthy of publication and assisting me with advice and displaying patience, which I deeply appreciate.

Finally, my thanks to my wife, Sarki, and to my daughters, Lior and Nitzan: my work would lack all savor without you.

Motti Golani
Haifa, March 2012

NOTE

1. Cunningham to Arthur Creech-Jones, Private and Personal, 12.4.1948, MECA, CP, B5, F4/90.

Abbreviations and Terms

AHC	Arab Higher Committee
CIGS	Chief of Imperial General Staff
C-in-C. ME	Commander-in-Chief Middle East
CSC	Chiefs of Staff Committee
CZA	Central Zionist Archives
Etzel	National Military Organization (Irgun)
Haganah (1920–1948)	Semi-underground militia of the Yishuv
GOC	General of Command
Lehi	Israel Freedom Fighters (Stern gang)
LHCMA	Liddell Hart Centre for Military Archives
MECA	Middle East Centre Archive
NA (PRO)	National Archives (formerly Public Record Office)
Palmah	"Shock Troops" (the Haganah's regular army)
UN(O)	United Nations (Organization)
UNSCOP	United Nations Special Committee on Palestine
WO	War Office
WZO	World Zionist Organization
Yishuv	Jewish community in pre-1948 Palestine

Palestine between Politics and Terror

Prologue
On the Road to Jerusalem

Alan Gordon Cunningham was born in Dublin, Ireland, on May 1, 1887, to a Scottish family. The fifth and youngest child of Elizabeth and Daniel Cunningham, he had two sisters and two brothers. Daniel Cunningham was a leading anatomist of the time and taught at the University of Edinburgh and afterward at the University of Dublin. Devoted to his work, he was an ardent and creative researcher, author, and teacher. Everything else took second place in his life, not least his children.

Alan Cunningham was born when his father was at the height of his academic and scientific career. Daniel inculcated in his children the virtues of self-discipline and hard work. The Cunninghams were an established family, confident of the future. The children were closer to their mother, who often acted as a mediator and protector in the face of their father's strict demands. Daniel served on many royal commissions of inquiry that investigated the treatment of diseases and injuries in the colonies and the armed forces. The children were thus exposed not only to stories about the medical world but also about the empire and its armed forces. Indeed, Daniel urged his sons to pursue a military career. He died suddenly, at age fifty-nine, when Alan was twenty-two and had recently embarked on lifelong army and national service.[1]

Alan Cunningham had his heart set on soldiering from an early age. He preferred the navy but was inducted into artillery. Educated at Cheltenham College and afterward at the Royal Military Academy, Woolwich, he was commissioned as an artillery officer in 1906, when he was nineteen. In the First World War, he served on the western front in the Royal Horse Artillery and apparently acquitted himself well. In 1915, he was awarded the Military Cross, and toward the end of the war, in 1918, the Distinguished Service Order. No less important for the career of a young officer, Cunningham was cited five times in the distinguished service list. Extraordinary among the members of his generation who spent the whole war on the front lines, young Cunningham emerged unscathed from the carnage. He had found his niche and remained in the army.

Those who pursued a military career in the interwar period often encountered a glaring disparity between their ambitions and the hard reality of what the imperial army could offer. Britain's reluctance to get involved in another armed conflict limited the options to two: service in one of the garrison forces scattered throughout the empire or service in the military training system. Those who chose the colonies found themselves performing what were essentially policing functions, quelling insurrections or coping with repeated waves of terrorism. Nor did service in the training units offer much of a challenge, given Britain's military stagnation. Promotion was correspondingly slow. Nevertheless, this was the world Cunningham knew, and no other profession seems to have appealed to him.[2]

In 1919, the young officer received an assignment that had nothing to do with the military profession but brought closer the fulfillment of his old but still passionate wish to serve in the Royal Navy. For two years, until 1921, he was posted to Singapore; afterward, he was accepted to the Naval Staff College. Despite completing the college successfully, he was posted to the ground forces' training system for what would become a frustrating fifteen-year stint. He spent most of this period at a small auxiliary weapons school at Netheravon. Unwillingly, he remained in artillery.

Cunningham rose through the ranks slowly. The only way to accelerate a stalled career was by obtaining a field command post. In 1937, now fifty years old and holding the rank of lieutenant colonel, Cunningham gained admittance to the Imperial Defense College, the highest institution for senior officers. In the same year, he was appointed commander of the First Division of the Royal Artillery, primarily an administrative position, with the division's units scattered across Britain. In 1938, as tension surged in Europe, he was promoted to the rank of major general and appointed commander of the Fifth Antiaircraft Division.

Though he spent most of the interwar years in Britain, Cunningham did not acquire property and did not marry. The army was his life. But he remained unknown to the public at least until the spring of 1941. The opportunity to scale career heights, out of reach in peacetime, arrived in the war that erupted on September 1, 1939. The British armed forces suffered a severe jolt and lessons were learned rapidly in the wake of the debacle in France in 1940. In the course of a year, as military units were expanded, manpower increased, and swift personnel changes ensued, Cunningham commanded several artillery and infantry divisions as necessity demanded. In October 1940, he was chosen by General Archibald Wavell, the commander-in-chief of the British Middle East Command (1939–1941), to lead the British expeditionary force in East Africa.[3]

On June 10, 1941, Italy declared war on Britain, Mussolini having been persuaded by France's fall to Germany and the evacuation of the British forces from Dunkirk to join Hitler. Italy's principal strength outside Europe resided in its control of Libya and in East Africa, where the Italians had conquered Ethiopia in 1936 and removed it from the British Empire's sphere of influence. That success, together with the hold on Italian Somalia to the south, provided Rome with a promising opening position in Africa. In July 1940, the Italians started to encroach on British-held territory in Sudan and Kenya; in August they conquered British Somalia, giving them effective control of the entire Horn of Africa. The threat to Egypt and the Suez Canal was palpable. These developments were compounded by the collapse of Western Europe in the spring and the Battle of Britain.

As its fortunes waned, London felt it urgent to dispatch a senior political figure to the African front to assess the situation in the overall context of the war and thereby aid the government's decision-making. Thus, on October 28, 1940, Britain's secretary of state for war, Anthony Eden, met in Khartoum, Sudan, with the prime minister of South Africa, Field Marshal Jan Smuts, General Wavell, and the senior officers in Sudan and Kenya. Smuts promised to back up a British offensive in East Africa with troops, air support, transportation, and logistical aid. On the day of the Khartoum meeting, the Italians attacked Greece. In response, the British and their allies decided to carry out targeted operations in Sudan and Kenya to retake the territories seized by the Italians, and to wait for the situation in Greece to clarify. In addition, the possibility was raised of taking Kismayu, the chief port city of Italian Somalia.[4]

It was at the Khartoum meeting that the voice of Major General Cunningham, who had just arrived in the region and had not yet assumed his post, was heard for the first time. Cunningham suggested that despite the logistical limitations in Kenya, the possibility should be examined of launching an invasion from Kenya into Italian Somalia as early as January 1941. This bold approach did not go unnoticed in London, and at the beginning of November 1940 Cunningham was appointed commander of the British East Africa forces.[5]

He took over in difficult conditions. Success was a virtual guarantee of rapid promotion, failure of immediate disgrace. In the meantime, he was not officially promoted but was given the rank of acting lieutenant general. After familiarizing himself with the operational conditions, the new commander suggested that the Kismayu campaign, which at his behest had been set for January 1941, be delayed. He now saw that it would be unwise to launch the first and main assault on Italian Somalia in the rainy season, which would last until the spring. The possibility of a column of forces with their logistics getting bogged down in the rain and mud while crossing the desert route was too great. Cunningham reached the conclusion that an attack would not be possible before May 1941, another key reason being the urgent need for additional forces, which were not yet available. It was, Cunningham believed, better to be safe than sorry and minimize the risks entailed in an incursion into Italian Somalia and southern Ethiopia.[6]

Wavell appreciated Cunningham's calculated restraint, which was consistent with his own approach. Not so Winston Churchill: the prime minister and minister of defense disdained Cunningham's approach in general and the postponement of the Horn of Africa offensive from the south in particular. The relations between the two men thus got off to a rocky start. Churchill wanted to exploit the momentum of the anticipated success of an offensive by the Western Desert Force under the command of Lieutenant General Richard O'Connor on the Egypt-Libya border in order to push into East Africa as well. This was the only region in which the British had any hope of victory at this stage of the war, as Germany and the Axis powers went from strength to strength. North and East Africa were no longer a sideshow but a critical strategic theater, militarily and politically as well as to boost morale. Success in Africa was essential as a potential deterrent in the light of reports about Japan's offensive intentions in the Far East. Churchill wanted the Italian episode in East Africa to be ended by April 1941. Wavell and Cunningham stood firm, though their adamancy came at a price: they received black marks in the ledger of the exacting prime minister.[7]

In the event, Cunningham soon realized that Churchill had been right, owing to the severe conditions in the Western Desert, the Germans' advance in Bulgaria, and the need to move forces from Africa to defend Greece. He therefore proposed to Wavell to move up the incursion into Italian Somalia, despite his misgivings. The change of plan was authorized. In January 1941, Cunningham acted swiftly to take Addis Ababa, Ethiopia, which surrendered to his forces on April 6, just as Churchill had insisted would happen at the end of 1940. Concurrently, the commander of the British forces in Sudan, General William Platt, completed the conquest of Eritrea. The Italians, squeezed between the forces of Platt and Cunningham, surrendered on May 16. Wavell summed up the thrust from Kenya through Italian Somalia to Addis Ababa in two words: "Brilliant campaign."[8]

In the meantime, however, the Germans, who had launched an offensive on March 30 in Libya from west to east, overran most of Cyrenaica (eastern Libya). Mainland Greece and Crete fell in April and May 1941, respectively. Vichy France gave the Germans access to its colonies in North Africa and the Levant, and a pro-Nazi revolt broke out in Iraq. Thus, in the spring of 1941 the British did not have a base (other than Malta) between the British Isles and Cyprus, Egypt, and Palestine. Britain's only victory was that of Cunningham and Platt in the Horn of Africa, and as such it was crucial at a stage in the war when Britain still stood virtually alone against Germany, Italy, the Soviet Union, and their allies.[9]

Despite the British defeat in the Western Desert due to the priority accorded Greece—to which forces were dispatched with the original goal of pushing back the Italians westward from Libya—the success in East Africa helped hasten the surrender of the Vichy France forces still stationed in Djibouti, in French Somalia, and contributed to the steadfast hold of the Tobruk enclave on the Mediterranean coast of Libya from April onward, the conquest of Syria and Lebanon from the Vichy French in June, and the suppression of the uprising in Iraq that month. The achievement by Cunningham and Platt resonated beyond the military context. Cunningham's performance was particularly surprising. Junior in rank to Platt and an unknown quantity, Cunningham waged a headstrong, inspired assault that was the polar opposite of the glumly ponderous manner in which he managed larger campaigns of this period. Churchill no longer had cause to berate the hitherto anonymous general, whose star now shone bright. Cunningham demonstrated that he was judicious but not a defeatist and was capable of mounting a decisive offensive. The defeats suffered by the Germans in the Western Desert, Greece, and Crete in the spring of 1941 threw Cunningham's success into bold relief. Toward the end of May, he was given the title of Knight Commander of the Order of the Bath. In mid-July, the Army Council cited his Ethiopia campaign and toward the end of August, King George VI extended his formal congratulations and showed the country's appreciation by titling him Sir Alan Cunningham.[10]

The Second World War accelerated the turnover rate in command posts within the British Army's senior officer corps. There were victories and defeats, and generals in turn gained glory or fell from favor, sometimes in the course of a single battle. This process is strikingly exemplified by Cunningham. On the eve of the war, he was the commander of an antiaircraft artillery division and was not promoted to the rank of major general until 1938; yet by the summer of 1941, he stood at the apex of the largest operative framework in the British Army at the time—the Eighth Army—for which the standard rank was general. The fact that such roller-coaster shifts of personal fortune were not exceptional did little to mitigate the emotional and professional turmoil that accompanied them.

In the wake of the loss of mainland Greece and of Crete in April and May 1941, large forces were massed by the British in Egypt and Palestine, which thus became the two major possible arenas of combat in the Middle East. General Claude Auchinleck, who had replaced Wavell as commander-in-chief of Middle East Command at the end of July, decided to organize his theater of operations within the framework of an army headquarters. The Ninth Army, under the command of Lieutenant General Henry Wilson, was responsible for Iraq, Transjordan, Syria, Lebanon, and Palestine. The Eighth Army was to operate in the Western Desert in Egypt, pushing toward Libya and Tunisia. Initially, a Tenth Army was also formed, to defend the Egypt-Libya border, but this mission was subsequently assigned to the forces in Egypt, which remained independent between the Ninth Army in the north and the Eighth Army in the west. Auchinleck wanted to reserve the army formations as operational headquarters exclusively on active fronts.[11]

On August 11, 1941, Auchinleck returned from a visit to London that, even though it had been forced on him, went well. He brought with him two unexpected concessions from the prime minister: first, that an offensive against Erwin Rommel's forces in the Western Desert would not be launched before November 1, rather than immediately, as Churchill had initially demanded; and second, Alan Cunningham's appointment as commander of the Eighth Army. Cunningham's fate had always been linked to the relations that prevailed between his commanding officer, Auchinleck, and Churchill. At the end of 1940, the prime minister had not wanted Cunningham as commander of the East Africa force. Now he demanded that command of the Eighth Army be entrusted to his confidant Wilson, who was identified with O'Connor's successes in the Western Desert during the winter of 1940–1941 and had led the forces that took Syria and Lebanon in June 1941. It was with unconcealed displeasure that Churchill finally agreed to leave the decision to the front commander.[12]

Auchinleck drew both praise and criticism for his performance during the year in which he headed Middle East Command (July 1941 until his removal in August 1942). One area in which he was roundly criticized was his choice of personnel, field commanders in particular. Some observers maintained that he had no understanding of people or of their suitability for specific posts. A flagrant case in point, these observers said, was the meteoric rise of Alan Cunningham. Auchinleck had never met Cunningham before the latter's arrival in the Western Desert. Initially, their bond was based on mutual admiration for Andrew Cunningham, Alan's brother and Auchinleck's navy counterpart. Auchinleck met Cunningham for the first time on August 16. The meeting reinforced the new regional commander's opinion of Cunningham, despite Churchill's adamant opposition to his appointment as Eighth Army commander. Auchinleck requested authorization from his superiors for the appointment, explaining that he had been impressed by Cunningham's bold blitz in Ethiopia. He failed to account, however, for Cunningham's inexperience in the massive movement of armor and large formations. What struck him was Cunningham's proclivity for mobile battle, as he had demonstrated in Ethiopia.[13]

Cunningham was named to lead the Western Desert Force before the Eighth Army was formed, even though the forces that were to constitute this army had been organizing for some time. Thus, he found himself in a position of being the army's founder but also having to accommodate himself to a situation in which it was already proceeding at a pace and along a track not of his making. This fact is worth mentioning, because Cunningham's name has been expunged almost completely from the history of the Eighth Army.

In August–September 1941, on the eve of the renewed campaign in the Western Desert, relations among the threesome then at the forefront of the major Allied push were far from harmonious. The prime minister was not pleased with his two senior generals in Egypt, and they, for their part, undoubtedly did not get the full backing they needed. That said, Cunningham was at the peak of his powers in August 1941, when he assumed his new post in the Western Desert. People who met him when he arrived in Cairo from East Africa described him as impressive, decisive, and energetic, and did not fail to mention his penetrating blue eyes. In short order, the view also circulated that he was overbearing, short-tempered, quick to anger upon hearing an opinion he found inconvenient—but also ready to give the matter a second thought.[14]

His period of grace was brutally short. He was thrust unprepared into a seething cauldron in which everything was in short supply: time, means, and, above all, experience—his and that of his superiors. Consequently, he felt inferior to his subordinates, whose experience and know-how in desert warfare generally surpassed his own: a serious problem for an officer in war, unless he possesses the qualities of a supreme commander or extraordinary charisma. The indications were almost immediately apparent. Even before he set out for the Western Desert at the head of the Eighth Army to execute the largest British action in the war to date—Operation Crusader, aimed at destroying Rommel's forces, or at least expelling them from North Africa—Cunningham was already exhausted.[15]

He arrived in Cairo in mid-August 1941, went back to Nairobi to settle his affairs there, and returned to Cairo again at the end of the month. On September 10, the Western Desert Force was established under Cunningham's command. His headquarters moved to the Western Desert on September 25, and the force officially became the Eighth Army on the night of September 26–27, with operative responsibility for all the desert forces, including those besieged in the British enclave at Tobruk.[16]

In addition to the need to familiarize himself with a new geographical region, Cunningham had command of forces on a scale far exceeding anything he had formerly undertaken. His situation was not facilitated by the fact that few of his colleagues, even those senior to him, had experience heading a formation of this size. This was for the simple reason that the British Army had not previously fielded operational combat troops on this scale in the war. The former artillery officer's experience in combat and logistical command amounted to four infantry brigades operating simultaneously in East Africa. Now Cunningham was the manager of two corps, consisting of eight divisions, nineteen brigades (some of them independent, five of them armored), a reinforced division in the Tobruk enclave, and administrative, maintenance, and logistical forces. All told, Cunningham's 118,000 soldiers and five hundred tanks outnumbered the forces of the Germans and Italians arrayed against him, which consisted of 113,000 troops and nearly four hundred tanks. The Eighth Army was the most highly organized and best equipped force deployed thus far by Britain in the war and possessed a substantial advantage over its foe, at least on paper. But numbers notwithstanding, it soon became apparent that the battle would be decided by stratagems, quick responses, and above all the ability to remain steadfast in conditions of uncertainty and pressure.[17]

Clearly, Operation Crusader would resonate far beyond the Mediterranean Basin. For the first time, the British pitted their finest armor on an open battlefield against the Germans' best. The idea was to create a precedent proving that the German war machine was not invincible. It took no great feat of the imagination in summer 1941 to realize the effect that the outcome of this battle would have on the allies of both sides, on the countries sitting on the fence, on the British public, and on the soldiers in every arena. As it happened, less than a month after Operation Crusader was launched, history veered onto a new course with the entry of the United States into the war; but the contemporaries did not know that.

The historical timing unavoidably generated soaring expectations. On the eve of the operation, the Eighth Army was the only British force about to enter into active combat with the Germans, and no effort was spared to equip it accordingly. The anticipation was heightened in part by a surge of exuberance. For a moment, Auchinleck, Cunningham, and their officers and men were in the world's spotlight. All eyes would be on Cunningham as he set out to prove that he could manage the vast array of troops, weapons, and equipment placed at his disposal. It was up to him to show that he was capable of arranging the unprecedented orders of battle into an organized, focused, and coordinated force, and, most important, capable of emerging victorious. Churchill himself spurred, and to a degree fostered, the high expectations for the campaign. The prime minister knew this was a critical crossroads in strategic, state, and historical terms. Under the scrutiny of public and political pressure, he had to explain to the British people and to Parliament why a British force of unprecedented scale, in which so much effort in human life, funding, and organization had been invested, was tarrying in Egypt. At the same time, he believed that the fraught expectations were buoying the soldiers and commanders who were about to engage the enemy on the field of battle.

As with expectations for the campaign itself, little imagination is required to grasp the effect of Churchill's comment on the eve of Operation Crusader—the Western Desert Army, he said, would likely "add a page to history which will rank with Blenheim and with Waterloo"—on those charged with writing that page of history. For Cunningham, such prophecies added a heavy burden, under which he was apt to buckle. Already working ceaselessly, his nerves stretched to the breaking point, he was now expected to prove himself the equal of the greatest field commanders in Britain's war-rich history. And in case anyone still had not got the message, Churchill added that failure was not an option.[18]

Operation Crusader was launched on November 18, 1941. On the night preceding the operation, a storm lashed the Egypt-Libya border. Torrential rain turned the desert sands into deep, viscous mud. The well-known quip, that when it rains the enemy also gets wet, could have been no consolation to Cunningham. Alone in his headquarters, the commander-in-chief of the Eighth Army suffered from eve-of-battle nerves, a well-known phenomenon in the military. The dismal weather, which created an uneasy atmosphere and threatened to wreak havoc on the battle plans, seemed to reflect his own uneasiness about bearing absolute responsibility for the events. Although there is little a supreme commander can do once all the planning and preparations have been completed, he cannot but contemplate the quality of his decisions, which, whatever the outcome, will be costly in human life: in this case, more than 200,000 troops stood ready on both sides of the front.[19]

The Eighth Army began to move westward before dawn and by early morning the first forces crossed the border into Libya. At first, Field Marshal Rommel, who led the German-Italian force in Libya, did not grasp that an all-out offensive was in progress. The initial absence of a response generated rumors in Cairo, and afterward in London, about a tremendous victory in the Western Desert. Cunningham did not initiate the rumors, but neither did he deny them. Finally, on November 22, after a few days in which Cunningham's nerves were severely frayed—he needed a German reaction before he could decide what orders to issue to his advancing forces—the Germans and Italians launched a counterattack. On the very first day of the offensive, 30 Corps, an armored formation, was badly mauled in a German trap and forced to retreat.

Meanwhile, Cunningham, in his headquarters in Fort Maddalena on the Egypt-Libya border, was unaware of that day's developments (November 22) and celebrated his "victory." At first light on November 23, he flew to the front in order to apprise his field commanders of his plans to exploit the supposed victory of the previous day. But within minutes of his return to Fort Maddalena later in the morning, his world collapsed around him. The reports, brutal and unembellished, about the events of November 22 had finally reached Eighth Army headquarters. Despite the battlefield disaster, Cunningham decided to continue the assault. At the same time, he cabled Auchinleck in Cairo with an urgent request that the latter come to his headquarters: he needed the backing of his superior. Although he did not modify his orders, Cunningham did not hide his consternation from his staff.[20]

Cunningham faced an excruciating dilemma: to press on with the offensive, with the possibility that his forces would sustain a mortal blow and the Germans would move into Egypt, or to pull back, regroup, and attack again later. From our perspective today, it appears that Cunningham's decision to summon Auchinleck saved the day, as the theater commander's steady demeanor and determination were crucial factors. However, from Cunningham's personal standpoint the move sealed his fate.

In their first—and decisive—meeting, on the afternoon of November 23, Cunningham assessed gloomily that he was now in an inferior situation in number of tanks and that, in principle, nothing could stop the Germans from advancing into Egypt. The advice he sought from Auchinleck was whether to call a halt to the offensive and deploy temporarily in a defensive posture, or to press on in the spirit of the orders he had issued that morning. In any event, he noted, the Eighth Army must not be left unprotected in the rear.[21]

The next day, November 24, Cunningham's worst fears seemed to be realized: flying to join his forces that afternoon, he saw a German column (led by Rommel himself, it later turned out) executing a characteristic blitz and then stopping (due to insufficient fuel) close to the Egypt-Libya border, only twenty-four kilometers from the Eighth Army's primary logistics base and about forty-five kilometers from Cunningham's own headquarters. While Cunningham visited his troops, Auchinleck acquainted himself with the situation. When Cunningham landed at his headquarters, deeply troubled by what he had seen from the air, Auchinleck handed him written orders that had nothing to do with his frame of mind or with the conclusions he had drawn from the situation; indeed, those conclusions were the very opposite of the orders Cunningham received.[22]

With the intuition of a supreme commander—a trait Cunningham lacked—Auchinleck grasped that the only way to avert defeat was to attack and to announce these plans. The theater commander understood that the British must take no action, even action that appeared logical at the time, that could give the impression of a German victory, even a temporary one. Not least, this was because beyond the basic question of morale, public relations and the media had become key weapons in the campaign. Accordingly, his order to Cunningham was not to retreat but rather to continue the assault with all the strength at his disposal, "to the last tank."[23]

Cunningham, though not certain that this was the right approach, obeyed the order and immediately issued directives in this spirit to his units. On November 26, Cunningham's forces succeeded in stabilizing—without a battle—the linkup with the Tobruk garrison that had been forged a few days earlier. This was the first stage in a process that in January 1942 would enable the Crusader forces to push back Rommel to the west.[24]

On the evening of November 25, Auchinleck returned to Cairo and immediately sent Cunningham a message relieving him of command. The theater commander was well aware of the implications of a mid-campaign dismissal—particularly when the campaign was being closely followed in

Britain and elsewhere—for the image of both the officer being removed and of the appointing officer. Consequently, a solution was found to meet the immediate needs: Auchinleck would keep Cunningham's dismissal a secret to the extent possible and explain that he had fallen ill. Cunningham would be hospitalized under an alias in a military facility far from Cairo for a very brief period and spirited out of Egypt secretly. Only when necessity dictated would an announcement be made of a change of command in the Eighth Army, citing the commander's illness, with any notion of a dismissal to be denied. To its devisers, this solution seemed fair to Cunningham as well. Thus, though Cunningham was relieved of command on November 26, 1941, the change of command was not announced until December 11, when the campaign in the Western Desert seemed to be tilting in the Eighth Army's favor. By then, Cunningham was on sick leave in Britain.[25]

The GOC Eighth Army was forced to step aside mid-battle and agree to be "convalescent" for nothing less than the fate of the war. He left his forward command post unceremoniously and flew directly to Military Hospital 64 in Alexandria. Lieutenant General (acting) Alan Cunningham, who led one of the last great battles (if not *the* last) in the pre-American period of the Second World War, now embarked on a very different war: a personal campaign to salvage his reputation.

Cunningham accepted the conviction but not the verdict. In his view, the only defensive measure he had taken was his order to ready the rear of his forces in case of a German raid. That had been necessary on November 24. All that remained was to request that at least his reputation not be tarnished and that his response, as expected of him, to Auchinleck's order to continue the offensive be acknowledged and made public. He insisted that he had not adopted a defensive posture, as Auchinleck claimed in the letter relieving him of command. His request was rejected. Cunningham was released from the hospital on December 4, 1941, and left Egypt clandestinely. His commanding officer promised that he would return. Auchinleck had no such intention; but Cunningham did.[26]

To aggravate the situation, the question of Cunningham's rank now arose. On December 16—some ten days after his return to Britain and less than a month after his dismissal—the War Office informed him that, because he had "vacated the command" of the Eighth Army on November 27 (in fact, he had been relieved of duty a day earlier), he was obliged to give up his temporary rank of lieutenant general. This was another punishment inflicted on Cunningham. He was deemed defensive in battle, purportedly sick, and now he was demoted to major general. The blow he suffered was both formal and symbolic, but it afforded him a specific target for his struggle. He needed to reclaim his rank in a meaningful command post, preferably a combat role, in order to prove that he was not defensive, still less defeatist.[27]

While Cunningham was still in Egypt, he was ordered by Middle East Theatre headquarters to send a report to the chief of the Imperial General Staff concerning his return to Britain. He did not send a report. A week after returning to Britain, and still without producing the report, he called on the chief of staff in the War Office in London. As it turned out, he could not have made a smarter move in the struggle to clear his name. At the end of November 1941, General John Dill had authorized his dismissal, but by the time Cunningham came to London, the Imperial General Staff was headed by General Alan Brooke.[28]

Brooke was five years older than Cunningham; both were artillery veterans. In 1938, Cunningham's division had been under Brooke's command when the latter served as commander of the Antiaircraft Corps. Their relationship grew closer after Cunningham's return from the Western Desert. The humiliated general felt free to share his feelings with Britain's top soldier. Brooke's impression was that Cunningham was "very depressed and hard to comfort." He described a second meeting, held a few months later, as a "painful interview." So sympathetic was he to Cunningham that by the end of 1945, on the eve of the latter's departure for Palestine, the solitary Cunningham, who had neither wife nor children, was like a member of the family in the chief of staff's home. The informal circle was also joined by Andrew Cunningham, Alan's brother, who returned to London from the Middle East in October 1943 to take up his new post as first sea lord. It is not clear whether Andrew was the reason for this friendship or its by-product.[29]

Brooke became convinced that Cunningham had been wronged and must be reinstated in a command post immediately. On December 7, 1941, just three days after Cunningham's return to Britain (and before he went to see Brooke), a week after assuming his new post, and on the day of the Japanese attack on Pearl Harbor, Brooke consulted with the secretary of state for war, Sir Percy James Grigg, on how to help Cunningham. But Brooke, high as he was, was not at the top of the pyramid. Between him and an order to reinstate Cunningham stood the prime minister, who used Cunningham's case as an example to his other generals of how not to behave as Britain fought for its survival.[30]

For many months, Churchill was adamant in his refusal to consider Cunningham for even a staff post, let alone training. Cunningham and his circle were compelled to face the fact that he had become the symbol of a commander who had failed in battle, without anyone of authority, or he himself, allowed to tell his version of the events in the Western Desert. After five months of waiting idly, Major General Cunningham was in a state of despair. He wanted his political-public fate to be decided, one way or the other. But Brooke refused to let him give up. He enlisted Grigg in the cause, and the two buttonholed Churchill in an informal moment at the conclusion of a cabinet meeting. Once more, in vain. Rather despairingly, Brooke wrote in his diary that whenever he brought up Cunningham's name, Churchill reacted as though they were discussing a dastardly criminal. In another cabinet meeting, in the same breath as Churchill decided, against the majority of the ministers, to dispatch a maritime convoy to the Soviet Union, he refused again to reconsider Cunningham's case. Brooke had no choice but to report to Cunningham that all his efforts had failed. Nevertheless, he did not give up. In his way, Brooke was one of the few who did not cringe in the face of Churchill's reactions.[31]

The turning point came in October 1942, from a somewhat unexpected quarter. It remains unclear whether Cunningham or perhaps Brooke conceived the idea. In any event, the shift was fomented by a high-ranking officer who had been instrumental in bringing about Cunningham's appointment as GOC of East Africa forces toward the end of 1940, on the eve of the invasion of Ethiopia, and afterward, in the summer of 1941, as commander of the Western Desert Force, which later became the Eighth Army. Brooke approached Field Marshal Jan Smuts, the prime minister of South Africa, a member of the British War Cabinet, and a figure of moral authority in Churchill's eyes. After some initial hesitation, as his ardent support for Cunningham in August 1941 had ended badly, Smuts relented and later persuaded Churchill to view positively the idea of Cunningham's return to active service, even if not in a combat unit.[32]

The passage of an additional few months provided other ousted commanders whom the prime minister could cite as examples not to be emulated. The most notable of these was none other than General Auchinleck; in August 1942, he was relieved of his double post as GOC Middle East Theatre and commander of the Eighth Army in favor of General Harold Alexander and Lieutenant General Bernard Montgomery, respectively. On October 30, Brooke informed Cunningham that his reinstatement had been approved. Brooke's stubbornness and Smuts's goodwill had done their part, but the unfolding events probably weighed more heavily in the decision. A week earlier, on October 23, the Eighth Army had launched its major offensive in the Western Desert, under Montgomery. Rommel's defeat seemed a certainty. Cunningham's ostracism no longer bore the significance that it did when the Eighth Army was on the brink of collapse. To a certain degree, it was Montgomery who, for reasons of his own, brought Cunningham out of the wilderness and back to active duty. It would be many more months before Churchill authorized a combat post for him, but toward the end of 1942 Cunningham was on the right path from his own point of view.[33]

Cunningham's first assignment returned him to the realm of training, in which he had spent most of his military career until 1937. The new post carried a certain prestige: his previous temporary rank (acting lieutenant general) was restored, his status was recognized, and perhaps there was a tacit admission of the injustice done to him. He was named commandant of the highly regarded Staff College at Camberley. After being accused of taking a defensive approach and of losing his nerve on the battlefield, Cunningham was now the commander and instructor of the new generation of staff officers.[34]

In July 1943, after Cunningham had been at Camberley for about eight months, the Germans were driven out of North Africa for good and Allied forces landed in Italy, the first landing of its kind on the European continent during the war. In this heady atmosphere of victory, Brooke felt he could act on his own in Cunningham's case. On July 23, the Imperial General Staff informed Cunningham that he was being returned to combat duty. The prime minister was not told of the move until five days later. The gamble paid off. Churchill acceded to Brooke's request and lifted another ban concerning Cunningham's employment: that on active command duty.[35]

With the reinstatement, Sir Alan was awarded permanently the rank of lieutenant general of which he had been stripped in December 1941. His new appointment was as Commander-in-Chief Northern Ireland. He took solace in the fact that although the command was small, it was interesting. Still, compared to the events of the war raging across the world, even a normally tempestuous arena like Northern Ireland was almost a calm backwater. Lieutenant General Alan Cunningham, along with his wellwishers, longed for his return to a combat command post, or at least one of major significance. He remained determined to restore his lost honor.[36]

Cunningham spent about a year and a half in Northern Ireland. In late

1944, with the end of the war looming on the horizon, and though the timing was not yet certain, Brooke informed him of a new appointment as chief of Eastern Command in Britain. This entailed a full workweek, almost like that of a clerk who returned home at the end of the day, and in Britain, to boot. There seemed no way that he could move forward from this assignment to being a full general. In October 1944, Sir Alan was already fifty-seven years old. The military pension laws in Britain required officers, apart from special cases, to retire when they were still usually in their prime, by sixty at the latest. Cunningham's satisfaction at obtaining the command post was tinged with disappointment, not least because it appeared that Eastern Command would be abolished when the war ended. In this sense, the termination of the global conflict—in Europe in May 1945 and in the Far East that September—was not good news for Cunningham on a personal level.[37]

Fate decreed otherwise. In July 1945, Churchill and the Conservative Party were, stunningly, voted out of office. Labour Party leader Clement Attlee became prime minister and Brooke stayed on as chief of the Imperial General Staff. Then, at the beginning of November 1945, after only a year as high commissioner of Palestine and Transjordan, Field Marshal Lord John Vereker, 6th Viscount Gort (1886–1946), announced that he would have to return to Britain. Since entering Government House in Jerusalem in October 1944, he had won praise from Jews and Arabs alike.

Gort himself had been chief of the Imperial General Staff since 1938 and still held the position when the Second World War broke out. In September 1939, he appointed himself commander of the British Expeditionary Force in France. As his forces were defeated, his posting to France was not extended. Others took the credit for his decision to evacuate his troops with their weapons from Dunkirk in June 1940, an operation that enabled the British Army to recover afterward. Although stripped of his high position, he refused to retire. Gort was governor of Gibraltar (1941–1942) and governor of Malta (1942–1944); the early part of his tenure in Malta included the ordeal of nonstop air attacks pummeling the island. Like the proverbial old soldier, he would likely have faded away, but considering Gort's successful performance in Malta, Churchill, in a last-minute gesture, promoted him to field marshal and afterward appointed him high commissioner to Palestine, which was a relatively calm arena in 1944.

Gort arrived in Jerusalem at a time of productive cooperation between the Yishuv—the Jewish community in Palestine—and the British administration. Moreover, the weak Arab community had not yet overcome the crisis it suffered following the suppression of its revolt in the second half of the 1930s. However, Gort's period in Palestine also witnessed a historic watershed: the end of the Second World War. The ensuing euphoria and the expectations of the Jews and the Arabs for a new world order, combined with the Yishuv leadership's active campaign against the terrorism of the breakaway groups (Irgun and Lehi), hurled Palestine back into the situation that had prevailed for the two decades before the war: that of a powder keg of conflicting aspirations that threatened to blow up at any moment. However, Gort did not get the opportunity to test his mettle in this environment. Working in his favor was his reputation as an effective military leader, which deeply impressed the local inhabitants. They were also taken by his affable character, his modesty, his ability to strike up informal relations with ordinary folk as well as dignitaries, and the fact that he did not surround himself with bodyguards. The Yishuv tended to view him as being sympathetic to the Zionist cause. It seems that only his illness kept him from confronting the two sides, particularly the Jews, and thereby of testing his capability in the crucible of the conflict.

Until the last moment, neither Gort nor his aides realized how serious his illness was. The high commissioner's right-hand man, Chief Secretary John Shaw, and the military commander-in-chief in Palestine, Lieutenant General John D'Arcy, did not become fully aware of his condition until after he returned from a medical visit to Britain at the beginning of October 1945. Despite an unwritten rule dictating absolute obedience to the person at the top of the pyramid, the two considered advising the Colonial Office privately that in their view Gort should return to Britain immediately for medical treatment. This was mandated by both the public and governmental interest in Palestine and Britain. In the event, they did not dare take that step, but life did the work for them.

At the end of October 1945, the two most senior officers in the British Army, Brooke and Montgomery, visited Palestine. Montgomery, who was still the commander of the British forces on the Rhine, was expected to succeed Brooke as chief of the Imperial General Staff in a little more than half a year. The two field marshals stayed at Government House. After dinner, as coffee was served, Gort lost consciousness before their eyes. Brooke's plane was immediately dispatched to Cairo in order to fly in the chief medical officer of the Middle East Theatre. He declared that Gort must be hospitalized immediately in Britain. Gort was forced to resign. On October 31, 1945, the secretary of state for the colonies accepted his resignation. Gort left Palestine for Malta on November 5 and was hospitalized in Britain the next day. As had happened the previous summer, he was replaced temporarily by the Palestine government's chief secretary, John Shaw.[38]

One consequence of this development was that Brooke was apparently involved once more in Cunningham's promotion and rehabilitation. This cannot be proven, but the fact is that Brooke was present when Palestine was left without a high commissioner, and his authorization would have been required to lend a senior officer of Cunningham's rank to the Colonial Office.[39]

A new high commissioner had to be appointed forthwith. Apparently, several candidates turned down the position before it was offered to Cunningham. The Colonial Office consulted with Churchill and Oliver Stanley, a former colonial secretary. It was certainly not Churchill's idea to appoint Cunningham—the history of their relations rules that out—and it is unlikely that he would have obtained the appointment if Churchill had been prime minister in November 1945. Still, it would be significant if the former prime minister did not object to the appointment. In later years, Cunningham claimed that Foreign Secretary Ernest Bevin had given him "exactly fifteen minutes" to respond to the offer. On another occasion, he related that on November 7, 1945, the colonial secretary, George Hall, approached him in the name of Prime Minister Attlee. Cunningham told a Yishuv delegation visiting him at Government House on November 23, two days after his arrival in Jerusalem, that he had been apprised of the appointment only a week earlier. However, this was not accurate, or perhaps David Ben-Gurion, who took notes, did not understand what he meant. In any event, on November 8 Cunningham was appointed high commissioner and commander-in-chief for Palestine and high commissioner for Transjordan. A sense of urgency attended the matter in London, and Alan Cunningham was the man of the hour.[40]

On November 9, three days after outgoing high commissioner Gort arrived back in Britain, Cunningham was announced as his successor. On the same day, even before he was officially appointed, Cunningham received a cable from Chief Secretary Shaw in Jerusalem, containing a declaration of loyalty on behalf of the administration in Palestine and a promise to work with him. To this, the high commissioner designate responded immediately and warmly. He was clearly eager to assume his new post, although the idea had never crossed his mind forty-eight hours earlier. On November 13, the colonial secretary informed Cunningham that the appointment had been endorsed by the king.

The next day, November 14, the new high commissioner met in the Colonial Office with Secretary George Hall and the ministry's senior officials to discuss the situation in Palestine. Beyond wishing him well, the participants replied to Cunningham's questions about Palestine, a country with which he was unfamiliar. The meeting offered a vivid example of the disparity between those who view the world through a military prism and officials engaged in civilian colonial affairs. Set me a clear mission, Cunningham told his new employers, and I will decide how to execute it. That is not how things are done here, they hinted to him in response.

Five days later, he received the official appointment, which stated that his formal tenure as high commissioner had begun on November 16. Without even meeting his successor as chief of Eastern Command in person, Cunningham left Britain. Time was pressing: he had to get to Jerusalem.[41]

Ignorant of the country for which he was destined but with an "open mind," as he put it, Cunningham arrived in Jerusalem on November 21, 1945, and immediately took office as high commissioner for Palestine and Transjordan.[42] Gort's condition and the short time between the appointment and Cunningham's departure for Palestine meant that briefings by the outgoing high commissioner and a formal handover of duties were almost nonexistent. Moreover, it was no small matter to step into the shoes of John Gort, a field marshal and former commander of the Imperial General Staff. Cunningham, who bore only a lieutenant general's rank, was cognizant of the historic occasion and of the opportunity. The perks of the job were alluring as well. The colonial secretary informed Cunningham that he would receive £4,500 per annum and an additional £1,500 for expenses. For a single man without a family, this was a handsome salary, the highest he had ever been paid. His salary as a lieutenant general in a home-front command was about half this amount, not to mention the living conditions, the aides, the servants, the meals, and all the other household expenses that would now be covered by the state. In terms of a government pension, the high commissioner was at a level equivalent to that of the heads of the armed forces, cabinet ministers, and the prime minister himself. However, what truly mattered to Cunningham was that in his new post in Jerusalem, he would be invested with the rank of full general—the status he would have achieved, in his view, if the November 1941 events in the Western Desert had not intervened exactly four years before his arrival in Jerusalem.[43]

On the night of October 31–November 1, 1945, about a week before Gort left Government House, the Jewish Agency Executive sent the Haganah, the official defense force of the Yishuv, to carry out a series of operations that were collectively called the "Night of the Trains"—the simultaneous detonation of 153 explosive charges on railway lines in Palestine. This was the opening shot in the Yishuv's rebellion against what it perceived as the British government's disappointing policy. Gort did not manage to respond to this first significant action by the Jewish Resistance Movement, as fashioned by the Jewish Agency. It would be up to his successor to cope with this uprising. Unlike his predecessor, Alan Cunningham did not receive what seemed to be an eve-of-retirement "resting place." Hard work awaited him. Still, he probably preferred this to the quiet obscurity of the Eastern Command in Britain in 1944. Cunningham had no thoughts of retiring; he still had a personal mission to complete along with his missions for His Majesty's Government in Palestine.[44]

NOTES

1. The biographical details about Daniel Cunningham have been culled from: John Strawson, "General Sir Alan Gordon Cunningham," Lord Black and C. S. Nichols (eds.), *The Dictionary of National Biographies* (*DNB*), 1981–1985, New York 1990, pp. 103–104; and John Winton, *Cunningham: The Biography of Admiral A. B. Cunningham*, London 1998, pp. 1–2.

2. The army's stagnation on the eve of the war is discussed extensively in, for example, Correlli Barnett, *Britain and Her Army, 1509–1970: A Military, Political and Social Survey*, New York 1970.

3. Strawson, "Cunningham," pp. 103–104.

4. The discussion of the war in East Africa draws chiefly on: I. S. O. Playfair, *The History of the Second World War, United Kingdom Military Series, The Mediterranean and Middle East*, Vol. I: *The Early Successes against Italy, 1939 to May 1941*, London 1954, pp. 391–450.

5. Ibid., p. 393; Richard E. Osborne, *World War II in Colonial Africa*, Indianapolis 2001, pp. 128–129, 134.

6. Playfair, vol. 1, pp. 396–405; Wavell to Cunningham, NAM/8303–104/10, May 14, 1941.

7. Playfair, vol. 1, pp. 393–395; Winston Churchill, *The Second World War*, Vol. III: *The Grand Alliance*, Boston 1950.

8. Playfair, vol. 1, pp. 396–405; NAM/8303–104/10, May 15, 1941.

9. Rommel himself reached Tripoli on February 12, 1941, and his offensive began more than a month and a half later.

10. Correlli Barnett, *The Desert Generals*, London 1960, p. 79; Wavell to Cunningham, NAM/8303–104/10, May 31, 1941; Order of the day, "Lieut. General A. G. Cunningham, General Officer Commander, East Africa Force," July 15, 1941, NAM/8303–104/10; Middle East Command to Platt and Cunningham, August 26, 1941, NAM/8303–104/10; Prime Minister to Wavell, March 1, 1941; Churchill, *The Grand Alliance*, pp. 85–90.

11. In time, as the army grew and was operatively united with the forces of the United States and other Allies, Auchinleck's method of forming army headquarters was increasingly used. Montgomery subsequently reestablished the Tenth Army and during the invasion of Europe in 1944 headed a formation called the Twenty-first Army Group.

12. John Keegan (ed.), *Churchill's Generals*, London 1991, p. 73.

13. Cunningham to Auchinleck, July 12, 1941, NAM/8303–104/10; Auchinleck to Cunningham, July 22 and August 16, 1941, NAM/8303–104/10; John Connell, *Auchinleck: A Biography of Field-Marshal Sir Claude Auchinleck*, London 1959, p. 286; Barnett, *The Desert Generals*, p. 79.

14. Barnett, *The Desert Generals*, p. 80.

15. Ibid., p. 90; Arthur Tedder, *With Prejudice: The War Memoirs of Marshal of the Royal Air Force, Lord Tedder*, London 1966, p. 196; Connell, *Auchinleck*, p. 287; "Eighth Army, Report on Operations, Sep. 10th –Nov. 17th, 1941," NA WO201/2693.

16. Playfair, *The History of the Second World War*, vol. I; I. S. O. Playfair, *The History of the Second World War, United Kingdom Military Series, The Mediterranean and Middle East*, Vol. III: *British Fortunes Reach Their Lowest Ebb, September 1941 to September 1942*, London 1960, p. 1.

17. Playfair, *The History of the Second World War*, vol. III, pp. 30–38.

18. Philip Warner, *Auchinleck: The Lonely Soldier*, Barnsley 2006, p. 11.

19. Cunningham's testimony in Barnett, *The Desert Generals*, pp. 86–89.

20. David Belchem, *All in the Day's March*, London 1978, pp. 98–99; Barnett, *The Desert Generals*, p. 94; "Record of conference—23/11 [1941], HQ 30 Corps," NA, WO169/998.

21. Cunningham to Auchinleck from Military Hospital 64, Alexandria, November 28, 29, 1941, NAM 8303–104/28; Auchinleck to Cunningham, November 27, 29, 1941, NAM 8303–104/28; Tedder, *With Prejudice*, pp. 194–200.

22. Barnett, *The Desert Generals*, pp. 111–112.

23. Auchinleck to Cunningham, November 24, 1941, NAM 8303/104–28.

24. Major General Frank Messervy, commander of the Fourth Indian Division, to Cunningham, November 26, 1941, NA WO169/999.

25. Auchinleck to Cunningham, November 25, 29, 1941, NAM 8303 104/28.

26. Cunningham to Auchinleck, November 28, 30, 1941, NAM 8303 104/28; Cunningham to Major General Arthur Smith, chief of staff to Auchinleck, November 30, 1941, NAM 8303 104/28.

27. Military secretary [not signed], War Office, to Lieutenant General Cunningham, December 16, 1941, and to Major General Cunningham, December 19, 1941, NAM 8303 104/28.

28. Dill was chief of the Imperial General Staff from May 1940 until the beginning of December 1941. He was appointed field marshal and posted to Washington, D.C., as the senior British military representative in the United States. He died there in 1944. Brooke became acting chief of staff on December 1, 1941, and officially held the post from the end of that month until late June 1946. Toward the war's end, he held the title of Field Marshal Viscount Lord Alanbrooke.

29. A. Danchev and D. Todman (eds.), *Field Marshal Lord Alanbrooke: War Diaries, 1939–1945*, London 2002, December 12, 1941 (p. 211), March 10, 1942 (p. 238), April 24, 1942 (p. 252), July 11, 1945 (p. 704), August 16, 1945 (p. 718).

30. Ibid., December 7, 1941 (p. 208).

31. Ibid., April 24, 1942 (p. 252), May 11, 1942 (p. 257), May 18, 1942 (p. 258), May 27, 1942 (p. 261).

32. Ibid., July 28, 1942 (p. 286), October 19, 1942 (p. 331).

33. Ibid., October 30, 1942 (p. 337).

34. Nicholas Smart, *Biographical Dictionary of British Generals of the Second World War*, Barnsley 2005, p. 25; Strawson, "Cunningham," p. 104.

35. Danchev and Todman (eds.), *Field Marshal Lord Alanbrooke*, July 23, 1943 (p. 433), July 28, 1943 (p. 434).

36. Military secretary in War Office to Cunningham, October 23, 1943, NAM 8303–104/28; Cunningham to Wavell, August 8, 1943, NAM 8303–104/28; Wavell to Cunningham, August 13, 1943, NAM 8303–104/28.

37. Danchev and Todman (eds.), *Field Marshal Lord Alanbrooke*, October 26, 1944 (p. 615). Cunningham to MP Lieutenant Colonel Colin Thornton-Kemsley, April 1, 1944, NAM 8303–104/28; Lieutenant General Sir Oliver Lees to Cunningham, December 5, 1943, MECA, CP.B6, F4/91. Lees, who succeeded Cunningham when the latter was posted to Palestine, wrote him about the discussions concerning the possible abolition of Eastern Command.

38. J. R. Colville, *Man of Valour: The Life of Field-Marshal the Viscount Gort*, London 1972, pp. 259–266; Viscount Montgomery of Alamein, *The Memoirs of Field Marshal Montgomery*, Barnsley (1958) 2007, pp. 51–66; Smart, *Biographical Dictionary of British Generals*, p. 124; "A High Commissioner Goes and a High Commissioner Comes, but the White Paper Still Exists," *Hatzofeh*, November 11, 1945; Hall to Gort, November 31, 1945, NA Co967/94; Shaw to Hall, November 5, 1945, NA Co967/94; and Gort to Shaw, November 6, 1945, NA Co967/94.

39. Colville, *Man of Valour*, pp. 264–266.

40. On Bevin's approach, see Avraham Rosenthal, "Last High Commissioner Reveals for First Time: 'Bevin Wanted Immediate Evacuation from Land of Israel, Montgomery Delayed It by Three Months'," *Yedioth Ahronoth*, April 23, 1958; Cunningham wrote to Foreign Secretary Douglas-Home in regard to Hall's approach on behalf of Attlee, July 15, 1971, NAM 8303–104/28; *Hatzofeh* correspondent in London, November 12, 1945; BGA, Ben-Gurion Diary, November 23, 1945; S. of S. for Colonies (Hall) to O. A. G. Palestine (Shaw), November 8, 1945, NA C0967/94.

41. S. of S. for Colonies (Hall) to O. A. G. Palestine (Shaw), November 8, 1945, NA C0967/94; Cunningham to Shaw, November 9, 1945, MECA CP, B5 F5/3; *Hatzofeh* correspondent in London, November 12, 1945; Hall to Cunningham, November 13, 1945, MECA, CP.B6, F5/94; "G. H. Hall, by His Majesty's Command, Commission Appointment to Be His Majesty's High Commissioner for Palestine and Trans-Jordan, November 19, 1945," NAM 8303–104/28; Conversation of senior officials in Colonial Office with Cunningham, November 14, 1945, NA C0537/1822. A letter sent by Cunningham's successor in Eastern Command suggests that they did not meet: Lieutenant General Lees to Cunningham, December 5, 1945, MECA CP, B6, F4/91.

42. Cunningham to Hall, November 21, 1945, NA C0967/94.

43. Lieutenant General Smith (formerly chief of staff, Middle East Command, who had been involved in Cunningham's removal and now held the equivalent post in India) to Cunningham, November 11, 1945, MECA CP, B6, F5/42; Hall to Cunningham, November 13, 1945, MECA CP, B6, F5/42; Cunningham to Douglas-Home, July 15, 1971, NAM 8303–104/28.

44. Some in the Yishuv thought that the Night of the Trains was the cause of Gort's departure. On November 6, 1945, *Ha'aretz* dismissed this conjecture and reported that the National Committee had announced with regret that the high commissioner was ill and that his successor was expected within a short time. On November 9, *Ha'aretz* reported on Gort's replacement.

A Political Process as Though There Is No Terrorism

November 1945–
December 1946

1   The Only Chance for Palestine Is Partition

Cunningham arrived in Jerusalem on Wednesday November 21, 1945, via the international airport in Lod. The official reception reflected the dual character of his mission: military and civilian. On the tarmac, he was welcomed by the chief secretary, the commander of the British Army in Palestine, and by air force and navy commanders in the Middle East; at the gates of Jerusalem, he was met by the Jerusalem district governor, the army commander, the chief of police, and the mayor; and on Julian's Way (now King David Street), the convoy was joined by mounted troops from the Transjordan Frontier Force and from the Palestine Police.[1]

The reception ceremony was to have taken place adjacent to the site of General Edmund Allenby's camp in the south of the city, near Government House. Cunningham was to have reviewed a guard of honor from the Highland Light Infantry Regiment, the unit that would provide his security during his two-and-a-half-year stay in the city. The chief secretary had planned to escort the incoming high commissioner under a canopy, where the district governor was to present the invited guests. The invitation mentioned "formal and informal guests," and they included both Jews and Arabs. However, rain forced the cancellation of the outdoor ceremony, so Cunningham, his close aides, and the mounted units proceeded straight to Government House at Jabel Mukaber (the traditional site of the Hill of Evil Counsel), which contained the high commissioner's residence and office.[2]

Government House was conceived in 1927, when Augusta Victoria, the former high commissioner's residence on Mount Scopus, was damaged in an earthquake. A new compound was built, which accommodated the high commissioner from the beginning of the 1930s and was also a symbol of the Mandate administration. The central building was designed by the British architect Austen Harrison, who also designed the Rockefeller Museum in the city's eastern section. In addition to the two-story main building—the ground floor devoted to offices and receptions, the private residence upstairs—the compound had accommodations for the administrative and grounds staff. Cunningham was delighted to discover that the main building was surrounded by a large, splendid garden, whose northern part offered a view of the Old City, including the Temple Mount and the Church of the Holy Sepulchre. There was also a space set aside by his predecessors as a cemetery for pet dogs.[3]

On the afternoon of Cunningham's arrival, the letter of appointment was read out in the ground-floor ballroom by the secretary of the executive council of the Mandate administration. The text was then recited in Hebrew and Arabic by the administration's chief interpreters. The guests obeyed the invitation and arrived in formal morning dress, complete with medals and decorations. Sir William Fitzgerald, the chief justice of the Supreme Court of Mandate Palestine, who was trusted by both Jews and Arabs, administered the oath of office to Cunningham. He supplemented his congratulations with a cautionary note. You will encounter here an atmosphere of civilian tension, he told the new high commissioner, which will call for extraordinary security measures aimed not only at the enemy storming the gates but also at destructive forces threatening from within.

In attendance were the mayors of the big cities, the heads of the Arab Higher Committee, and the leaders of the Jewish National Council and the Jewish Agency, among them David Ben-Gurion, who had returned from a visit abroad earlier in the day. The ceremony was aired live by the Palestine Broadcast Service, with commentary provided by the station's director, Edwin Samuel, the son of the first high commissioner to Palestine. There was no unusual activity in the streets of Jerusalem that day.[4]

Cunningham thanked the guests briefly. He was touched that both the written congratulations he had received at the airport and the spoken comments at the ceremony cited his past activity positively. He also thanked the Mandate administrative staff, who were responsible to him, and the officers and soldiers under his command, and noted that even though he had not yet doffed his uniform in his new post, he was taking his leave of the army. He had come to fulfill what was, above all, a civilian function. He said that the collective British memory and his awareness of the postwar geopolitical situation taught him that a zero-sum game was being played out in Palestine: Britain would have a hard time getting the adversaries to consider a possible political solution. In light of this, he reminded those present that it was Britain and its allies (and, implicitly, Cunningham personally) that had saved Palestine from a German invasion. His principal goal was to ensure a good future for everyone; to this end he wished to instill in his new place of service the consensual atmosphere that had prevailed among the Allies during the war, and he would be ready to cooperate with all well-intentioned people. Cunningham reminded his listeners of the British government's early November announcement that the United States had agreed to take part in the committee of inquiry whose members were en route to Palestine. This last point was an allusion to the possibility of a political solution aided by the Americans, an option then preoccupying the Colonial Office in London. Cunningham also cautiously alluded to the Jewish revolt, which was then in its nascent stage and was still viewed by the British as a random series of violent events perpetrated by the Yishuv. His brief remarks make it clear that he knew he faced a difficult mission. He wanted it to be known that he had come to Palestine with little knowledge of the country but without prejudice and that he was determined to help it blossom.[5]

Six days later, on November 27, 1945, Cunningham attended the ceremony of his other appointment: high commissioner and supreme commander of the armed forces of Transjordan. (This second title, held by each high commissioner in Jerusalem since 1928, expired in May 1946, when Transjordan became independent.) Cunningham spent only six hours in Amman, and dined with the Emir Abdullah. He was escorted by the two senior British figures in Transjordan, Sir Alec Kirkbride, the resident minister in Amman, soon to become the ambassador to the Hashemite Kingdom of Jordan, and Lieutenant General Sir John Bagot Glubb, the commander of Transjordan's Arab Legion.[6]

On December 14, the new high commissioner and supreme commander of the armed forces in Palestine and Transjordan reminded the War Office that he should be promoted to the rank of general, commensurate with his new duties. He did not wait for the routine procedures; waiting could be detrimental to his interests. Prior to his appointment, the Colonial Office had informed him that as high commissioner he would have to retire from the army. However, he was reassured by the War Office that the extension of his service for one year, in order to bring about his promotion, was being positively considered—promotion would be impossible if he were retired or did not have at least a year of service ahead of him. Indeed, his term of service was extended until October 30, 1946. In January 1946, the War Office informed him that the rank of general had been approved for him retroactive to October 30, 1945. An announcement to this effect would appear on January 29, 1946, in the *London Gazette*, the official newspaper of record in the United Kingdom. Cunningham thus gained the recognition—formal, at this stage—for which he had longed since the fiasco in the Western Desert five years earlier. At the end of September 1946, the War Office duly informed him that, effective October 30, he would conclude his active service and be transferred to the reserves until May 1, 1949, unless he was otherwise informed. After that date, he would be fully retired. The letter concluded on a formal note, though not without personal significance for him: the secretary of state for war thanked him at the king's directive for his long and devoted military service.[7]

Holding the rank of general also bore practical significance for Cunningham's Palestine service. It was clear to both him and to London that the high commissioner's rank and status in Britain contributed to the way he was perceived in the country under his authority. In the case of Palestine, this was particularly important in his contacts with the Yishuv, which was in the midst of a confrontation with the Mandate administration. Indeed, the president of the National Council, Yitzhak Ben-Zvi, congratulated Cunningham on his promotion. Ben-Zvi's message was a formal one, on behalf of the body he headed, but at the same time very personal. At that point, General Cunningham did not know that the National Council and its leader had long since ceased to be a meaningful factor in the Zionist movement's national and international politics. The Jewish Agency and its head, David Ben-Gurion, did not extend congratulations. Cunningham's emotional response to Ben-Zvi's gesture shows how unusual this letter was in the relations between the Mandate authorities and the Yishuv at that time.[8]

The Yishuv knew very little about the new high commissioner. So little, in fact, that at first the Jewish community made much of an unconfirmed episode supposedly showing that the commander of the southern sector of the British campaign in Ethiopia in 1941 was a close friend of Major General Orde Charles Wingate. Wingate, an innovative British officer who served in Palestine during the period of the Arab Revolt, was pro-Zionist and revered by the Yishuv. The story went that Wingate told Cunningham, during their joint expedition from Kenya to Addis Ababa, of his aspiration to establish a Jewish state. This connection ostensibly boosted Cunningham's prestige in the eyes of the Yishuv. In reality, it is not clear what sort of relations existed between Wingate and Cunningham. Certainly, the two were not together during the push to Addis Ababa, though they did meet afterward in the Ethiopian capital. Cunningham removed Wingate from Ethiopia for the same reason that he had been removed from Palestine earlier: excessive independence.[9]

Two days after his arrival in Jerusalem, Cunningham met with a Yishuv delegation for a get-acquainted talk. The participants, representing a cross section of the Jewish community, were personally invited by the high commissioner's advisors so that he could hear a range of approaches. In the event, David Ben-Gurion spoke and the others assented. The chairman of the Jewish Agency Executive praised the high commissioner as the king's representative and a "freedom-fighting soldier," but without giving him a moment's grace noted the rift between Britain and the Zionist movement: "The blow is most bitter when it comes from a friend—the English people, our friend." Ben-Gurion said he could not promise to act against the violence emanating from the Yishuv—for which the Jewish Agency refused to accept responsibility—unless the regulations of the 1939 White Paper were rescinded. "We parted tensely and courteously," Ben-Gurion wrote in his diary after his first meeting with Cunningham.[10]

The *History of the Haganah*, the closest work to an official Yishuv history, which reflected the approach of the leadership of the organized Jewish community, offers an unfounded appraisal of the new high commissioner, probably gleaned from Ben-Gurion himself. It shows wishful thinking, expresses regret at Gort's departure, and alludes to the Western Desert episode:

> The British began to prepare for riots that were liable to break out in the country following a public declaration of their policy [Bevin's address to the House of Commons on November 13], and this time on the part of the Jews. Lord Gort, who refused to accept the new policy line, resigned as high commissioner "for reasons of health." He was replaced by another army man, Lieutenant General Sir Alan Cunningham, "a fair man but weak" (D. Ben-Gurion).[11]

In contrast, the Yishuv press, particularly the nonestablishment papers, took a generally positive approach to the new high commissioner. As in the past, a high commissioner with a military background was perceived as the antithesis of the bureaucracy of the Colonial Office, which was generally considered hostile to the Yishuv.[12] The fact that the appointment had been made within two days of Gort's resignation was taken as evidence of the importance that London attached to Palestine. And the fact that a military man had been chosen was seen as reflecting awareness of the problematic nature of Palestine and as proof that the political question would be resolved in London and other capitals, not in Jerusalem. According to this point of view, the Mandate administration had the temporary role of imposing order until a political solution could be found.

The new high commissioner would only carry out orders. His arrival thus dovetailed with the Yishuv's growing expectation of the establishment of a Jewish state and a period of quiet and security, internal and external. According to the contemporary Yishuv press, not everyone applauded the Jewish Agency's declaration of the Jewish Resistance Movement in October 1945. In contrast, the Palestine Arabs, according to their newspapers, believed that a military figure had been appointed in order to deal with Zionist violence.[13]

Along with this positive spin by the Yishuv press, an implicit threat was also discernible, originating mainly in labor movement newspapers but probably reflecting a broader outlook. In this view, the new high commissioner would be given a chance, but his ideas would be judged from a strictly practical point of view: it made no difference whether he was personally likable. The press abstracts read by Cunningham suggested that the Yishuv was determined to fight the policy advocated by the 1939 White Paper and that its battle was not with Britain and its troops but with British policy. These were not mere words, as Cunningham was to discover immediately.[14]

———————

On November 13, 1945, the day on which Cunningham's appointment was approved in London and a week before his arrival in Jerusalem, British foreign secretary Ernest Bevin informed the House of Commons that an Anglo-American Committee of Inquiry had been established to examine and recommend an agreed policy for Palestine by the two powers. The next day, a stormy rally against British policy in Palestine was held in Tel Aviv, with the Yishuv reacting furiously to the foreign secretary's statement that the White Paper policy would not be revised at this time and to his comment that the question of the Jewish refugees must be solved in Europe, in their places of origin. Six demonstrators were killed and many wounded. On November 25, in reaction to the British interception of the *Berl Katznelson*, a ship carrying illegal immigrants, Palmah commandos blew up the shore-patrol stations at Sidna Ali, next to Herzliya, and at Givat Olga, outside Hadera. In response, the British security forces systematically searched suspects, along with imposing a curfew and closure of the Sharon area, north of Herzliya. The security operation targeted the agricultural hinterland of Herzliya and Hadera, the Palmah's staging ground. The British moves triggered an unguided and uncontrolled popular response. Thousands tried to break the curfew imposed on Kibbutz Shfayim and on the farming village of Rishpon, north of Herzliya, and the Jews acted with even more intensity in the area of Kibbutz Givat Haim and Kibbutz Hogla, south of Hadera, in order to hamper the search operations. Eight people were killed by police and army fire—and not a week had passed since Cunningham took office.[15]

A perusal of the Hebrew press could have indicated to the new high commissioner that the Yishuv placed very high hopes—perhaps too high—on Britain and its new senior representative. The Resistance Movement was already a reality, though incipient; its implications had not yet been fully grasped, either by the Yishuv or by the administration. This new reality was also expressed in the form of critical remarks from some quarters, alongside the generally favorable reception accorded Cunningham. On the right, the newspaper *Haboker* threatened that the high commissioner would find a community on the brink of its patience; while on the left, *Mishmar* lamented, "This is not how we envisaged the arrival of the first high commissioner in peacetime, the first under the rule of the Labour Party in Britain."[16]

Overall, the foreign secretary's announcement of the creation of the Anglo-American Committee, and, foremost, the content of the announcement, threw a damper on the Yishuv's reception of the new high commissioner. On the day of Cunningham's arrival, *Ha'aretz* noted that, in light of the committee's establishment, it appeared that the high commissioner had been appointed to lead a transition period toward a trusteeship regime, but he would find it difficult to gain the cooperation of the local population. Accordingly, the paper editorialized, the high commissioner's personal behavior would assume surpassing importance: he would need to be friendly, sociable, and not be a nuisance. Many in the Yishuv were under the sway of the one-year tenure of Cunningham's immediate predecessor, Gort, whom they perceived as a likable old fellow who was not involved in weighty policy issues and was seen as the polar opposite of his hostile predecessor, Sir Harold MacMichael (1938–1944). No one believed in the goodwill of the British government. Accordingly, the Yishuv wanted, at the least, for its new representative, like Gort before him, to project a positive approach until a desirable political decision was made, undoubtedly with American intervention.[17]

The declared mission of the Anglo-American Committee was to recommend to the British government a desirable policy to be coordinated with the United States, a senior ally with which it was at odds on the Palestine question. For half a year, from November 1945 until the following April, the committee's work stifled the political debate and curbed the handling of Jewish terrorism. In this situation, no other diplomatic initiatives could be put forward, but at the same time the committee's efforts brought about restraint by both London and the Mandate administration vis-à-vis Yishuv-perpetrated violence.

The political-military paralysis that the committee's work imposed on the high commissioner constrained his ability to respond to events on the ground, but was also a blessing in that it disinclined him from taking rash measures before acquainting himself with the intricacies of the situation and articulating a position. By the time the committee completed its work and published its report, on April 20, 1946 (the report was officially submitted to the two governments on May 1), Cunningham had been in the country long enough to form an opinion on the local conflict. Immediately upon his arrival in Jerusalem, he had to cope with events that would repeat themselves numberless times in the next two years; that is, to respond astutely to resistance activities that were part popular, part establishment, part fomented by trained guerilla groups, part by terrorists. The very first incidents were harbingers of what would preoccupy him in his contacts with the Yishuv: illegal immigration, popular reactions, and above all, political disagreement.

Amid this scene, a crucial problem began to emerge that largely overshadowed the serious challenges posed by the Yishuv. It became necessary to issue clearer directives to the security forces about how to behave in the face of the demonstrations and the violence originating in the organized Yishuv. The eight civilians killed on November 26, 1945, were still an "appetizer," coming on top of the six who were killed in the demonstration against Bevin's speech, two weeks earlier. The Mandate security forces clearly lacked a guiding hand, and equally obvious was the substandard professional level of police operating as an army, and worse—of an army operating as a police force.

On November 29, Cunningham visited the Jewish communities for the first time. One stop was at Beit Eshel, in the northern Negev, where he took an interest in agricultural experiments being carried out in desert soil. He went on to pay a lightning visit to Kibbutz Negba, which had been established as part of Zionist-British cooperation at the end of the 1930s, during the Arab Revolt. The tour was a response to a remark in the press, whose translation he had read on the eve of his arrival, that visits to Jewish communities by high commissioners had stopped almost entirely since the term of General Arthur Wauchope, who left Palestine in 1938.[18]

On December 4–5, he visited Haifa, the most salient example of a mixed Jewish-Arab city. The first part of the visit was devoted to the British presence in Haifa: the port, the oil refineries, the train station, and of course a call on the district governor. Cunningham then met with the Municipal Council, a mixed body, reflecting the city's ethnic makeup, under the mayor, Shabtai Levy. In his remarks, Cunningham noted that he was the first high commissioner appointed after the war—an expression of the great expectations being held out for him by all the country's inhabitants. Mayor Levy explained to him that in Haifa, he and the city's residents rose above "political considerations" involving relations between Jews and Arabs and between the municipality and the district and central administrations. This was undoubtedly meant as a comment on the relations between the Yishuv and the administration, which had soured against the background of the resistance actions in general and the events of the past month in particular. In Haifa, Cunningham found a desirable model of governance throughout Palestine. Indeed, the city, a vital Middle Eastern site for the British Empire, could have been the mainstay of its rule and a potentially successful model for a political solution acceptable to both Jews and Arabs—a success to which Cunningham aspired. In his remarks, he forecast a brilliant future for the city. He and his superiors were perfectly sincere about this sentiment.

Cunningham paid a first visit to an Arab city—Nablus—on December 15. Probably only routine greetings were exchanged. In any event, Cunningham's staff did not transcribe his remarks on this occasion.[19]

On December 18, Cunningham undertook a key visit, in terms of his work with the Yishuv, to Tel Aviv, the "first Jewish city" and the largest in the country, the political, economic, and cultural hub of the Jewish community of Palestine. However, the height of the expectations was matched only by the depth of the disappointment in the actual visit. This Jewish bastion took little account of the new head of government in the country. Cunningham himself, curious about the most modern city in Palestine, came for a visit to get acquainted and learn. Yet the mayor, Israel Rokach, did not spare him withering criticism, possibly giving personal offense and projecting a spirit contrary to that of Zionist-British cooperation which transcends narrow interests. The mayor expressed his regret at the departure of the ailing Gort, whom he called a "well-known soldier," whereas Cunningham was only a "bold soldier." The mayor obviously had no idea how sensitive his guest was on this point. Worse, Rokach used the term *bitterness* in describing his feelings about the administration's approach to the richest city in the country, which, he said, the British authorities milked for its money without doing anything for its development, even though the war was over. This remark, honest but far from polite in the circumstances, provoked Cunningham to lose his patience in public for the first time. Officers who had served under him in the Second World War were only too familiar with his outbursts, but now he forgot that he was no longer on the front and that the speakers were not his soldiers. He pointed out that nothing good would come of this style of speech, only to restrain himself immediately. As head of the supreme civilian authority, he knew that a moderate tone was essential if he wanted to succeed. In the tense atmosphere of Palestine at the time, style was substance. He declared that the visit to Tel Aviv was meaningful for him. He also lost no time in dealing with Rokach's complaints. In the spirit of British imperialism, he linked the good of the local population with the good of the empire and suggested to his superiors that they make a loan to the Tel Aviv municipality. The idea was given favorable consideration, but it soon became apparent to the high commissioner that matters were not so simple, owing to the general deterioration in the Yishuv's relations with the administration. When he learned that administration-appointed local authorities were collecting money for the Jewish illegal immigrants, he froze their budgets.[20]

Before the end of 1945 and within less than a month of taking office, Cunningham visited the principal urban centers of the Yishuv and the rural periphery. He came away from these visits with the certain knowledge that none of his interlocutors on the Jewish side, including the critics of British policy, denied the authority of the Mandate administration or of Britain itself. He had been addressed like the envoy of a familiar landlord and showered with complaints and requests for a revision of policy and a rethinking of the general approach to the Yishuv. In the same spirit, the Jewish Resistance Movement sought a change of policy by Britain, not a change of administration. Grasping this, Cunningham, in his meetings and contacts with the Jewish public at the start of his term of office, emphasized that he was the first high commissioner in peacetime; that his personal mission was to manage the country properly and see to its development; and that he sought to bring about a political agreement between the Jews and the Arabs (though he had not yet addressed this last point concretely).[21]

Did Cunningham not feel the ground shaking under his feet? The anti-British violence by the Jews, which had ceased in 1939 when the war broke out, erupted again in October 1945. The first months of the new high commissioner's tenure were very turbulent. The peak was the murder of seven British soldiers in their sleep at a parking lot in Tel Aviv by members of Lehi on the night of April 25, 1946. The carnage badly rattled the administration.

By the end of January 1946, it was apparent to Cunningham that the Yishuv constituted the dynamic element in the country: its actions shaped the local agenda. He was able to distinguish between majority and minority in the Yishuv, both quantitatively and qualitatively, between the organized Yishuv and the extremist minority that had broken away from it, between terrorists and the Haganah semi-underground organization and within it the Palmah, the Haganah's strike force, which carried out most of the resistance operations. Cunningham also understood the public's emotional opposition to Britain, along with the inherent duality of Zionist policy, which desperately yearned for the Britain of the Balfour Declaration and sought a reason to abandon terrorism. It had not taken Cunningham long to discern these subtleties. This awareness would be the prelude to Cunningham's difficult and painful relationship with the Yishuv, whose leadership, and still more the Jewish public, was neither willing nor able to grasp that he increasingly sympathized with its cause.

Though Cunningham's focus was the Yishuv—and ever more so as time passed—he did not ignore the Palestine Arabs. Increasingly, however, he perceived them as a community that did not take the initiative but instead responded to the Jews' actions. In the winter of 1946, he believed that the Arabs were showing signs of incipient communal organizing that, in the best case—if they accepted the economic advantages of the Mandate and rehabilitated their economy, which had not recovered from the Arab Revolt of 1936–1939—would enable them to help bring about calm in the country. In the worst case, he thought, they were likely to clash with the Jews and with the administration but with no chance of a significant achievement.[22]

At the end of April 1946, Cunningham believed he could sum up the present situation and future intentions of the Palestine Arab community. His first report on this subject, though reflecting his superficial thinking and scant knowledge, drew on the experience of more than two decades accumulated by the Mandate administration. The high commissioner addressed the question of whether the Palestine Arabs intended to or had the capability to generate a violent confrontation. His conclusion was that the majority of Palestine Arabs were disinclined to resort to politically motivated violence; the evidence suggested that violence might flare up under certain circumstances. Overall, the Arabs of Palestine were still reeling from their defeat in the Arab Revolt and were heartily fed up with gang wars, extortion, and murder. In Cunningham's view, they were anxious about the future and weary of the events of the recent past and of the adversity inflicted on them by the British security forces.[23]

Cunningham sometimes showed a patronizing, prejudicial approach. Thus, he found the transition by the local Arabs—from flagrant hostility during the uprising in the 1930s to an enthusiastic welcome for the administrative personnel after the Second World War—embarrassing and typical of a Semitic population. "Even when they [British officials] are not armed, they are received in the villages with great honor," he noted, whether innocently or superciliously. His explanation for this shift was the dramatic improvement in the economic situation, in particular of the landless fellahin. Before the war, they were at the mercy of the landowners, whereas now they enjoyed security, rights, and a market for their produce. This, together with the relentless suppression of the revolt, he believed, had left the majority of the country's Arabs uninterested in politics and had halted the wartime popularity of those supporting the mufti, Haj Amin al-Husseini, and the Nazis. In Cunningham's view, the Palestine Arabs knew that, in contrast to the situation under Ottoman rule, the British colonial system and the boon to Palestine in the wake of the Second World War ensured a more equitable distribution of the country's resources.[24]

Nevertheless, there was disquiet among the Palestine Arabs, caused by their fear of the Zionist movement's dominance and the Jewish Agency's constant invocation of the Biltmore Program of 1942 (adopted at the Biltmore Hotel in New York), which demanded the whole country for the Jews. This situation, he noted, stirred no enthusiasm within the Arab public. At the same time, the Arabs of Palestine would not rise up unless they were presented with a political initiative that they considered especially threatening. As for the Arab Higher Committee, Cunningham assessed that even if its members were usually at odds with one another, a significant political crisis could unite them in a joint national struggle. Proof of this came with their response on the eve of the publication of the Anglo-American Committee's report, in April 1946. In the works were a boycott, demonstrations, and a general strike under AHC auspices. Nevertheless, Cunningham had his doubts whether members of the Palestine Arab leadership would again be willing, as in the 1930s, to pay a personal price in the form of expulsion or imprisonment. In any event, the high commissioner considered those two forms of punishment effective weapons against local Arab leaders—and, as would soon become apparent, against Jewish leaders too.

From the outset, the Palestine Arab press made it clear to the new high commissioner that the point of departure for any future political agreements was the Arabs' majority status in the country. Accordingly, any such agreement was to be based on a ratio of two thirds for the Arabs and one third for the Jews. In retrospect, we can see that Cunningham underestimated the depth of the Arabs' enmity for Zionism and also their ability—and will—to act. He believed that the Arabs could be brought around to a solution that they would find at least tolerable, even if temporarily.[25]

The fact that no significant Arab activity occurred until the fall of 1947 adversely affected the administration's analysis of the Arab community's intentions. The documents in the Mandate administration's thin dossier dealing with the AHC in 1946–1947 are mainly requests for information from intelligence agencies about Palestinian personalities and their politics. In August 1947, Cunningham acknowledged that for information about the AHC he depended almost completely on the Arab press. This approach was in stark contrast to his interest in Zionist politics, even if his knowledge of the Yishuv did not always improve his analyses. Furthermore, his focus on internal political struggles with his former British Army colleagues in Palestine and with the Yishuv left him less interested in the Arab community and, hence, less well informed. Increasingly, he adopted a policy of assuagement, believing that the Arabs' ability to move from talk to deeds was limited and that, in any event, they should not be given reasons to try. Cunningham stuck by this assessment until August–September 1947, when Arab violence surged.[26]

By the end of January 1946, Cunningham's initial optimism had all but vanished; his mission now seemed impossible. The intensifying Jewish terrorism was compounded by the Jewish Agency's general backing of the acts of terror and, more significant for Cunningham, by the activity of the Anglo-American Committee, which arrived in Palestine at the beginning of March after spending most of the first two months of 1946 in Europe.

The high commissioner summed up the situation as he saw it in January 1946, after two months in Jerusalem, in a personal letter to the colonial secretary:

> I think it is my duty to bring to your notice . . . the following: We are trying, in between outrages, to carry on a normal administration under

"peace" conditions. The conditions however are nearer those of war than of peace. Most of the Jewish population is against the government in sentiment, while the terrorists and the unlawful organizations, heavily armed, equipped, well-trained and holding the initiative as is necessarily the case, periodically exploit the situation by force of arms with greater or less success to themselves and loss of life and property to the Government. So long as these conditions persist it is inevitable that risks have to be taken which might be susceptible of elimination if the Government could come out into the open and face the situation, by giving up all pretense of normal administration (as was indeed done to some extent in the Arab rebellion of 1938/9), concentrating essential activities in wired perimeters etc., and directing all its resources and energies to the forcible suppression of the armed opposition to the Government. I do not suggest that these measures should be taken at present, and indeed it would be impossible to take them and at the same time to receive the international Committee in the country. But I do think it is advisable that the issue as above should be squarely placed before you. The General Officer Commanding [D'Arcy] is in agreement with my views.[27]

Even at this early stage, then, Cunningham saw clearly that he could not afford to give even a semblance of concession or surrender. His analysis offers a broad albeit not-yet-cohesive indication of the measures he would take in the months ahead. This followed a short but intensive period in which he sought to place the Mandatory entity under his rule on a course of rehabilitation and peacetime development. In general, a certain lassitude affected the postwar British colonial administrations, compounded by a sense of the empire's looming dismantlement. The new Labour government in Britain believed that the only chance to preserve the country's status as a world power lay in the colonies' economic, social, and political rehabilitation and in an effort to work with them as partners, not as vassals.[28]

In Palestine, however, the high commissioner was hamstrung by the operations of the Jewish Resistance Movement and, more significantly, the work of the Anglo-American Committee. Repeatedly targeted in terrorist attacks yet unable to strike back forcefully because of the activity of the joint committee, the administration found that this state of affairs also made it impossible to press ahead with development projects. The problem was that the committee was not under the control of the Mandate administration or under the full control of the government in London; Washington was now also in the thick of things, at London's behest. With an official American fact-finding mission in the country, the use of military force was ruled out. As long as the committee was in Palestine, Cunningham was prohibited from initiating operations against Jewish terrorists and from generating a political discussion.

Cunningham had been appointed by a newly installed government. In large measure, his mission, and his knowledge of and approach to the Palestine question, developed in a learning process parallel to that of the Labour government itself, in some instances involving disagreement with the government. The new high commissioner did not come to Jerusalem with a full-blown doctrine. In the few days between his agreement to assume the post in Jerusalem—despite his ignorance of the region and its conflict—and his departure, even before the appointment formally took effect, he ensconced himself in the Colonial Office for a crash course on the country he was about to govern. He was particularly struck by two of the documents he was shown, one containing the gist of Colonial Secretary Hall's approach to the Palestine question, the other outlining Foreign Secretary Bevin's policy on the subject. Between them, the two documents highlighted the main contours of the disagreements within the government over Palestine and set the political direction for a solution. Together, they constituted the anvil on which the new Labour government and the new high commissioner forged their policy.[29]

On the day of Cunningham's arrival in Jerusalem, the London *Times* devoted its editorial to the Palestine quandary. Despite the difficulty and sensitivity entailed in Sir Alan's task, the paper noted, the Jews' and Arabs' shared dependence on the West heightened the prospect of finding a solution. At bottom, this entailed the partition of Palestine. The paper took a wider perspective, placing the Palestine issue within the framework of the shaping of the international reality after the Second World War and what would soon become known as the Cold War. From this point of view, the *Times* argued, the only possible solution was partition based on the principles of the 1937 Peel Commission report. Violence would not serve anyone, including the British. The peaceful completion of the mission (i.e., partition) would benefit not only Britain but also the international order and, as such, help achieve the goals for which the world war had been fought. The editorial also devoted considerable space to the newly formed United Nations, noting that the nascent international organization could help promote a two-state solution.[30]

Underlying this evaluation was the assumption, also held by Cunningham, that success, as envisaged at the end of 1945, resided in a political plan acceptable to the parties to the dispute in Palestine, to Britain, and above all to the United States—and under British-American auspices. That assumption remained basically unchanged until the beginning of 1947, and in large measure even afterward, until the decision by the British government in September 1947 to leave Palestine. If, as is likely, the high commissioner read the *Times* editorial, he would have discerned that if the paper's opinion differed from that of the government majority—which backed a binational solution—it was close to that of his immediate superior, Colonial Secretary Hall.

Hall was the first to propose to the Labour government a policy on the Palestine question. His approach was formulated already in August 1945, in a memorandum he submitted to the new government after studying the issue for several weeks. The memorandum is notably free of the constraints that would characterize the language of future proposals, to the consternation of the policy-making echelon. In fact, what Hall proposed was basically identical to the Palestine clause in Labour's platform in the elections just held. Thus, in August 1945, Hall maintained that British policy in Palestine stood no chance of success if it failed to account for the radical differences between the two sides in character, culture, society, religion, and language, along with the contradictory nature of their political ambitions. What was good for the one was bad for the other. Moreover, neither side had a moral commitment to a one-state solution or any desire for that outcome. Consequently, a binational state was out of the question. It followed, Hall wrote, that British policy in Palestine should be based on separation or partition. Hall, though, did not dare propose the creation of two nation-states, in the spirit of 1937, but thought in terms of local or provincial autonomy. The Mandate administration, he proposed cautiously, would continue to stand above the autonomous provinces, be responsible for external affairs, defense, and national infrastructures, and supervise the work of the local-regional authorities. Jerusalem would remain under British responsibility. Hall believed that an India-like administrative division of powers, based on shared economic resources, stood a chance of success.

Partition along these lines, Hall maintained, would enable Britain to meet its dual commitment as enshrined in the Balfour Declaration (1917) and the Mandate (1922–1924). Hall's memorandum suggests that in the summer of 1945, some senior British officials, at least in the Colonial Office, were not eager to go on ruling Palestine. However, the government was not yet ripe for a return to the two-state partition concept. Hall thus confined himself to invoking partition/separation as a principle; the colonial secretary was a year ahead of the government. In any event, this approach marked a retreat from the policy espoused in the White Paper of May 1939. The high commissioner's emergent approach showed that he appeared to have internalized Hall's viewpoint.[31]

In addition to absorbing Hall's views, Cunningham took note of the policy enunciated by Foreign Secretary Bevin in his memorandum of November 1, 1945, and his statement to the House of Commons two weeks later. Bevin's approach was in the main a response to American policy on the Palestine question, which sought the absorption of as many refugees as possible. His address set forth Britain's official opening position upon the establishment of the Anglo-American Committee. Bevin was out to counterbalance and perhaps annul altogether the partition approach suggested by the colonial secretary. His address to Parliament should be seen in the context of the Foreign Office's effort to become the decisive voice in setting government policy on the Palestine question in particular and the colonies in general. These power relations between the Foreign Office and the Colonial Office were firmly grounded in the empire's decline on the one hand and the recognition of an emerging East-West confrontation on the other. Bevin's policy on Palestine, which boiled down to the creation of a binational state in one form or another, became the British government's policy at least until the beginning of 1948, when Britain secretly started to promote the country's partition between the Kingdom of Jordan and the future State of Israel.[32]

Hall did not accept this policy and paid for his intransigence by being removed from office a year later. Cunningham himself leaned toward his minister's opposition stance. Bevin's speech in the House of Commons, which showed no readiness to meet the Zionists' demand for a return to the Balfour Declaration policy, and equally his announcement that the government would not differentiate between the Palestine question and the problem of the Jewish displaced persons, unleashed a new level of violent protest by the Jews. From Cunningham's window in Government House, London seemed to be cooking its own goose. He agreed that nothing good would come of riling the Arabs, but why do it to the Jews, and more so to the Americans? At this early stage, he had more questions than answers.

As the Anglo-American Committee went about its business, it appeared to Cunningham that everyone connected with the Palestine question was in the wrong. Not only his government, under the American aegis, had erred in setting a Palestine agenda consisting more of propaganda than substance; after a few months in the country, Cunningham was also critical of the path chosen by the Arabs and especially by the Jews.

The Jewish Agency was unaware of the internal government debate in London. Its expectation was of a dramatic and positive change in British policy. When those hopes appeared to be dashed, violence ensued. Statements made by the Jewish Agency's leaders in the heat of the struggle against British policy disquieted Cunningham. Such statements were, he believed, largely responsible for the anti-British mood among the Jewish public, which had intensified since October 1945. The Jewish leadership claimed that the Yishuv was capable of overcoming the Palestine Arabs alone, without British or American aid. This conflation of reality with an inflated image of the Haganah was intended to reduce the Jewish public's fear of the Arabs' reaction if Jewish refugees were permitted to enter the country or a decision to partition the country was made. The Jewish Agency's reactions to the work of the joint committee were a source of substantial information for Cunningham about the Yishuv leadership's aggressive mind-set and its self-confidence.[33]

It was clear to Cunningham that young Jews were chomping at the bit to engage in anti-British activity, so much so that the leadership was apt to lose its authority by curbing them. The direct beneficiaries of this state of affairs, in Cunningham's view, were Etzel (Irgun) and Lehi (Stern gang). Nevertheless, he believed that at bottom, despite the Jewish public's growing sympathy for terrorism perpetrated under the auspices of the Jewish Resistance Movement and the breakaway organizations—which ordinarily were ostracized—the organized Yishuv and its leadership sought a political solution with all their might. That solution, he understood, was partition, even if these leaders did not admit this publicly. As early as February 1946, amid the Jewish terror offensive and a radicalization in the statements of the Yishuv leaders against both Britain and Cunningham personally, the high commissioner wrote to Hall, "It is perhaps worth mentioning that there are increasing signs that the Jewish leaders would accept partition as a solution. . . . [A]ny other solution would probably not result in easement of the tension for it is the extremist tail that wags the dog."[34]

This, the high commissioner's first explicitly positive comment on partition as a preferred political solution, came two months before the

Anglo-American Committee quashed the idea in its report. Beginning in the spring of 1946, then, his mission was to persuade his government and the Jewish Agency that partition into two nation-states was the preferred option, and of course to demonstrate that the Palestine Arabs would agree to such a solution.

The Anglo-American Committee arrived in Palestine on March 6, 1946, and spent three weeks in the country, until the twenty-eighth of the month. Terrorism was by now a major issue for Cunningham. He, along with the senior officials of the administration and the ranking officers of the security forces, was among those invited to testify before the committee. In the case of the high commissioner, the committee met with him at Government House. One of the committee's American members, Bartley Crum, a pro-Zionist who seemed to want partition more than the Zionists themselves at the time, was impressed by Cunningham's sincerity. The high commissioner left him with the clear impression that he, in contrast to his superiors, supported partition. Crum was aware that the high commissioner could not openly advocate a policy that was unacceptable to his government, but nevertheless the committee understood that Cunningham supported a partition plan that would be more generous to the Zionists than the Peel Commission plan of 1937.[35]

The high commissioner's testimony was different in spirit and content from that of the British officials and politicians in London and Palestine. They argued that the Jewish Agency should be dismantled and that its existence as a "state within a state" was intolerable. The first secretary, John Shaw, told the committee that he would agree to accept 100,000 Jewish refugees (the opening demand of the United States) only if the Jewish Agency and the Haganah were dismantled. Cunningham, in contrast to his position in his first weeks in office, vehemently opposed the dissolution of the Jewish Agency. More than three months before the administration's limited punitive operation (Operation Agatha; see chapter 3), the high commissioner told the joint committee that he would not want to see the Jewish Agency's eradication. He was not one of those who belittled its importance, he said. The administration might not be fond of the Jewish Agency, he added, but could not ignore it. The agency was a force that must be considered and with which the administration must work. In any event, there was no possibility to eradicate it. Cunningham felt that in the unstable conditions prevailing in Palestine the Jewish Agency most closely resembled the conception of governance that he espoused. It was with good reason that Moshe Shertok, the head of the Jewish Agency's Political

Department, later inveighed against the high commissioner for viewing the agency as though it were built in the image of the British governmental system.[36]

Based on Cunningham's testimony to the committee, it can be inferred that in March 1946, just four months after his arrival in Palestine, the high commissioner thought that only a political solution held out the hope of outlasting British rule in the country. To achieve a political—as opposed to a military—solution, he needed to know that those he interacted with wielded authority within their community. This he found in the Jewish community, less so among the Arabs. Their attempts to put forward the mufti, Haj Amin al-Husseini, as a recognized and representative leader were unrealistic after the Arab Revolt and the mufti's stint in Berlin during the Second World War. Here, then, was another reason for the high commissioner's tilt toward the Jewish side in Palestine. However, neither Cunningham nor Crum—the dominant figure on the joint committee delegation that met with the high commissioner—fully reflected the sentiments of the decision-makers. Neither the British government nor the majority of the committee was willing to countenance the idea of partition at this stage. If Cunningham and the advocates of partition on the committee viewed one another as a possible prop, it was a very shaky one.

The committee's report, issued at Lausanne, Switzerland, on April 20, 1946, was an American victory. Washington, which was not yet deeply involved in the Palestine situation, could feel a sense of satisfaction. It was not by chance that the report played up its declarative aspect—the immediate transfer of 100,000 Jewish refugees from Europe to Palestine—alongside a vaguely worded formulation regarding a binational state. No one bothered to examine the feasibility of this refugee transfer, but the round, principled number was President Harry Truman's declarative achievement. What was a success for the Americans was a threat to the British. The entry of tens of thousands of Jewish refugees into Palestine, or even only a discussion of this possibility, would create the danger of a civil war and deliver a mortal blow to Britain's standing in the Arab world, whereas not allowing the entry of such Jews meant entanglement with the United States and stepped-up Jewish terrorism. In short, the British government did not like the report; its recommendations were hardly what the committee's initiators—Attlee, Bevin, and their allies in the government—had wished for or expected.[37]

A furor erupted in Britain. Anger gripped everyone, from the prime minister and officials in the ministries and departments involved with

Palestine down to the last of the envoys in the Middle East. Their wrath was aimed in particular at the United States and its president for putting spikes in the wheels of an already rickety Britain. In May 1946, Attlee, doing his best to control his emotions, assailed the United States for aggravating Britain's situation without lifting a finger to assist it. Bevin, who was less diplomatic than Attlee, prepared a propaganda campaign that mixed anger at the United States with antisemitic sentiments. Even Bevin's ostensible success, his quid pro quo from the United States for the inclusion of the declaration about the Jewish refugees—namely, the report's lack of an explicit reference to the political future of Palestine, together with its recognition that Palestine alone could not solve the problem of the Holocaust survivors—damaged British interests. Practically speaking, the report meant that the political fog would continue, leaving the arena open to pressures from many quarters, including more terrorism. The report was forged from the internal balance of forces in the committee—though not necessarily in a division of Americans versus Britons—and from the determination of those on both sides to arrive at a joint conclusion almost at any price.

From the point of view of the high commissioner and his administration, what counted was the end result, and in the end the committee's recommendations were not viable, either in regard to the Jewish refugees or in terms of a political solution. The Arabs objected to the former, the Jews to the latter. After the report's publication, the British government, which was more concerned about its relations with the United States than about a solution in Palestine, pursued the discussions with the Truman administration about an agreed policy in Palestine while making it clear that the report was unacceptable. But during the long weeks in which the powers bandied words, violence in Palestine surged. This was the situation that confronted Cunningham.[38]

Fundamentally, the British position was that, contrary to the American view, the problem of the Jewish refugees and the desired solution in Palestine were inseparable. Cunningham disliked the report for reasons other than those cited by London. From his vantage point, the recommendations constituted working guidelines, if London gave the word to act on them. The key recommendations were, in addition to permitting the entry of 100,000 Jewish refugees, the temporary continuation of the existing Mandate until Jewish-Arab enmity ended, a trusteeship agreement of unclear character, actions to raise the Arabs' standard of living to help ensure equitable self-government by both communities, and an agreement on the issues of immigration and a future political solution (a binational state). Other recommendations entailed the lifting of the 1940 restrictions on land purchases by Jews and the introduction of alternative regulations that would protect Arab tenant farmers and fellahin, encouragement of the Jewish Agency's development plans in cooperation with the Palestine Arabs and the neighboring Arab countries, the improvement of education (in particular, the Jewish schools, which "are imbued with a fiery spirit of nationalism," the report states), and a demand that the Jewish Agency cooperate with the Mandatory administration to suppress terrorism and illegal immigration. From the high commissioner's viewpoint, all these recommendations and guidelines were, in large measure, written on the wind, because they were portrayed as independent goals rather than important results of a comprehensive political solution. At the same time, their publication was enough to trigger anew the same sort of unrest that had greeted Cunningham on his arrival in Jerusalem the previous November.[39]

Like the British government, whose disappointment in the report stemmed from its overreach and likelihood of setting off an explosion in Palestine that the administration would be unable to contain, the Jewish Agency was equally disappointed, but in its case because the report did not go far enough: it said nothing about the possible establishment of a Jewish state. After Attlee's address in the House of Commons on May 1 and Bevin's remarks on the twelfth of that month at the Labour Party convention, it was clear that the government opposed the report. Bevin, in his usual blunt manner, pinned the blame squarely on the Jewish lobby in the United States. Hall, the colonial secretary, gave expression to the feeling in London from the perspective of the Mandate administration. He argued that to bring about the limitless expansion of the Jewish national home by means of immigration contrary to the explicit will of the Arabs meant that Britain would have to rule Palestine by force of arms. This analysis was not without foundation: the remarks by Attlee and Bevin rekindled the despair of the Zionist movement's leaders at the possibility of a solution under a British aegis and revived the gloom that had existed on the eve of the appointment of the Anglo-American Committee. The upshot was that the Jewish Agency Executive continued to pursue a combined struggle: encouraging American pressure on Britain and waging a violent struggle, which reached its peak in the middle of June 1946.[40]

The report's tumultuous aftermath strengthened Cunningham's opinion that partition into two separate states was the only solution for the

Palestine problem. Although not the first to arrive at this conclusion, in the first half of 1946 he was the only official British figure who dared say it aloud. The high commissioner thereby became the most unwavering senior British advocate of partition by agreement and in a planned political process. He was more determined to bring about partition than even the Colonial Office, and in particular the colonial secretary, as they were increasingly under the sway of the Foreign Office, which rejected partition. That Cunningham was more determined in this regard than the senior officer corps goes without saying, but his advocacy of partition was more insistent than that of the local population as well—certainly the Arabs and even most of the Zionists. At the same time, the latter were a source of inspiration (even if he did not always admit this) for his recognition of the superiority of partition as a realistic political solution.[41]

It did not take long for Cunningham to realize that his pro-partition stance was not being well received either in London or by his staff in Jerusalem. He remained concerned about his image, particularly about its perception in London. Support for partition seemed to be at odds with personal image-building, unless he was imbued with the same conviction that this was the right solution for Britain as he was determined to rehabilitate his reputation.

The high commissioner's growing distress in the light of what he perceived as the government's political insensitivity, the stubborn insistence of the Jews and the Arabs on ignoring each other, and his own determination not to crack under the pressure led him to solicit advice from people whose opinion he valued and whom he viewed as a possible political allies.

From the middle of April 1946 on, the Hebrew press carried reports that General Sir Arthur Wauchope, the former high commissioner, was about to visit Palestine. Behind the expected visit lay Cunningham's desire to find an interlocutor of identical rank, experience, and, above all, approach. Indeed, Wauchope, like Cunningham, was a Scot with no family who had come to Government House from the military and preferred a political solution to the use of force—and had on one occasion clashed sharply with the army over this last question, presaging Cunningham's similar confrontation. It was during Wauchope's term as high commissioner that the Peel Commission for the first time formulated the recommendation on which Cunningham now drew: the partition of Palestine into two nation-states. Both Wauchope and Cunningham saw spiraling terrorism wreak havoc with the political prospect. In both cases, the Jewish Agency was the likely candidate for cooperation to calm the atmosphere and promote the political orientation. Like Cunningham, Wauchope, too, had to cope with an open revolt—though in his case, the insurgents were the Arabs. Both found their ability to respond constricted by inquiry commissions: the Peel Commission and now the Anglo-American Committee. Wauchope himself likened his period as high commissioner to Cunningham's. (He also noted, under the impression of a visit to India, the similarities between the two countries.) And then, as now, the British government did not take the principle of partition all the way to the end.[42]

Wauchope, in Egypt following a visit to India, was to arrive by plane at the Dead Sea, be greeted by Cunningham's representative, and then proceed to Government House and afterward tour Galilee. Both old soldiers found their service in Palestine, and in Government House in particular, highly congenial. Before departing for Palestine, however, Wauchope, exhausted from his trip to India, suffered a heart attack and was ordered to rest. The visit to Palestine was canceled. Cunningham expressed his regret but wrote to Wauchope that perhaps the cancellation was for the best, as the rumors on the Jewish street were that Cunningham had requested the help of a popular predecessor and the result could have proved embarrassing and counterproductive to him. Indeed, given the mood in the Yishuv and within the Arab community after the publication of the Anglo-American Committee's report, the visit could have been more harmful than beneficial. Nevertheless, Cunningham kept up his ties with Wauchope and added a courtesy correspondence with the first high commissioner, Lord Herbert Samuel, a Jew and a Zionist. Their advice and support were important to him. Equally significant was the fact that he did not seek the friendship of two other past high commissioners, Sir John Chancellor and Sir Harold MacMichael. They were less sympathetic to the Zionist project, though MacMichael was not basically opposed to the partition idea.[43]

In this trying period, caught between pressures emanating from London and from the local arena, Cunningham gained the support of a well-known figure of great importance to him: Chaim Weizmann, the president of the World Zionist Organization. In April 1946, Weizmann learned that the prime minister of South Africa, Jan Smuts, would stop over briefly in Egypt on his way to Britain. Weizmann suggested to Cunningham that he invite Smuts to visit Palestine, even for a few hours. "It is important for us," Weizmann wrote, "and I dare say for you as well."

Weizmann's interest was to enlist the support of the high commissioner, a general and statesman who was admired in Britain, in dealing with the crisis relating to the Anglo-American Committee's recommendation to establish a binational state. But as with the proposed Wauchope visit, this visit, too, could have been an embarrassment, although in this case for Smuts, who, because of London's attitude toward the report, could not publicly express support for the Yishuv and the high commissioner (together or separately). Accordingly, Cunningham suggested to Weizmann that Smuts be invited to stop over in Palestine on his way back from London, in the hope that the situation would be calmer by then. Greater calm was not to be, however, and the visit did not take place. Cunningham, for his part, took advantage of the opportunity to underscore his wartime relations with Smuts, which both the Yishuv and certainly Weizmann would appreciate.

While understanding that he could not invite Smuts to visit, Cunningham asked the colonial secretary to convey his personal good wishes to the statesman, who was in London on the occasion of South Africa's Independence Day, May 24. In return, he received a gift in the form of a note to "The Military Governor, Jerusalem," in which Smuts wrote exactly the words that the high commissioner needed in this period: ". . . Best wishes for your success in most difficult but not hopeless task." It is not only by chance that the figures mentioned here were known for their empathy toward Zionism.[44]

Cunningham received political and moral support, albeit not direct, on the partition issue from a famous figure—though if it had been up to this figure, Cunningham would have been tending his garden in some remote corner of Britain. Sir Winston Churchill, responding to a note from Attlee at the beginning of 1946, wrote that he supported the use of force against Jewish terrorism in Palestine. At the same time, and without contradiction, the wartime prime minister added that he continued to uphold Britain's commitment in the spirit of the Balfour Declaration, which now could have only one interpretation: partition. Surely no one could have better formulated the policy that Cunningham was trying to pursue from Jerusalem. Attlee needed Churchill's political and moral support because of the rift with the United States over the Palestine issue and the exceptional operation the government had authorized a few days earlier (Operation Agatha). With this in mind, Attlee replied—though privately—that he and his party were committed to the Jewish national home. They would not accept a solution that would disavow the 1917 commitment (and, implicitly, would also reject the report of the Anglo-American Committee). "In this connection," he wrote, "I note your view that Partition may still be the remedy."[45]

Did Cunningham know about this exchange? Possibly. In any event, the remarks about partition in Churchill's letter and in the prime minister's reply were forwarded to the Colonial Office, which customarily passed on correspondence about Palestine to Jerusalem. By July 1946, then, the high commissioner was probably operating in a less hostile environment than previously. He also found a surprising partner in the Foreign Office mission in Cairo. At the end of August 1946, Brigadier Iltid Clayton, the advisor on Arab affairs to the resident minister in Cairo (the British government's senior representative in the Middle East, who bore ministerial status), wrote that he thought there was a chance for a political move that would lead to Palestine's partition into two states. Until then, Clayton, like his colleagues in the Foreign Office, had considered the White Paper of 1939 a good compromise, as it met the Arabs' demands and would also increase the number of Jews in the country by means of the immigration quotas it granted the Yishuv. And like his colleagues, he, too, had been opposed to the partition idea and to the policy of the colonial secretary and his high commissioner in Palestine. However, at the end of 1946, it was clear to Clayton that the Zionists would never accept the White Paper or any other plan less than partition. Accordingly, Clayton argued—drawing on the precedent of Ireland from the early 1920s—partition could be accepted by the Arabs as a solution, even a temporary one, that would afford everyone involved a breathing spell. The Zionists, Clayton maintained, would not be able to spurn the establishment of a state in part of Palestine and would suppress their extremists as a by-product. As for the Arab states, if the mufti were neutralized, they would dare to accept any idea that would tone down the conflict.

Clayton was not the first to reach this conclusion: Cunningham, as we saw, was months ahead of him; and his opinion, in contrast to Clayton's, was not voiced in back rooms but spelled out in messages to the colonial secretary. Those that were not of a personal character were circulated among the relevant officials in the government and in the Middle East missions. Cunningham agreed that it was impossible to promise unreservedly that partition would succeed. Still, he was more optimistic than Clayton. In his view, partition had the best prospect of bringing about an ultimate Jewish-Arab peace in Palestine. He also preceded Clayton in making the comparison to Ireland, his native land, which was partitioned in 1922. The hope was that, as in Ireland, the moderates who preferred to get something rather than nothing would prevail and ultimately form a government and suppress the extremists.[46]

The difference between the two lay in perspective: when Clayton referred to "Arabs" he meant the Arab states, whereas Cunningham was talking about the Palestine Arabs. The historical perspective shows that the gamble was an equal one in both arenas. The important question, then, is not what the Arabs or the Jews said but what the British thought. At this stage, their attitude was still of importance not only in terms of managing their affairs in the Middle East and Palestine; it also influenced the positions taken by the parties to the conflict.

Almost expectably, Clayton's backing for partition was short-lived: he soon fell into line with the mood in the Foreign Office. After August 1946, when it looked as though the Jewish Agency were returning to the partition concept amid mounting Arab objections to it, Clayton reverted to his original approach, namely, that a binational state possessing an Arab majority was the most favorable solution for Palestine and for British interests. Cunningham remained almost alone in espousing partition; his ally was Colonial Secretary Hall, whose political power was waning.

Contrary to his expectations, Cunningham did not find support in the Jewish Agency, certainly not in the period of April to June 1946, immediately after the Anglo-American Committee issued its report. This, he believed, was a tremendous missed opportunity: the Jewish Agency could have exploited the committee's looming failure by taking a positive approach and putting forward an alternative idea, one that was acceptable to both world Jewry and the United States and had support in London and Jerusalem—a return to the partition ideas of the 1930s. Instead, the Jewish Agency, seeing the British government's open hostility toward the Anglo-American Committee report, renewed its violent struggle against British policy and against the Mandate administration and its head. It seemed to Cunningham that the only viable prospect for him and the Colonial Office lay in persuading the Jewish Agency to save itself from itself.

The Jewish Agency, for its part, generally chose to play up the political weakness of the Colonial Office and its envoy in Jerusalem, rather than trying to empower them. In 1946, they and they alone were the opening through which the Jewish Agency could have breached the thick wall of British opposition to a reasonable Zionist solution, namely, partition. Moreover, the Jewish Agency tended to translate the political weakness of the senior Colonial Office personnel into weakness of character. The support the high commissioner received from the Zionist movement was limited to the assumption that "he's all right, but weak."[47]

In August 1946, Ze'ev Sherf, the secretary of the Jewish Agency's Political Department, wrote to the department's head, Moshe Shertok, that a conversation with the high commissioner had been "worthless."[48] In November, Shertok told Cunningham frankly:

> I know that the new colonial secretary [Creech-Jones] is sincerely interested in facilitating the situation as far as possible within the sphere in which he is able to act, but I know as well that the decision depends neither on him nor on the high commissioner, with all their good intentions. The decision is made at a higher level, and the prevailing notion among our public is that fundamentally the decision has already been made—that the Foreign Office and the services [the army] are determined to abandon us.[49]

NOTES

1. "Program for the Arrival and Reception of His Excellency Lieutenant General Sir Alan Cunningham," November 21, 1945, MECA CP, B6, F5/95.

2. Ibid.; on the planned reception ceremony, Cunningham to Chief Secretary John Shaw, November 21, 1945, MECA CP, B5, F5/96; *Ha'aretz, Mishmar*, November 22, 1945.

3. David Kroyanker, *Jerusalem Architecture*, New York 1994, pp. 148–150; author visits to the site in March 2005 and June 2011, courtesy of the United Nations Truce Supervision Organization.

4. *Ha'aretz, Mishmar*, November 22, 1945; the Executive Council, which was established in 1922, was a kind of toothless cabinet, as the high commissioner possessed overriding powers. Fitzgerald (1894–1989) was the last president of the Mandate Supreme Court and the senior justice on the court (1944–1948); David Niv, *Campaigns of the Irgun Zvai Leumi [Etzel]*, Part IV: "The Revolt (1944–1946)," Tel Aviv 1973 (Hebrew), p. 190; Shabtai Teveth, *Kinat David* (David's Jealousy), *The Life of David Ben-Gurion*, vol. 4, Jerusalem and Tel Aviv 2004 (Hebrew), pp. 624–626.

5. Cunningham to Shaw, November 21, 1945, MECA CP, B5, F5/96; High commissioner's words of thanks at the appointment ceremony, NAM 8303-104/28.

6. The visit to Transjordan: "Program for Amman Visit—Tuesday 27th November 45," MECA CP, B6, F3/14.

7. Exchange of correspondence between Cunningham and the War Office concerning his rank, December 14, 1945, January 3, 1946, September 30, 1946, MECA CP, B6, F5/66-104; War Office writ of appointment to rank of general, January 26, 1946, MECA CP, B6, F4/89.

8. Ben-Zvi to high commissioner, January 31, 1946, MECA CP, B6, F4/15; Cunningham to Ben-Zvi, February 6, 1946, MECA CP, B6, F4/16.

9. *Hatzofeh*, November 12, 1945; Avraham Akavia, *With Wingate in Abyssinia*, Tel Aviv 1944, p. 34 (Hebrew).

10. BGA, Ben-Gurion Diary, November 23, 1945.

11. Yehuda Slutzky, *History of the Haganah*, Vol. III, Part 2: "From Struggle to War," Tel Aviv 1972, p. 809 (Hebrew).

12. Cases in point are Field Marshal Lord Herbert Plumer (1925–1928), General Arthur Wauchope (1931–1938), and Field Marshal John Gort (1944–1945). Sir John Chancellor (1928–1931), though a former army man (holding the rank of lieutenant general), arrived in Jerusalem with rich experience in the colonial service—and acted in that spirit. Sir Harold MacMichael (1938–1944) came from the Colonial Office and did not have a military background. Lord Herbert Samuel (1920–1925) was a statesman, politician, and former cabinet minister as well as being a Jew and a Zionist and the first high commissioner in the golden age of relations between Britain and the Zionist movement.

13. *Ha'aretz*, November 11, 1945; *Mishmar*, November 11, 1945; "Review of the Palestine Press, No. 264, December 11, 1945," MECA CP, B6, F5/264.

14. "Review of the Palestine Press, No. 264."

15. Bevin, parliamentary statement, MECA CP, B6, F3/77; Slutzky, *History of the Haganah*, III, 2, pp. 862–865.

16. *Haboker*, November 22, 1945; *Mishmar*, November 11, 1945.

17. *Ha'aretz*, November 22, 1945.

18. "High Commissioner's Visits, November [19]45–October 1947," MECA CP, B6, F3/1–5; "Visit of H.E. The High Commissioner to Beth Eshel, 29th of November 45," MECA CP, B6, F3/1–5; *Ha'aretz*, November 30, 1945.

19. "High Commissioner's Visits, November [19]45–October 1947"; "Haifa Visit, 4th and 5th December [19]45, 15th December [19]45," MECA CP, B6, F3/17; Shabtai Levy's remarks at the reception for the high commissioner in Haifa, December 4, 1945, MECA CP, B6, F3/19; *Davar*, December 5, 1945.

20. "Mr. Rokach's Speech and Note on the High Commissioner's Reply, Tel Aviv Municipality, 18th December 45," MECA CP, B6, F3/20–21; Barnett, *The Desert Generals*, p. 80; George Gater (Colonial Office) to Cunningham, January 30, 1946, MECA CP, B1, F1/29; Cunningham to George Hall, colonial secretary, September 26, 1946, MECA CP, B1, F2/65.

21. For example, in his remarks on Christmas, December 25, 1945, MECA CP, B6, F5/97.

22. Cunningham to Hall, February 19, 1946, MECA CP, B1, F1/30.

23. "High Commissioner for Palestine, Note on Potential Arab Political Violence in Palestine (April 1946)," NA C0537/2416.

24. Ibid.

25. Ibid.; "Review of the Palestine Press, No. 264."

26. "Review of the Palestine Press, No. 264"; Arab Higher Committee file for 1946–1947, NA CO537/2417; Cunningham to Colonial Secretary Arthur Creech-Jones, August 14, 1947, NA CO537/2417.

27. Cunningham to Hall, "secret and personal," January 26, 1946, MECA CP B1 F1/29.

28. Roger William Louis, *The British Empire in the Middle East, 1945–1951*, London 1984, pp. 7–8.

29. Hall memorandum: "A New Policy for Palestine, Memorandum to the Palestine Committee," August 20, 1945, MECA CP, B4, F3/51; Bevin memorandum: "Parliamentary Statement," November 1, 1945, MECA CP, B4, F3/77.

30. Editorial in the London *Times*, November 21, 1945.

31. Hall memorandum, MECA CP, B4, F3/51.

32. The British-American dispute over the Palestine question is elaborated in Amikam Nachmani, *Great Power Discord in Palestine: The Anglo-American Committee of Inquiry into the Problems of European Jewry and Palestine, 1945–1946*, London 1987.

33. The committee of inquiry was indeed persuaded of the Yishuv's military, economic, political, and societal superiority. *Report of the Anglo-American Committee of Inquiry into the Problems of European Jewry and of Palestine*, Lausanne, April 20, 1946, Parliamentary Document 6808, Jerusalem 1946, pp. 4–7; Joseph Heller, "Zionist Policy in the International Arena after the Second World War—The Affair of the Anglo-American Committee 1945/6," *Shalem* 3 (5741), pp. 257–259 (Hebrew).

34. Cunningham to Hall, February 19, 1946, MECA CP, B1, F1/30.

35. Bartley C. Crum, *Behind the Silken Curtain: A Personal Account of Anglo-American Diplomacy in Palestine and the Middle East*, New York 1947, pp. 223–225.

36. Ibid.; Cunningham to Hall, December 29–30, 1945, NA CO733/457; Richard Crossman, *Palestine Mission: A Personal Record*, New York and London 1947, p. 164; Heller, "Zionist Policy," p. 265; Moshe Sharett, *Imprisoned with Paper and Pencil: Letters of Moshe and Zipporah Sharett during His Detention by the British at Latrun, June–November 1946*, Tel Aviv 2000, Appendix 15: "Report on a Conversation with the High Commissioner," November 19, 1946, p. 429 (Hebrew).

37. *Report of the Anglo-American Committee.* The number of Jewish DPs in 1946 was far higher than the number proposed for emigration; on that number as both a mythic and practical concept, see Louis, *The British Empire*, pp. 10–11, 386–390.

38. Attlee to Crossman, May 6, 1946, quoted by Louis, *The British Empire*, p. 419; see also Louis for Bevin's reaction (p. 428) and elaboration (chapters 2 and 3).

39. *Report of the Anglo-American Committee.*

40. Heller, "Zionist Policy," pp. 275–281; Hall to Cunningham, April 27, 1946, MECA CP, BI, F1.

41. Cunningham to Hall, February 19, 1946, MECA CP, BI, F1/30.

42. On Wauchope's handling of the Arab Revolt and on his differences with the army at the time, see Yigal Eyal, *The First Intifada: The Suppression of the Arab Revolt by the British Army in Palestine, 1936–1939*, Tel Aviv 1988 (Hebrew).

43. Wauchope to Cunningham, April 22, 1946, Cunningham to Wauchope, April 25, 1946, Wauchope to Cunningham, December 11, 1946, Cunningham to Samuel, December 12, 1946, MECA CP, B6, F5/26, 60–62; Avraham Rosenthal, "Revelations of the Last High Commissioner," *Yedioth Ahronoth*, April 23, 1958.

44. Weizmann to Cunningham, April 23, 1946, WA, 2653; Cunningham to Weizmann, April 23, 1946, WA, 3653; Cunningham to Smuts via colonial secretary, May 19, 1946, Smuts to Cunningham, May 31, 1946, MECA CP, B6, F4/43–4.

45. Prime minister's private secretary to Colonial Office, and Attlee to Churchill, July 4, 1946, NA Co537/1714.

46. Louis, *The British Empire*, pp. 447–449, 451–456; Cunningham to Hall, September 20, 1946; Louis, *The British Empire*, p. 449.

47. Slutzky, *History of the Haganah*, III, 2, p. 809.

48. Sherf to Shertok, August 14, 1946, CZA, S25.10016.

49. Sharett, *Imprisoned with Paper and Pencil*, p. 431.

2 Toward a Clash with the Yishuv

In the spring of 1946, with the mission of the Anglo-American Committee completed, the high commissioner enjoyed greater freedom of action. The waiting period mandated by the committee's work had the effect of tempering his approach—which sprang from his military experience—and enriching his experience of the situation.

Now placing the emphasis on the civil-political-diplomatic aspect of the high commissioner's office, Cunningham moved to deal with the Jewish Agency's stance regarding a political solution and Jewish terrorism. He was determined to moderate the approach of the agency's leadership.

Initially, Cunningham, who was learning on the job, had supported an effort at dismantling the Jewish Agency. Afterward, he accepted a recommendation from the Colonial Office not to discuss policy issues with the agency's leaders. Adoption of this posture had first been broached toward the end of 1945, but the government rejected plans put forward by the Colonial Office, the high commissioner, and the army to take direct and vigorous action against the Jewish Agency, maintaining that such an effort would strengthen the extremists at the expense of the moderates. (By "extremists," the British meant not the breakaway groups Etzel and Lehi but "activists," as David Ben-Gurion, Moshe Sneh, and their colleagues were known in Zionist argot.)

By June 1946, Cunningham had a different perspective. He now believed that the alternative to a large-scale military operation and civil noncooperation with the Mandate administration lay in restoring to the moderates in the Zionist leadership the power they had lost as Yishuv-perpetrated violence and terrorism surged beginning in the autumn of 1945.[1] The contemporary reader may be wondering why the British were preoccupied with the question of who would lead the Yishuv and the Zionist movement. In the reality of the time, it was understood by both the British and the Zionists, in the spirit of the Mandatory approach, that the latter would choose their own leadership. On the other hand, neither side could ignore the thorough involvement of the government of Britain and the Mandate administration in both security and the question of a political solution, and also their say in matters of principle and personnel, such as the leadership of the Jewish Agency. (The agency's existence derived from the Palestine Mandate received by Britain from the League of Nations after the First World War.)

The question in dispute was how far the legal authority of the Mandate administration and of the Jewish Agency extended. The legality of the Mandatory power and the Jewish Agency was not in dispute. And beyond any legalistic quibbles that might nevertheless arise, the two sides were interdependent. Cunningham, like Weizmann and Ben-Gurion—the head of the Jewish Agency at the time—understood this, each in his way and from his particular vantage point. Each side might reject the legality of the other's actions, but not its existence as such.[2]

The road to upgrading the moderates' status naturally passed through Chaim Weizmann. There is no need to elaborate here on the ties that Weizmann—a British citizen and president of the Zionist movement whose reputation as both a statesman and a scientist preceded him—had developed with the British authorities since the First World War. His approach, with variations, was shared by others in the Zionist leadership on both the right and the left, from Ze'ev Jabotinsky to David Ben-Gurion. Its gist was that the Zionist movement's alliance with the Great Power that had issued the Balfour Declaration and was responsible for validating the idea of the Jewish national home was the elixir of life for the Zionist movement. But Weizmann's quest for a moderate policy was informed, particularly in his second term as head of the Zionist movement (1935–1948), by his Anglophile inclinations. Zionism, he believed, should pin its hopes on relations with Britain and the United States as an alternative to resorting to violence. Weizmann held violence to be both morally repugnant and concretely counterproductive.[3]

In his major biography of Ben-Gurion, Shabtai Teveth writes about a "strong friendship" that supposedly developed "very quickly" between Weizmann and Cunningham beginning at the end of 1945. In practice, the relations between the two men were complex. They were certainly not marked by friendship, let alone intimacy. Weizmann habitually prefixed letters to friends and those he was close to with the salutation "My dear. . . ." This phrase does not appear in any of his letters to Cunningham; instead, they are studded with honorifics and apologies to a dignitary whose time is precious. Nevertheless, even if the two were on opposite sides of a constantly growing barrier, the common viewpoint they shared on certain key issues induced a mutual effort by each to advance his causes with the other's help.[4]

Cunningham made Weizmann's acquaintance immediately upon arriving in Palestine at the end of 1945. The two became closer in the first half of 1946, the period during which Cunningham thought it would be possible through a political move to return the moderates—Weizmann and his supporters—to the center of the leadership of the Zionist movement and the Jewish Agency, at the expense of Ben-Gurion and his camp. Weizmann spent five months in Palestine in 1946, from late February until mid-July. His relations with Cunningham continued afterward as well, though less intensively, then faded even before the expiration of the Mandate, when they could no longer be of help to each other.

Cunningham was more aware than Weizmann that their relations might also be harmful: to him in London and to Weizmann among his colleagues in the leadership, who at the time did not believe in close ties with the Mandate administration. Weizmann was less cautious in this regard. From his lofty perch in the Zionist arena, he saw no reason to apologize for his relations with the high commissioner. He invited Cunningham to the opening of the biophysics and organic chemistry unit at the Sieff Research Institute (the forerunner of today's Weizmann Institute of Science) on June 3, 1946, including a luncheon at his home in Rehovot. Cunningham replied that he would be delighted to accept but felt he should refrain from attending ceremonies at which speeches would be made, even if the events were meant to be nonpolitical. He added that he hoped for more natural relations between the two men in the future. Weizmann pressed him, but Cunningham could not allow himself to make the visit, given the looming crisis over the Anglo-American Committee and the surge of terrorism. Nor, however, could he allow himself to cause affront to Weizmann, who was a very valuable asset. In the end, the chief secretary, John Shaw, and the head of the financial department, Julius Jacobs (a Jew and a Zionist), attended the event.[5]

Cunningham's polite rejection of the invitation attested to his awareness of Weizmann's political weakness and, more crucially, indicated the emerging necessity of taking action against the Jewish Agency in order to induce it to combat terrorism and adopt a political solution in the form of partition. On May 4, Cunningham wrote to Hall that he had the impression that the Jewish Agency leaders were deliberately distancing Weizmann (whether to ensure that he didn't interfere or to protect him) from the ugly side of the Jews' violent political actions. In a meeting with Weizmann on June 19, Cunningham addressed the WZO president as though he were an envoy who would deliver a message "to those who are now in control of the Yishuv's fate." Weizmann's response suggests that he understood that the high commissioner saw him as no more than a "postman." With this, any possible friendship that might have developed between the two dissolved. In any event, Cunningham wanted Weizmann's policy to be implemented even more than Weizmann himself did, though without alienating the Jewish Agency Executive, the target of his blandishments.

The uncomfortable relationship between the two surfaced in three discussions they held in June–July 1946: one after the "Night of the Bridges" (June 16–17), the second on the day Operation Agatha began (which is remembered in the Jewish collective memory as "Black Sabbath," June 29),[6] and the third on the eve of Weizmann's departure from Palestine in the middle of July. He doesn't know much and it looks like he is not making any efforts to know, the frustrated high commissioner wrote to the colonial secretary on June 21. Through Weizmann, Cunningham had wished to exploit the momentum of Operation Agatha in June and July to bring about the moderation of the Zionist leadership. The distress of the WZO president, who met with the "enemy" because he sincerely believed that such a meeting would avert violence between the administration and the Yishuv—and who was weakened politically for his efforts—showed clearly which side could gain and which could lose from these semiformal contacts. Weizmann, sensing that the high commissioner was effectively using him to reach the Yishuv leaders who were behind the Jewish terrorist acts, neither forgot nor forgave. He paid the high commissioner back in the same coin and snubbed him during the last months of Cunningham's tenure. In any event, by the winter and spring of 1948, the high commissioner was no longer of relevance for the embryonic Jewish state.[7]

Weizmann counseled ongoing practical and political work vis-à-vis Britain. His approach was undermined by the actions of the Jewish Resistance Movement, in particular the terrorism by Etzel and Lehi, and also the Haganah's increasingly aggressive operations. Though Weizmann was still the titular head of the Zionist movement, the violence demonstrated clearly "that his moderate policy had been rejected altogether, and in its stead the way of Ben-Gurion was accepted, as executed by Sneh"—namely, the violent campaign against Britain's White Paper.[8]

Cunningham discerned the growing rift between the advocates of moderation and the hard-liners in the Zionist leadership. Within the Zionist movement, the violence of the Yishuv's struggle against British policy exacerbated the debate between the activists and the moderates. The high commissioner was attuned to these voices. Some Zionist leaders thought, after the eruption of the violence in October 1945, that the Jewish public grasped that cooperation with Britain had ended. This was the obstacle Cunningham faced.

One exponent of this viewpoint was Moshe Sneh, a member of the Jewish Agency Executive and the head of the Haganah National Command. He said as much ten days before Cunningham's arrival, in a discussion at the Jewish Agency Executive about whether the Yishuv should cooperate with the Anglo-American Committee.[9] Accordingly, he argued vigorously—and Ben-Gurion cautiously—that the Yishuv should boycott the committee. Moshe Shertok, the head of the Jewish Agency's Political Department and a leading moderate, took the opposite stance. Zionism in the Land of Israel could not afford to ignore the political power that could determine the movement's fate, he maintained. A violent insurgency was not off the mark; large national groups such as the Indians or the Arabs could allow themselves to foment "actions" (i.e., violence) and to boycott political efforts, but not the Zionist movement and still less the Yishuv.[10]

This was the essence of the debate, the wedge Cunningham tried to broaden. Nevertheless, in 1946 he probably had an exaggerated view of the strength of the moderates in the Zionist leadership. Still, with his fresh approach he could see the political potential possessed, at least in theory, by moderates such as Eliezer Kaplan, Nahum Goldmann, Joseph Sprinzak, Moshe Shapira, Eliahu Epstein (Eilat), Yitzhak Ben-Zvi, and even Moshe Shertok, whom the administration categorized as an activist because of his senior status in the Jewish Agency Executive but whose approach was clear. The high commissioner made his viewpoint known to Colonial Secretary Hall and to his deputy, Creech-Jones. At the conclusion of Operation Agatha, on July 11, the British cabinet adopted a policy aimed at bolstering Weizmann and the policy he stood for.[11]

Was Cunningham's approach wishful thinking? Was he wrong about the Jewish Agency's political orientation? Probably not. In the end, his mistake, which he himself realized too late, lay in his analysis of the people involved rather than of the Jewish Agency's political thrust. In fact, the agency's main thrust was a return to the idea of partition, as became apparent that summer under the leader whom the British in general and Cunningham in particular had labeled an extremist: David Ben-Gurion.

As of June 1946, Cunningham had held few meetings with the activist leaders in the Jewish Agency. He met with Ben-Gurion three times in November–December 1945, before Ben-Gurion left the country for an extended period, other than very short visits. In any case, no meetings with the high commissioner would have been possible after June 1946, when Ben-Gurion was categorized as an escaped fugitive by the Mandate administration. Shertok, too, spent much time in Europe, and when he returned to Palestine for his son's bar mitzvah he was arrested. Sneh was immersed in illegal activity and was hardly available for talks with the head of the administration, which was the target of his actions. In the absence of the operative leadership, Cunningham was left with Weizmann, who, unusually, as we saw, was in the country continuously from February to July 1946.[12]

From the high commissioner's viewpoint, the Zionists' disappointment in the report of the Anglo-American Committee, and even more so in the British government's reaction to the report, meant that almost the entire Zionist leadership was now firmly in the opposition camp and must be dealt with accordingly. Indeed, "Britain's anti-Zionist line very much facilitated the narrowing of the gap between the moderates and the extremists in the Zionist camp."[13] The moderates now consisted of a weak minority (Weizmann and also, at a different level—of political nonrelevance—Ben-Zvi, the president of the National Council). In short, Weizmann was a feeble ally at this time. Cunningham quickly found that his rebukes about extremism had been spoken to the wrong interlocutor: with Weizmann, he was preaching to the converted.

By June 1946, Cunningham was ready to use force to impose change on the Jewish Agency. He had not been indifferent to the concentrated Jewish violence that marked the first months of his tenure. However, his initial reaction was conditioned by the attitude of a determined general who drew on his military experience but seemed out of place in the present circumstances. In his first meeting with the senior staff of the Colonial Office, on November 14, 1945, in London, he declared that his top priority would be to deal harshly with anyone who bore arms illegally. He did not heed the advice of those who cautioned that the issue was complex and that it was more important to engage the Jewish Agency, the lawful leadership of the organized Yishuv, in dialogue. Indeed, at the end of December 1945, he proposed that British security forces seize the Jewish Agency's offices and detain some of its leaders.

Cunningham was not acting in a vacuum. A week after his arrival in Jerusalem, against the backdrop of the Yishuv's furious reaction to Bevin's anti-Jewish and anti-Zionist statement in Parliament on November 13, an internal memorandum of the Colonial Office addressed the question of the Jewish Agency's responsibility for the surging violence in Palestine. The conclusion drawn by the memorandum's author, Sir John Martin, the assistant undersecretary of state for the colonies—as well as former secretary of the Palestine Royal Commission (the Peel Commission) in 1936–1937 and Churchill's private secretary during the war—was that striking at the Jewish Agency would be imprudent at this time, even though the agency's responsibility was clear. This was the first written affirmation by a senior Colonial Office official of the assumption that the Jewish Agency was behind the revolt in Palestine. As suggested earlier, the colonial secretary accepted the recommendation not to strike at the Jewish Agency but suggested to the high commissioner that he reduce his political contacts with the body as an expression of the government's opinion of its leaders' behavior. The high commissioner and the colonial secretary also urged that extensive arms searches be conducted at key locales in the Yishuv.[14]

The cabinet, in consultation with the Chiefs of Staff Committee (the highest military body in Britain), blocked this aggressive approach. The reasoning: it would have a boomerang effect and would only augment the strength of the Zionist extremists. More important, the last thing Britain wanted was to provoke a harsh American response as the work of the Anglo-American Committee got under way. The delay gave Cunningham time to study the situation more closely. As we saw, he subsequently declared that using force against the Jewish Agency would be wrong, a view to which he held at least until summer 1947. Should the situation become untenable, action must be undertaken in a controlled manner. Moreover, until June 1946, Cunningham's friend and benefactor Alan Brooke (now Field Marshal Lord Viscount Alanbrooke) was chief of the Imperial General Staff. He had been able to curb the high commissioner's aggressive tendencies, though he himself was concerned about the effect of the wave of terrorism on army morale. Alanbrooke taught the high commissioner a lesson in calculated moderation.[15]

The situation changed in May–June 1946. Violence raged again in Palestine, but now the high commissioner took a more confident and measured stance vis-à-vis the new chief of the Imperial General Staff, Field Marshal Bernard Montgomery, who was eager to retaliate with force. For his part, Montgomery had not forgotten Cunningham's debacle in the Western Desert three and a half years earlier. He even invoked that memory in the confrontation that developed beginning in spring 1946 between the Mandate administration and the army over how to deal with Jewish terrorism in Palestine (see next section of this chapter).

Even before he was fully acquainted with the Yishuv reality, and before fully formulating his position, Cunningham drew a distinction (albeit not as sharply as he would afterward) between the violence perpetrated by the organized Yishuv against the administration and the army and seemingly similar operations carried out by the breakaway organizations, Etzel and Lehi. Although he branded every act of violence against the administration "terrorism," he took a different attitude toward the uprising of the organized Yishuv as compared with the terrorism of the two groups. The situation began to clarify for him in the spring and summer of 1946. As Jewish violence spiraled at the end of April 1946, the high commissioner was able to identify the different trends in the Yishuv, and certainly the difference between the organized Jewish community and the groups that had broken away from it. The general Jewish public's negative reaction to Lehi's murder in Tel Aviv on April 25, 1946, of seven British soldiers as they slept taught him an important lesson about the difference between a revolt in which violence was a secondary tool and one in which it was the only tool. That essential difference bolstered him in advancing his political approach and in doing battle against Jewish terrorism, mainly by urging the Jewish Agency to take action against the practice.[16]

At the beginning of March 1946, even before Cunningham had decided how to address the Jewish revolt, two institutions helped him crystallize his personal approach: the Jewish Agency and the army, namely, the Chiefs of Staff Committee in London and the Cairo-based Middle East headquarters. The Jewish Agency (under its cover name at the time, "Headquarters of the Jewish Resistance Movement") announced its plans to stop the insurgency as of March 6, the date of the Anglo-American Committee's arrival, in order to create a congenial atmosphere for the Zionist cause. This turned out to be a mere declaration; there was no respite in the uprising. In the meantime, the army, reeling under months of relentless terrorism, prepared to act against the Jewish Agency. Neither the agency nor the army, each for its own reasons, took into account the views of the new high commissioner. But they ignored him at their peril. Cunningham harnessed military action to political will. His aim was to hasten a change in the Jewish Agency's policy, and he considered the army's approach a means toward achieving that aim. The effect was to block the Jewish Agency's slide deep into terrorism and the army's aim of dismantling the Jewish Agency, a statutory body, immediately and by force.

Even though Cunningham was plunged directly into the Yishuv revolt, he sensed that serious interlocutors existed on the Jewish side. He put this impression to practical use, albeit not always successfully. He grasped that even though the Yishuv, leadership and public alike, sympathized with the terror tactics, its members also viewed Britain as a supportive power, even an ally. In other words, the high commissioner explained to his superiors, the struggle was against Britain's policy, not against the fact of its rule in Palestine. Moreover, he viewed with satisfaction the Yishuv leadership's political rejection of terrorism, though he also believed that this same leadership had not only initiated the terror campaign but was also fully informed about specific operations before they were launched, however much this was consistently denied. With this in mind, he had arrived at two working assumptions by spring 1946: that the Jewish Agency leadership could be brought back to supporting a political solution entailing a compromise (i.e., partition) and that the organized Yishuv and its leadership could be mustered for a campaign against terrorism. Between these poles, he had to prove beyond a doubt that the legal leadership of the Jewish Agency was in practice behind the revolt, particularly its violent aspect.[17]

The army, for its part, whether assessing that the terrorism would only intensify unless Britain moved resolutely to quash it or seeing which way the wind was blowing on the eve of Montgomery's expected appointment as chief of the Imperial General Staff, completely reversed its opinion. If, toward the end of 1945, it thought aggressive action against the Jewish Agency would be counterproductive for Britain, from the spring of 1946 on, the army believed that such action was essential. Some background is necessary to explain this policy reversal.

In the period covered by this book, 1945–1947, the army (namely, the War Office and its dominant body, the Chiefs of Staff Committee) was the most conservative of the British government bodies that dealt with Palestine. This was not an inevitable state of affairs. In November 1945, just before Cunningham's arrival in Palestine, his brother Admiral Andrew Cunningham, the commander of the Royal Navy, strongly advocated the view that the key to British activity in the Middle East lay in cooperation with the United States; this, he argued, overrode cooperation with any of the Arab states separately or with all of them together. The Foreign Office accepted this analysis; it was not by chance that the establishment of the Anglo-American Committee was announced in that same month. Field Marshal Alanbrooke, whether due to sheer exhaustion or to the excessively long period (October 1945–June 1946) of the handover of command to his successor, Montgomery, could not prevent the army from reverting to an approach that was by then totally anachronistic. In short, Montgomery continued to believe in bayonet hegemony, as though the war had changed nothing.

Just before taking over as CIGS, Montgomery visited a number of flash points throughout the empire. In June 1946, he stopped over briefly in Palestine twice, on his way to India and en route back to England. The first visit lasted less than two days, from the fourteenth to the sixteenth of the month, and the second, on June 22, only a few hours. The fact that Montgomery had spent time in Palestine before was both an advantage and a disadvantage for Cunningham. Montgomery viewed the developments in Palestine through the prism of the glory he won in the Second World War and through his combat experience as a division commander in Palestine in 1938–1939, during the Arab Revolt. The two visits in June 1946, however brief, were ordeals for Cunningham. The two men had not met previously, but there was no need to talk about the military record each brought to the meeting: both were well aware of that history.

Montgomery was adamant that the army should take the lead in restoring Britain's authority in Palestine. Only the army, not the civil administration, could accomplish this goal, he insisted. It infuriated him that the elite reserve unit of the Imperial Army, the Sixth Airborne Division—posted in Palestine and ready to be dispatched westward or eastward as the need arose—was engaged in policing activity at the expense of training and on-call readiness. That was not the unit's mission. The humiliation caused by Lehi's murder of the seven soldiers, themselves members of the Sixth Airborne Division, still burned. In the background lay Montgomery's imperial conception of Palestine as an essential base to preserve Britain's standing in the Middle East and, accordingly, his belief that the British military presence there must be bolstered. His gaze seemed fixed more on the Western Desert in the period when Palestine served as a logistical rear and as a base for reserve forces to train and rest—and less on the postwar political reality, in which Palestine ceased to fall exclusively within the British purview once its future became subject to an Anglo-American decision.[18]

David Charters, in his study of the British Army's attempts to suppress the Yishuv's struggle and the terrorism of the breakaway groups—and of the Haganah, during a certain period—terms the events a military *insurgency* and the army's response the Palestine Campaign. Whether or not these characterizations are apt, Charters's study, which covers the period 1945–1947, reflects faithfully the viewpoint of the army, which entered the campaign (or was supposed to) in order to quell the uprising. Both the army and Charters tried to apply the experience of dealing with the Arab Revolt in the previous decade to the new situation, though it was not necessarily relevant.[19] The high commissioner was well aware of the difference between the wide-scale Arab uprising in the 1930s and the limited struggle of the Yishuv in the following decade.

Cunningham did not invoke terms such as *insurgency* or *campaign*, because they did not reflect his views of his relations with the Yishuv—neither during June–July 1946, when his relations with the Jewish Agency were at a nadir, nor in the spring and summer of 1947. For the same reason, he did not launch an all-out campaign against the Yishuv. Beyond the operational-tactical debate about how to deal with the Yishuv and the Jewish Agency, Cunningham's approach and that of Montgomery and the army represented two radically different points of view.

Amid the complex constellation of relations among the Foreign, Colonial, and War Offices, ad hoc coalitions sprang up. Everyone agreed that Egypt was the most essential territory for Britain in the postwar Middle East. The Foreign Office and the War Office took a unified stand against the Colonial Office in opposing partition in Palestine; this, they believed, would weaken Britain's hold in the region and particularly in Egypt. The two ministries thought in terms of regional defense. At the same time, and more important, the Foreign Office and the Colonial Office realized, in contrast to the War Office and the military, that conditions had changed. The Second World War was over, the Cold War and the supremacy of the superpowers loomed, and the glory days of the empire were gone forever. These developments called for a new policy. Ultimately, as Roger Louis, the leading historian of the end of the British Empire noted, the severe economic crisis was the dominant factor that dictated policy in postwar Britain.[20]

Montgomery-style anachronism was very damaging; in this context, it is not surprising that on the eve of his appointment, and certainly afterward—at least until the summer of 1947—the Cairo-based headquarters of the Middle East Land Forces regained some of its wartime powers. The military's approach was undoubtedly influenced by Egypt's centrality and by the conclusion reached by the chiefs of staff that the primary problem facing Britain was rising Arab nationalism, which threatened the freedom of movement of the armed forces, of merchandise, and of Middle East oil.

This is the necessary perspective for viewing the shift in the army's attitude toward the Jewish revolt, from restraint to blatant aggression. Despite the recommendations of the Anglo-American Committee in April 1946 and of an Anglo-American experts' commission (as formulated in the Morrison-Grady plan, July 1946) that dovetailed with a revised government policy—all indicating that Britain was prepared to forgo Palestine and that Egypt's status was declining—the military continued to view Egypt and Palestine (together with Transjordan, Iraq, Syria, and Lebanon) in monolithic terms. The military in both Cairo and London exerted constant pressure to regain its former prestige, even arguing, somewhat bizarrely, that the climate in Palestine and the Levant (Syria and Lebanon) was more amenable for training than elsewhere. Churchill, who was still prime minister in May 1945, offered a one-word riposte: "Nonsense."[21]

Facing a surge of violence, the high commissioner, in his capacity as supreme commander of the British forces in Palestine, worked more intensively with the senior military echelons in Cairo and London than with the Foreign Office (in his capacity as civilian governor). He disagreed with the approach of both, but the Yishuv insurgency demanded immediate handling before a discussion of long-range policy. Cunningham's concern was that an encounter between excessive Jewish Agency–sponsored violence and a disproportionate response by Montgomery would destroy the possibility of a political compromise. In the meantime, the Jewish Resistance Movement, and even more flagrantly the breakaway groups, played into the hands of the anachronistic Montgomery school of thought. While the government was busy coping with the recommendations of the Anglo-American Committee, and the resulting fallout between London and Washington, the army acted as though there were no option for a political solution.

Intelligence evaluations rely not only on the quality of the available information and unbiased professional analysis but also on the spirit informing the analysis and, even more important, the spirit in which it is received—in the case at hand, by the Chiefs of Staff Committee (CSC). At the beginning of March 1946, Security Intelligence, Middle East (SIME), submitted to the CSC what amounted to an "indictment" of the Jewish Agency. The aim: to set forth the military, political, and legal background for an operation against the agency. The document effectively summed up the case of those in the military who advocated an immediate, drastic operation against the Jewish Agency in order to remove the Jewish revolt from the British agenda in the Middle East. The intelligence appraisal contains clear echoes of the November 1945 "Martin memorandum," which had blamed the Jewish Agency for the wave of violence in Palestine, although this earlier document had recommended against taking action at the time. Now, in March 1946, the SIME report, which was forwarded to Cunningham, recommended a strike against the Jewish Agency.[22]

SIME cited nine points supporting an operation on an unprecedented scale against the Jewish Agency. The report's authors were aware of the Haganah's potential strength, and not only because of the quality of its weapons and its mobilized fighting force (the Palmah). What impressed the British was that the Haganah was not an ordinary underground terrorist group but an organized, disciplined illegal army, displaying the characteristics of regular army management, and was accountable to a legally elected civilian political authority (the Jewish Agency Executive). Indeed, as the British well knew, the Haganah's military capabilities had in no small part been forged by its fruitful ties with the Mandate administration and army during the Arab Revolt and the Second World War.

The SIME document is less important as an exact catalogue of the Haganah's weapons and troops than for the understanding it shows of the Haganah's mode of operation and its source of authority. The British intelligence personnel in Cairo accurately portrayed the Haganah's new operative orientation, which had shifted from a saliently defensive posture to guerilla and even terrorist activity. The change entailed professional units and working methods and, not least, guidelines issued by the authoritative body, namely, the Jewish Agency. At the same time, the document's authors failed to discern the extent of the operative and strategic self-destruction caused by the Jewish Agency, Haganah national headquarters, and the General Staff in terms of the ability to defend the Yishuv against the Arabs by reducing the "army in the making" to a perpetrator of guerilla attacks, executed largely by the Palmah. This new role was pursued at the expense of training and preparing the other units, such as the Field Corps, the Guard Corps, military intelligence, and the military industries.[23]

Of particular interest was SIME's analysis of the Jewish Agency–Haganah's methods of control and obtaining matériel. In this non-sovereign national society, a high level of engagement was able to force acceptance of the leadership's decisions through education, "information" (propaganda), internal discipline, boycotts, and the like. British intelligence discerned that this social pressure was applied against those whose national orientation was suspect: anti-Zionists, non-Zionists, ultra-Zionists, and people uninterested in the national goals. Similarly, the authors, like the vast majority of the administration, distinguished between the illegal armed force (the Haganah and its regular army, the Palmah) and the terrorists (Etzel and Lehi). Perceptively, they also noted the operative coordination between the Yishuv and the breakaway groups as the Haganah was propelled onto the path of terrorism.

The document concluded that the strength of the Jewish Agency and the Haganah, which was accountable to it, lay in the political and military exclusivity they possessed, respectively, in the organized Jewish community. This, the central British working hypothesis, was shared by Cunningham, who would also later try to make use of it. According to the document's authors, the Jewish Agency was responsible for the acts of terrorism, certainly of the Haganah but also of the breakaways, since the onset of the wave of violence in October 1945. The Jewish Agency consistently denied a connection—not only between the Jewish Agency Executive and the Haganah but also between those two bodies and the amorphous entity known as the Jewish Resistance Movement and certainly with the breakaways. The British did not believe the denial.

Basically, the document shows that British military intelligence had an accurate picture of the mood in the Jewish Agency at the time. Even if the Cairo-based personnel did not fully grasp the duality that underlay the agency's attitude toward the revolt, they did perceive that it was effectively undermining its own legal foundation by flouting the powers granted it under the Mandate and acting against the entity from which it drew its authority. The conclusion was clear with regard to the Jewish Agency: "Its efforts are more akin to the anarchic outrages of the terrorists than to the responsible acts of a public body." From here, the path was short to outlawing the agency and its subordinate bodies, arresting its leadership, and taking broad military and police action against the Haganah—in other words, an operation against the Yishuv using methods similar to those used to suppress the Arab Revolt in the previous decade, including the destruction of its political, social, economic, and security capabilities. All such activity needed the assent of the high commissioner in Jerusalem and the principled authorization of the government in London.[24]

At the request of the theater commander in Cairo, General Bernard Paget, the intelligence assessment was transmitted to Cunningham in March 1946, through the army commander-in-chief in Palestine, Lieutenant General John D'Arcy. Paget, who adopted the conclusions of his intelligence personnel, made it clear that the document was not for circulation, unless a decision was made to act against the Jewish Agency. From the army's viewpoint, the agency's culpability was clear. The legal and political arguments described earlier were needed only in order to ground a recommendation for action that would be submitted to London and Jerusalem.

Cunningham responded to the intelligence assessment toward the end of March. He rejected its underlying approach but agreed that it would be of tactical use when the need arose. This "indictment," he wrote to Chief Secretary John Shaw, who was known to favor the Jewish Agency's dismantlement, is excellent in its analysis of the Haganah's military activity, but is politically deficient. He wanted consideration to be given to the preparation of a more comprehensive survey of the situation for use when needed—a document that would necessarily be more balanced and responsible in terms of analyzing the complexity of Yishuv politics, with its potential risks and prospects. Cunningham found the simplistic portrayal of Jewish Agency totalitarianism inaccurate and, more important, irresponsible when it came to the Yishuv leaders' will to resolve the conflict, as well as to prove the justice of their cause. Despite the fraught atmosphere, Cunningham believed that neither the Jewish Agency nor the Yishuv as a whole considered Britain an enemy; in his view, the agency also favored partition. However, he agreed that the Jewish Agency was acting against its own best interests, certainly since his arrival in the country. It was clear to him that there was only one way to eradicate Jewish terrorism, namely, the method that had been successfully tested during the so-called Saison, or "hunting season,"[25] in 1944–1945, when the Yishuv took action against Jewish terrorism. The Jewish Agency will act against terrorism far better than all the army's sophisticated intelligence branches, special units, and firepower, the high commissioner noted.[26]

Cunningham's response to the army's proposals set in motion a pattern for the months ahead: the active civilian governor overcame the latent military man. Even though he was still in uniform, and had only recently been awarded the coveted rank of general, Cunningham took a civilian perspective, as the envoy of the Colonial Office, not as the supreme commander of the armed forces in Palestine and the envoy of the War Office. Of the two branches that were subordinate to him, the political (Office of the Chief Secretary) and the military (army headquarters in Palestine), he gave primacy to the first.

To ensure he would be ready in case action were needed, Cunningham kept in close touch with the senior officials of the Colonial Office, the theater commanders in Cairo, and as far as possible the leaders of the Zionist movement and the Yishuv—less so with the Arab population. An extensive web of contacts, he believed, would prevent loss of control. From this point until the start of Operation Agatha, on June 29, 1946, Cunningham maneuvered between his awareness that influencing the Jewish Agency through violence would be wrong and his powerful desire not to be seen again as the advocate of a defensive approach.

In mid-April, the high commissioner transmitted to the colonial secretary the principles for military action against the Yishuv as agreed with the commander of the Middle East Land Forces: searches for illegal weapons and the detention of the commanders of the Haganah and the Palmah and, if necessary, also the members of the Jewish Agency Executive. This last target would be unprecedented in Britain's relations with the Yishuv. The colonial secretary accepted the method but delayed the execution; Cunningham willingly agreed. The minister reminded him that even if there were good reasons to take action against the Yishuv, such action would not be feasible until the cabinet reviewed the situation in light of the recommendations of the Anglo-American Committee. In other words, the government of Britain was unable to act independently in Palestine, even to mount a purely military operation. In case a flare-up made action necessary, London would consider the matter with all dispatch. In the meantime, the colonial secretary allowed Cunningham to propose the detention of selected leaders; the authorizations would be considered as circumstances merited.[27]

Toward the end of April, when the political-security situation began to deteriorate, compounded by disappointment in the report of the joint committee, the Mandate administration and army were ready. From their point of view, the truce requested by the Jewish Agency was meaningless. The violence erupted again and again, first sparked by the breakaway groups and later also by the Jewish Resistance Movement, in the form of clashes with the army and police in Tel Aviv on "Wingate Night"[28] in Tel Aviv (March 25–26), ahead of the possible arrival of a ship carrying illegal Jewish immigrants. In fact, there was no truce at all.[29]

At the beginning of May, the army began to circulate among its commanding officers in Palestine an extensive plan of action against the Jewish Agency and the Haganah. The operation would target the Yishuv's political-security leadership and attempt to destroy the Yishuv's military force—the same strategy that had been applied against the Palestine Arabs a decade earlier. The high commissioner, for his part, had already made it clear that he would not authorize a plan of this scale, which he believed departed from the spirit of the mid-April agreements between him and the theater commander. The plan was not implemented but remained a platform of ideas from which the principles of Operation Agatha were later extracted and formulated more stringently by the high commissioner himself.[30]

In the meantime, Cunningham sought to exhaust fully the possibility of persuading the Jewish Agency to cooperate in the effort against terrorism and embark on the path of political compromise. In this connection, the report of the Anglo-American Committee was a boon to him—and to the army, which urged the use of force. The report noted that the Jewish Agency was the largest nongovernmental organization in Palestine—and in the entire Middle East—but nevertheless was, for all practical purposes, a government alongside the appointed government and wielded vast influence over the Jewish public. At the same time, the report urged the agency to work with the administration in combating illegal immigration and terrorism. "Private armies ought not to exist if they constitute a danger to the peace of the world," the report stated. Deliberately or by mistake, the committee accepted the Jewish Agency's position of noninvolvement in Haganah operations within the framework of the Jewish Resistance Movement, but turned the mistake into a weapon against the agency. The committee did not distinguish between the Haganah and the breakaway organizations, maintaining that the latter had split from the Haganah, not from the Yishuv. In this view, all three organizations, including the Haganah, were illegal and the Jewish Agency was enjoined to fight them. The British officials in both Jerusalem and London knew that this was not the case—that unlike Etzel and Lehi, the Haganah was under the authority of the Jewish Agency.[31]

Cunningham believed that if the United States, the report's cosigner, were to add its weight to the pressure being exerted on the Jewish Agency, then the agency would ultimately help suppress terrorism and agree to a political compromise. He viewed the Jewish underground terrorist organizations (Etzel and Lehi, not the Haganah) as spikes in the wheel of the diplomatic process that must be removed in order to bring about a compromise in the form of partition. However, London, like the Jewish Agency, took a different view, though at least until the beginning of May both parties tried to play up the report's positive elements. However, it quickly became apparent that all the parties, including the United States, were prisoners of their expectations—expectations that were incompatible, not to say in conflict, with those of their counterparts. Tensions on the Washington–London–Jerusalem axis rose again. In the second half of May, the British government asked the Jews and the Arabs for their response to the report's recommendations. The Jewish Agency viewed this step, fundamentally anti-American in its thrust, as deliberate foot-dragging aimed at blocking implementation of the recommendations and, in particular, the absorption of 100,000 Jewish refugees. A new outbreak of violence loomed.[32]

The Jewish Agency decided to take action that would be painful for the British authorities in both Jerusalem and London. On the night of June 16–17, the Haganah blew up the bridges that connected Palestine with its neighbors. In terms of the Haganah's strength and experience at the time, Operation Markol (the "Night of the Bridges," in popular parlance) was an impressive feat. Overnight, eleven bridges along the country's borders were dynamited; ten of them were damaged. The Palmah lost fourteen men in the operation, and a British officer was also killed. The act was symbolic: Palestine was not cut off by land, as no deep rivers or broad canyons separated it from its neighbors. The Jewish Agency wanted to show that it could cause the Mandate administration serious trouble, as a reminder to London that it could not be ignored in any discussion about the future of the country. According to Shertok, the bridges operation was part of a combined plan in which the Jewish Agency sought to intertwine American pressure on Britain with pressure from below through resistance actions. The usually moderate Shertok found encouragement for this approach in the broad (though not total) agreement to the operation within the American Zionist movement and also, to the high commissioner's great embarrassment, in the ruling party in Britain. Just before the Night of the Bridges, Richard Crossman, a young pro-Zionist Labor member of Parliament who had served on the Anglo-American Committee, suggested to Shertok, with the knowledge of two ministers whom he did not name, that the Jewish Agency do all it can to make itself feared.[33]

Immediately after the Night of the Bridges, Etzel and Lehi joined in, lest they seem to be lagging behind the organized Yishuv. On June 18, Lehi, in coordination with the Haganah, attacked the Haifa railroad workshops; nine of the operatives were killed and twenty-two arrested. On the same day, Etzel, acting independently in response to a death sentence given to two of its activists, abducted five British officers. Two other officers were wounded in a second abduction attempt in Jerusalem, and one went missing. The abducted officers were likely to be murdered if the death sentence were carried out. Not for the last time, Cunningham had to choose between the security of his personnel and the overall British interest as he understood it.[34]

The dynamiting of the bridges compelled Cunningham, as the head of the civil system, to send the army, which eagerly awaited the call, into action, even though a military operation might weaken the status of the civil branch. On the night of June 18–19, under the harsh impression of the attacks on the bridges and the operations of the breakaway groups, Cunningham implored London to give him freedom of action. The request bore a dual aspect: an urgent necessity to respond and Cunningham's desire to control the character and scale of the response, rather than give the army free rein. On June 18, in the course of searches carried out following the bridges operation, three residents were killed in Kibbutz Kfar Giladi, in Upper Galilee. It was clear to Cunningham that the retaliatory method in force since his arrival in Palestine (encirclement, closure, searches, arrests, quelling civil resistance) had failed, not least because it resulted in casualties and did not advance his twin goals of achieving deterrence and cooperating with the Jewish Agency. Cunningham explained to his superiors that there was no guarantee that vigorous and effective action by the security forces would produce the desired result: persuading the Jewish Agency to accept a compromise plan and to cooperate in the campaign against terrorism. At the same time, he had to work fast to free the abducted soldiers, for fear of spontaneous outbursts of rage from the army and police. Cunningham noted that the Jewish community in Palestine was sympathetic to the criminals or was afraid of their reaction to collaboration with the British authorities. The "hunting season" was over.[35]

Cunningham understood the message of the Night of the Bridges as the Jewish Agency had intended—as a symbolic military action—and sought to respond in kind. Though aware of the need to act, his reservations about turning to the military and his preference for political pressure spawned a reaction that reflected his competing impulses. He knew the use of force would undercut his ability to function as the head of the civil system, and he grasped the advantage of cooperating with the Jewish Agency, but at the same time he knew that action was essential to create deterrence, boost the security forces' morale, and emphasize an offensive orientation. His conclusion: political pressure backed by a violent operation was the most efficient means both to bring about future cooperation with the Jewish Agency and to free the abductees.

Cunningham recommended to the colonial secretary to immediately break off the talks with the Jewish Agency about the entry of 100,000 refugees into the country and to approve an operation against both the illegal organizations and the Jewish Agency at a time the high commissioner himself deemed appropriate. Apparently frightened by his own bluster, he added that the threat of action alone might be enough to improve the situation, though without authorization to act he could not even issue a threat. Moreover, Weizmann had been invited to a private meeting with Cunningham on the evening of June 19, and it was important for Cunningham to have London's reply to his proposal beforehand so that he could articulate a clear position. "I can assure you," Cunningham wrote to Hall, "that should I see any way of avoiding the use of extreme measures I am and always have been the most anxious to do so."[36]

Even before Cunningham sent his emotional cable, London responded to his earlier requests in which he sought the freedom to decide whether to take action. The colonial secretary informed him that in consultation with the chiefs of staff, agreement was emerging to submit to the cabinet a draft resolution empowering the high commissioner to act when he saw fit, on a scale and using a method of his choosing, in coordination with the commander of the Middle East arena.[37]

To this, Cunningham reacted neither happily nor with a sigh of relief but ambivalently, and with anger that in the meantime abated: "I hope it was clear that what I asked was not permission immediately to put the plan into operation but merely to be in a position to do so should I think it was essential in the interests of public safety." Indeed, he retracted his request to take action. Until the eve of Operation Agatha, at the end of June, he consistently explained to his superiors and subordinates alike why this was not the time to act. With responsibility for a full-scale operation against the Jewish Agency falling on Cunningham for the first time, the high commissioner mustered short-term operational military arguments against an operation, counterbalanced with long-term policy grounds in favor of an operation. Duality, not to say confusion, marked his response.[38]

The high commissioner noted that, as a result of the recent events, the measures taken by the security forces were now more stringent and more thorough than in the past: extensive, painstaking searches had led to the seizure of wanted individuals, though no weapons as yet. This being so, Cunningham wrote with barely concealed satisfaction, the new (since May) GOC Palestine, Lieutenant General Evelyn Barker,[39] had apprised him that he wanted to reconsider the operational plan against the Jewish Agency and the Haganah and to put forward new ideas. "I agreed," he reported. In line with his general approach of separating the political from the military and not burning all his bridges, he suggested to Barker that he examine the possibility of differentiating between the operation to cripple the Jewish Agency—by arresting high officials and politicians—and action against members of military organizations (including the breakaways) or those suspected of possessing weapons.

Cunningham grasped the complexity of the situation: a military approach was needed in the short term, a diplomatic orientation was essential for the long term. To explain his approach to Secretary Hall, he cited Barker, an underling but useful in this context because of the military's vaunted eagerness to act. Yet even the new GOC, he noted, had doubts about the usefulness of arms searches, a posture that strengthened Cunningham's opinion that the illegal arms issue would be resolved only in a political agreement. Indeed, the imminent large-scale operation against the Jewish Agency did not include such searches. Even as the high commissioner had enough evidence to justify the operation, it was increasingly clear to him that sending the army into action should serve primarily the political-diplomatic goal; that is, it should be basically a policing action, to arrest leaders and uncover incriminating material, and not involve arms searches or a military offensive against the illegal armed organizations.[40]

On the evening of June 19, Cunningham met with Weizmann. Even as their conversation took place against the attacks by the Haganah and the breakaway organizations, the high commissioner emphasized that the only viable solution was a political one. Yet the Jewish Agency's military operation (the Night of the Bridges) had drenched its hands in blood. Cunningham accused the Zionist Yishuv leadership of having, by its deeds, thrust the military to the forefront of relations between the Yishuv and the administration.[41]

Weizmann, who was opposed to the operation against the bridges and still more to abductions of soldiers, told Cunningham that the violence marked a response to cumulative evidence of a negative shift in British policy toward Zionism: Bevin's hostile speech at the Trades Union conference on June 12, the mufti's return to the region, death sentences meted out to Jews, remarks by former Arab Legion commander Glubb Pasha that he was ready to participate in an operation against the Jewish Agency, and the blacklist of wanted activists, which the army had apparently leaked deliberately and had been pasted on walls in Palestine's big cities. As for the last item, Cunningham did not like the army's independence in this matter but thought the leak might be for the good: the Yishuv should know that the British were well informed, knew who was who, and intended to act. To Weizmann's protest against the publicizing of the list of names, the high commissioner retorted angrily that it was typical of the Jewish mentality to be surprised and astounded when the British prepared a violent response to their violence. This was no more an antisemitic generalization than Weizmann's threat, according to Cunningham, that he was concerned the list would reach the United States, "with most unfortunate results for us [the British]." Weizmann, as usual, did not hesitate to invoke the Jews' close ties with the United States and their influence there when he thought it needful.[42]

Weizmann's arguments did not persuade the high commissioner; in his view, the Jewish Agency's violence was hurting not only Britain, the administration, and him personally but also—and mainly—the Yishuv itself. At this time, Cunningham sought the common interests of the administration and the Yishuv. He found Weizmann's assumption that the Mandate administration, along with the high commissioner, would slide down the slippery slope together with the organized Yishuv to be poor consolation. For the Yishuv, he told Weizmann, the crash was apt to be the last one; for Britain it would be a painful blow, no more.[43]

In London, the cabinet approved Cunningham's request for authorization to act on the very day on which the high commissioner formulated his objections to his own proposal. The authorization was granted not only in response to pressure from the military in London and Cairo and from the Mandate authorities in Jerusalem but also in view of the diplomatic-political background: Britain's rift with the United States over the report of the joint committee as well as a diminished fear of the implications of the rift for urgent American economic aid to Britain, as the legislative process in Congress had reached a stage where the aid was assured. The British government also took into account the reaction of its Arab wards to the Anglo-American Committee's report. All these factors helped lower the barriers to the authorization of an operation against the Jewish Agency. On June 20, the cabinet, in consultation with the Chiefs of Staff Committee, authorized an operation under the aegis of the high commissioner, to be coordinated with the army, at a time he would deem appropriate.[44]

As the high commissioner saw it, the authorization was based on political and practical considerations, combined with London's respect for his clear point of view. He understood that the use of force, even if successful, would adversely affect the future ability of his administration to function. The good cooperation between the administration and the Yishuv was a stabilizing factor in Palestine. The army could break the Yishuv's strength, but if so the Yishuv would no longer be capable of cooperating with the administration to manage the country even if it wished to, in the absence of effective national institutions. Thus, a full-scale and excessively thorough military operation could bring about the end of the civil administration in Palestine, and with it the end of the high commissioner's power as the supreme civilian authority, and hence his overall prospects of success.

Accordingly, Cunningham's view in late June was that a limited operation against the Jewish Agency, with purely political goals, should be mounted. The cabinet decision of June 20 allowed him to act in that spirit. It is not an exaggeration to say that the high commissioner's personal history worked in favor of the Zionist cause here. The Jewish Agency, for its part, "rewarded" him by stepping up the violence, for the first time pushing him to center stage of the British presence in Palestine. He did not intend to allow the Jews to ruin either their part or his in the unfolding drama.

NOTES

1. Cunningham to Hall, December 29–30, 1945, NA C0733/457; and May 4, 1946, NA F0371/52528.

2. On the duality of Ben-Gurion's approach, see, e.g., Teveth, *Kinat David*, p. 703. Recognition that the Jewish Agency was both essential and legal, along with the total rejection of its path, is seen precisely in the green light given by the cabinet to act against it. Cabinet meeting, June 20, 1946, NA CAB128/5.

3. Weizmann's early approach is discussed in Jehuda Reinharz, *Chaim Weizmann: The Making of a Zionist Leader*, New York 1993; on Weizmann's moral stance vis-à-vis Jewish terrorism, see Norman Rose, *Chaim Weizmann: A Biography*, New York 1986, chapter 19.

4. Teveth, *Kinat David*, p. 717. This theme is a thread through the book, notably in chapter 26, "Sneh Appears in Paris"; a similar account appears in Naomi Shepherd, *Ploughing Sand: British Rule in Palestine, 1917–1948*, London 1999, p. 227. In contrast, Rose's *Chaim Weizmann: A Biography* describes a confrontational relationship between the two.

5. Weizmann to Cunningham, May 17, 1946, WA, 2659; Cunningham to Weizmann, May 23, 1946, WA, 2660; Weizmann to Cunningham, June 2, 1946, WA, 2662; Shaw to Weizmann, May 29, 1946, WA, 2662.

6. On the Night of the Bridges, see later in this chapter; Operation Agatha is discussed in chapter 3.

7. Cunningham to Hall, May 4, 1946, NA F0371/52528, and also June 18, 1946, MECA CP, B1, F1/109, June 21, 1946, MECA CP, B1, F1/110, June 29, 1946, NA C0537/1713/93869.

8. Teveth, *Kinat David*, p. 711.

9. Heller, "Zionist Policy," pp. 225–227.

10. Ibid., p. 226.

11. Joseph Heller, (ed.), *The Letters and the Papers of Chaim Weizmann*, Vol. XXII, Series A, May 1945–July 1947, Jerusalem 1979, p. 163, note; Teveth, *Kinat David*, p. 891; Cabinet meeting, July 11, 1946, NA CAB128/5.

12. Teveth, *Kinat David*, pp. 626, 677, 689; Shertok, *Imprisoned with Paper and Pencil*, p. 15. The British sought to arrest the senior officials of the Jewish Agency starting at the end of June 1946, with the onset of Operation Agatha (see chapter 3). If Weizmann was too busy to see him, Cunningham made do with the Jewish Agency's legal advisor, Dov Joseph; the two met on May 20, 1946, CZA, S25/7706.

13. Heller, "Zionist Policy," p. 282.

14. Meeting of the senior staff of the Colonial Office with Cunningham, November 14, 1945, NA C0537/1822; John Martin to Hall, November 27, 1945, NA C0537/1742; Cunningham to Hall, December 29–December 30, 1945, NA C0733/457; Hall to Cunningham, January 2, 1946, NA C0733/457.

15. Cabinet meeting, January 1, 1946, NA CAB128/5; report of the Chiefs of Staff, "Situation in Palestine," November 19, 1945, MECA CP, B5, F4.

16. On the murder of the seven soldiers and the Yishuv's reaction, see David Ben-Gurion, *Toward the End of the Mandate: Memoirs, June 29, 1946–March 1947*, Tel Aviv 1993, p. 3.

17. Cunningham to Hall, December 29–December 30, 1945, NA C0733/457, and also February 19, 1946, MECA CP, B1, F1/3.

18. Montgomery, *The Memoirs*, pp. 420–424, 426; Charters, *The British Army and Jewish Insurgency in Palestine, 1945–47*, London 1989, p. 100.

19. Charters, *The British Army*.

20. Louis, *The British Empire*, pp. 3–21.

21. This description is a development of Louis's approach, ibid., pp. 21–27, and is based on an analysis of Montgomery's viewpoint, as elaborated in the chapters that follow.

22. "The Jewish Agency," SIME/700/XI/2, March 1, 1946, MECA CP, B4, F4/33.

23. Ibid.; Yoav Gelber, *The Emergence of a Jewish Army—The Veterans of the British Army in the IDF*, Jerusalem 1986, pp. 11–15 (Hebrew).

24. "The Jewish Agency," MECA CP, B4, F/4/33–4. Gelber shows that the British Army's intelligence information about the Haganah, particularly the numerical data, was generally inaccurate. Yoav Gelber, *Growing a Fleur-de-Lis: The Intelligence Services of the Jewish Yishuv in Palestine, 1918–1947*, Tel Aviv 1992, vol. 1, pp. 293–295 (Hebrew).

25. Referring to the collaboration between the Mandate administration and the organized Yishuv to suppress the terrorism perpetrated by Etzel and Lehi. There was also a previous "little hunting season," in 1942, in which the Jewish Agency dispatched Etzel—which joined the war effort against Germany—to take action against Lehi. In the "big hunting season" of 1944–1945, the Jewish Agency operated against Etzel, and did so again in summer 1947, following Etzel's murder of two British sergeants (discussed later).

26. Cunningham to Shaw, March 25, 1946, MECA CP, B4, F4/32.

27. Cunningham to Hall, April 15, 1946, Hall to Cunningham, April 23, 1946, MECA CP, B1, F1/67.

28. The Yishuv's operation that night in support of illegal immigration commemorated Major General Orde Charles Wingate's friendship to the Jews and military leadership in Palestine from 1937 to 1938. Wingate was killed in Burma in 1944.

29. Slutzky, *History of the Haganah*, III, 2, p. 879, notes that the truce began upon the publication of the report. Immediately afterward (p. 880), the author writes that the truce had been in effect "since the Anglo-American Committee started its work." (The text does not make clear whether this refers to the end of 1945, when the committee arrived in Palestine, or the beginning of March 1946.) In any event, the British could only react to events that had occurred, and there was no truce in that regard. The truce argument has been accepted in the historiography as well, e.g., Meir Avizohar's introduction to David Ben-Gurion, *Toward the End of the Mandate*, p. 4 (Hebrew).

30. LHCMA, SP, 6/4; Cunningham to Colonial Office, April 24, 1946, NA F0371/52516.

31. Report of the Anglo-American Committee of Inquiry, pp. 14, 33–35.

32. Cunningham to Colonial Office, April 24, 1946, NA F0371/52516; Heller, "Zionist Policy," p. 282.

33. Slutzky, *History of the Haganah*, III, 3, Appendix 35, pp. 1931–1932 (Hebrew); Zerubavel Gilad (ed.), *Book of the Palmah*, Tel Aviv 1955, I, pp. 650–655 (Hebrew); and Slutzky, *History of the Haganah*, III, 2, pp. 880–888; Shertok to executive of Zionist Action Committee, June 17, 1946, CZA, S25/355.

34. Slutzky, *History of the Haganah*, III, 2, pp. 886–887; Cunningham to Hall, first of two cables from the high commissioner to the Colonial Secretary, June 19, 1946, MECA CP, B1, F1/10.

35. Slutzky, *History of the Haganah*, III, 2, pp. 886–887; Cunningham to Hall, first of two cables, June 19, 1946.

36. Cunningham to Hall, second cable (see previous footnote), following the Night of the Bridges, the attack on the railway workshop, and the spate of abductions, June 19, 1946, MECA CP, B1, F1/109.

37. Hall to Cunningham, June 18, 1946 (received June 19 at 4 a.m.), MECA CP, B1, F1/102.

38. Cunningham to Hall, June 20, 1946, MECA CP, B1, F1/108.

39. Barker (1894–1983) was the GOC British forces in Palestine from May 1946 until February 1947. He had previously served in Palestine during the period of the Arab Revolt as a regimental commander. In the Second World War, he took part in the Normandy landing and in the conquest and occupation of Germany, all under Montgomery's command. Upon his return to Britain, he was appointed head of Eastern Command, the same post Cunningham held until his departure for Palestine. Barker retired from military service in 1950.

40. Cunningham to Hall, June 20, 1946, MECA CP, B1, F1/108.

41. Cunningham to Hall, June 21, 1946, MECA CP, B1, F1/110.

42. Cunningham to Hall, June 20, 1946, MECA CP, B1, F1/108.

43. Ibid.

44. Ibid.; Cabinet meeting, June 20, 1946, NA CAB128/5.

3

Saving the Jews from Themselves
Operation Agatha

On Saturday June 29, 1946, the Mandatory administration sent the army into action to carry out the largest operation mounted against the Yishuv during the British period of rule in Palestine. The operation, which ended on July 11, was aimed at the legal and semilegal institutions of the organized Yishuv, which functioned under the auspices of the British authorities and in coordination with them. The Yishuv was stunned by the scale of the offensive. The first day of the operation, with its shock of surprise, would be engraved in the collective memory of the Jewish community, which dubbed it Black Sabbath. The British, more mundanely, code-named it Operation Agatha, without any special known reason.

For Cunningham, the operation was a tool in the service of his policy. It was launched with his consent, but more important, under conditions he laid down. Limited in scope, the operation had a broader political aim: to help the Jewish Agency help itself, for the agency's own best interests, as the high commissioner viewed them, and for the sake of the British interest. The Jewish Agency would avoid becoming embroiled in a hopeless war against the British and would return to the road leading to partition and a state. Britain would gain quiet and the prospect of steering the Mandate to a termination desirable both for itself and for the West as a whole, in the light of the Cold War: two states, Jewish and Arab, that would remain in the West's sphere of influence. Cunningham also needed these results—suppression of the violence and a political solution beneficial to Britain—for his struggle to restore his image. Everyone would see that the so-called "defensive" general was advancing his policy by means of a saliently offensive move.

The British cabinet's decision of June 20, 1946—to take action against the Jewish Agency in a controlled manner and with limited responsibility, and with a timetable set by the high commissioner—was Cunningham's first victory in the intra-British arena and confirmation that the stage of adjustment to his new mission had ended. London was no less critical an arena than Palestine itself. After the Colonial Office and the high commissioner retracted their demand in late 1945 for action to be taken against the Jewish Agency, the army led the call for an offensive. Now, with Cunningham's original proposal up for discussion, and no new ideas put forward by the army, the cabinet approved the high commissioner's plan.[1]

In the meeting, the ministers were asked to consider a memorandum submitted by Colonial Secretary Hall, who led the discussion. Hall took verbatim Cunningham's ideas as they appeared in the cable he had drafted on the evening of June 18 and sent in the predawn hours of June 19. He did, however, delete the hesitations Cunningham expressed. The high commissioner wished to defer the discussion about the entry of 100,000 Jewish refugees into Palestine until the officers abducted by Etzel were released. He requested authorization to take action against the illegal Jewish organizations and against the Jewish Agency according to a plan whose principles had been articulated in mid-April with the army. Special emphasis was placed on the necessity of demonstrating a connection between the Jewish Agency and the rampant terrorism. On June 29, in the very first hours of the operation, Hall had Cunningham send him an interim summation of the findings of the searches (particularly of the documents seized in the Jewish Agency headquarters in Jerusalem) and a situation assessment ahead of a statement that the prime minister was to make in the House of Commons on July 1. Hall was especially interested in findings proving that the Haganah had taken illegal action, which would thereby convict the Jewish Agency, to which the Haganah was accountable.[2]

The cabinet took a broader view than that of the high commissioner. This was a useful lesson to the latter, who was a novice in the field of statesmanship. Thus, the cabinet rejected his request to postpone the discussions about the 100,000 refugees until the return of the abducted British officers, because the British government could not allow itself to act under the threat of Etzel (however significant the threat might be in terms of public opinion). Indeed, from the government's perspective the question of the abducted soldiers was far overshadowed by the issue of relations with the United States. On this subject, Hall added, somewhat convolutedly, that if the discussion about the 100,000 were deferred because of terrorism, this would be as though Britain were accepting the number and now arguing only about the conditions of their arrival in Palestine.

Others in the meeting added that Britain must on no account suspend the discussion of the Palestine question in general while London was expecting the arrival of the American members of the joint committee of experts—the Morrison-Grady Committee, which had been formed in order to pry open the Anglo-American channel through which London sought to reach a political solution. That channel seemed to be blocked at the end of June, owing to the sharp disagreement between the two powers over the report of the joint committee of inquiry. The Morrison-Grady Committee submitted its recommendations for the division of Palestine into semi-autonomous regions toward the end of July 1946. The British government accepted them and kept them on file until the following spring, when it returned the Mandate to the United Nations in despair.

In the meantime, the cabinet, spurred by the urgent necessity for secrecy, and contrary to the opinion of the foreign secretary—who, though not present at the meeting, requested that the Americans be informed immediately, in writing, of whatever decision was made—decided to wait as long as possible before apprising Washington of the planned action against the Jewish Agency. There was concern about possible leaks and about pressure by the American Jewish community on the White House if the plan became known.[3]

Cunningham's request for authorization to take action against the terrorist organizations—Etzel and Lehi—and against the Haganah (Palmah) and the Jewish Agency was approved. Here, too, the cabinet, under Hall's guidance, helped Cunningham reword his proposal to better reflect the desirable mix of a military operation having a political purpose. Hall exploited the moderating presence of Alanbrooke, the outgoing chief of the Imperial General Staff—he would be succeeded by Montgomery a week later, on June 26—to assert that this was the time to act, before the British troops in Palestine took matters into their own hands. Revenge wreaked by even a few soldiers for their buddies' death would be extremely damaging to Britain's status in Palestine and the entire Middle East.

Alanbrooke, for his part, explained that if the current uncertainty persisted the military commanders in Palestine would be apt to lose control of their troops. He probably had in mind Montgomery's militant visit to Palestine a week before the cabinet meeting (June 14–16). Montgomery met briefly with Cunningham but claimed that the high commissioner was incapable of making decisions. He spent most of his time with his aides and with the commander of the Middle East arena, who accompanied him on the visit. His aim was to prepare the new GOC Palestine, Lieutenant General Barker, and with him the many soldiers who listened to his speech at the Sarafand base, for "a war on the Jews." On June 19, the day before the cabinet meeting, a Jewish passerby was murdered in Jerusalem by a British officer, apparently in reaction to Etzel's abduction of the officers. The troops could well misconstrue the approach of the new chief of staff. Accordingly, Alanbrooke recommended that the cabinet accord greater freedom of action to the high commissioner and to the Middle East commander (in that order) and thereby enable them to initiate action to deter the Jewish Agency and pacify the army. The recommendation had the support of the secretary of war, who was also present at the meeting.[4]

One aspect of the cabinet decision was identical to Cunningham's approach and as such represented his greatest success: the ministers instructed him to bear in mind that the Yishuv had created its military force not to fight against British policy but to defend the Jewish community against possible Arab violence. Arab leaders' declarations made it clear that such violence was likely to recur, the ministers noted. It was not by chance that in this meeting the cabinet also decided to probe how the mufti, Haj Amin al-Husseini, had reached Egypt from France, and to make his stay there conditional on his shunning politics. The Jews, in short, must be able to defend themselves, so the operation should not aim to disarm them. Nor should the Jewish Agency be destroyed, the cabinet emphasized.

At the same time, though the cabinet believed that the Jewish Agency was behind the violence, the allegation needed to be substantiated. Accordingly, the cabinet decided on a raid of the agency's headquarters in which documents would be seized in order to prove its responsibility for acts of terrorism. Additionally, some senior Jewish Agency officials would be taken into custody, as a warning and deterrent measure. The aim here was to strengthen the moderates in the Yishuv leadership. The cabinet decision noted further that because the Jews had organizations that were capable of operating against the administration, it must be made clear that the British government would not tolerate such activity by either the Arabs or the Jews and that the operation was not meant to curry favor with the Arabs.[5]

The decision-making process prior to the implementation of Operation Agatha bolstered Cunningham's status. For the first time since he took office, in concrete operative terms rather than just in theory, he was identified clearly as the supreme commander of the armed forces in Palestine. This was of critical importance for his highly charged relations with the War Office and the military. On the eve of the decision to authorize the high commissioner to act, the colonial secretary, in consultation with the Chiefs of Staff Committee (CSC), laid down the chain of command in Palestine: the cabinet would decide in principle to act after consulting with the csc; the minister of defense would decide whether to implement the decision; and the goc Middle East would submit for the high commissioner's approval a proposal for a specific operation, or the high commissioner would propose a plan to him that would require their joint agreement. The authority to order the armed forces into action and the decision about the scale and composition of the troops naturally resided with the arena commander, in accordance with the responsibility vested in him. However, the order would not be given without the high commissioner's consent to the character and orientation of the operation and, above all, its timing. To ensure clarity, Hall wrote to Cunningham: "In these circumstances, final responsibility rests with you as head of civil Government. . . ." That authority found clear expression in the cabinet decision of June 20.[6]

Even though the high commissioner was the supreme commander of the military forces within his realm of jurisdiction, his superiority over the commander of the Middle East arena was not clear. The problem had first arisen for discussion in 1937, when the decision was made to commit forces to suppress the Arab Revolt. From June 1920, when the British military government was abolished, until 1937, no significant troop deployment occurred in Palestine. At the beginning of 1937, High Commissioner Arthur Wauchope raised the question of where supreme authority to send forces into action lay, in the event of differences between him and the goc Palestine. His authority as supreme commander was recognized by the government, though it was emphasized that he was not the forces' direct commander. If differences arose, the government would decide. In October 1938, the cabinet reaffirmed that supreme power lay with the high commissioner.[7]

The problem was that between 1937–1938 and 1946 a world war intervened. On the eve of the war, in May 1939, a new command function was established: Middle East Command, headquartered in Cairo. The state of war deprived the high commissioner of his military supremacy in favor of the arena commander. Moreover, the high commissioner beginning in 1938, Sir Harold MacMichael, did not have a military background, and Palestine was a jumping-off point for military operations (such as the conquest of Syria and Lebanon in June 1941) and also a training and relaxation site for troops. As the domestic scene in Palestine was relatively quiet until October 1945, Field Marshal Gort, who succeeded MacMichael in autumn 1944, did not have to make use of the armed forces. Hall had good reason to focus his recommendation to the government on the relations between the high commissioner and the Middle East commander-in-chief. The GOC Palestine was not even mentioned in the debate between the Colonial Office and the military in 1946.

Hall and Cunningham could not have known that the cabinet decision of June 20, 1946, did not end the dispute. Indeed, it soon became apparent that the decision marked only the start of the campaign to enshrine the high commissioner's status vis-à-vis the army. Just a week later, the new CIGS, Montgomery, contrary to Alanbrooke, his predecessor, was unwilling to accept the supremacy of the high commissioner in general and of Cunningham in particular. On the day he assumed office in practice, June 27 (the appointment formally took effect the previous day, but he returned that day to Britain from the imperial tour just described), and after it had been decided to launch the operation against the Jewish Agency on June 29, Montgomery instructed General Miles Dempsey, the new Cairo-based commander-in-chief of Middle East Land Forces, to strike powerfully, rapidly, and decisively at the "fanatical and cunning" Jewish "enemy."[8] Categorizing the Yishuv as an enemy was foreign to British conduct until then and to Cunningham's approach in particular. Beyond reflecting Montgomery's style—that of a hard-core soldier devoid of political sophistication—the move might have been expected in light of the violence in Palestine and on the eve of an unprecedented operation against the Jewish Agency. However, neither Montgomery nor Dempsey, both of whom took office only a few days before Operation Agatha, was aware of the high commissioner's status in the spirit of the cabinet decision. Indeed, even if they had wished to modify the guidelines of Operation Agatha, as they were agreed between Cunningham and the GOC Palestine, and approved by their predecessors, Alanbrooke and Paget, they would have been unable to do so. It was simply too late, both because of the short time that remained until the start of the operation and because eliminating the high commissioner's involvement required negotiations with the Colonial Office and, effectively, a revision of the cabinet decision.

It is no accident that contemporaries who later tried to measure the success of Operation Agatha through the prism of Montgomery's guidelines viewed it as a failure of the military. The Haganah was not trounced, because that was not the purpose of the operation. The army provided forces, equipment, procedures, and reports—not much more. Its control of the operation, in terms of both aims and management, was limited.[9]

The decision to entrust the high commissioner with supreme authority for the operation was of precedent-setting importance for Cunningham, allaying his fears about the collapse of the civil administration and the transfer of its powers to the army. His differences with the army had surfaced in May–June 1946, before Operation Agatha. They revolved around the question of whether Britain's rule in Palestine was based on political agreement, in particular with the Yishuv, or on military force. Cunningham was now embarking on an operation that might usher in a period of quiet enabling political activity or generate a bloodbath with unforeseeable consequences. What is clear is that his words and deeds on the eve of the operation showed the importance for him of reassuming, even if only momentarily, the mantle of the general capable of using force.

Although the declared reason for Operation Agatha was the connection between the Jewish Agency and Jewish terrorism, the operation was actually mounted in large measure to prove that connection. Not everyone on the British side, whether in London, Cairo, or Jerusalem, was convinced of the connection, which the Jewish Agency consistently denied. And, as noted, another goal, no less crucial for the long term, was to bring about the moderation of the Jewish Agency's leadership. These larger goals were channeled into a series of concrete tasks, in descending order of importance: finding and impounding documents linking the Jewish Agency's legal leadership to terrorism; taking the agency's leaders into custody; and, to prevent possible resistance, arresting senior Haganah and especially Palmah officers.

On June 25, following a consultation between Cunningham and Barker, the operation's main points and projected time frame were transmitted to British military headquarters in Cairo. The operation was set for the predawn hours of Saturday June 29, as this would facilitate the primary operative objective: to seize documents and arrest leaders. Its conclusion was left open-ended, depending on developments. The aim was to cripple the Palmah, which the British viewed as the most effective and most dangerous organization in the short term. Raids on the Palmah's command posts would be conducted to detain as many "officers and ORs [other ranks]" as possible. Members of the Haganah, the Palmah's parent body, would not be arrested unless they actively resisted.

Cunningham understood the character of the Yishuv's revolt, which consisted mainly of guerilla and terror acts carried out by the Palmah, while the main force of the Haganah—consisting of the militia-like field corps and most of the command structure—took no part in the resistance. The breakaway organizations, Etzel and Lehi, were not mentioned in the operational plan. From the outset, Cunningham sought to eradicate Jewish terrorism by cooperating with the Jewish Agency: by persuading it to return to the "Saison" of World War II, when the agency succeeded in silencing the breakaways almost completely. Arms searches would be a byproduct of the arrests and uncovering of documents, not a goal in their own right. Emphasizing this point, Cunningham and Barker agreed that the operation's success depended on absolute secrecy. That same day, June 25, the GOC Middle East transmitted the plan to the CSC in London.[10]

At 4:15 a.m. on June 29, 1946, the British forces began moving toward the primary target of Operation Agatha: the offices of the Jewish Agency and others connected with the agency in Jerusalem, Tel Aviv, and Haifa, as well as kibbutzim at which the Palmah was based. In order to mask their true intention, the security forces also conducted searches in nine randomly dispersed kibbutzim in the northern valleys, the Sharon region, the south, and the Jerusalem area, leaving the Jewish Agency and the Haganah confused about the purpose of the operation. The kibbutzim chosen to serve as decoys in the operation's first stage were Yagur, Sha'ar Ha'amakim, Mizra, Kfar Gideon, Geva, Ein Harod, Tel Yosef, Beit Hashitta, and Ashdot Ya'akov. A little later, concurrent with the takeover of the Jewish Agency compound in Jerusalem, Kibbutz Ramat Rachel, at the city's southern edge, was also raided. Simultaneously, British forces entered three more kibbutzim: Ma'abarot, Givat Haim, and Givat Brenner. As of 8 a.m., no reports had surfaced of significant resistance. Those first hours saw the arrest of three members of the Jewish Agency Executive: Moshe Shertok, Yitzhak Gruenbaum, and Rabbi Judah Fishman-Maimon. Among other senior agency figures taken into custody later that day were David Remez, David Hacohen, Dov Yosef (Bernard Joseph), and Berl Raptor. At 8 a.m., on the assumption that the surprise had played itself out, an official announcement was issued about the operation that mentioned some of the kibbutzim raided by the army, referred to the arrests, and added that the high commissioner would be making a "very important announcement" to the entire public in Palestine, Jewish and Arab alike.[11]

At 10:50 a.m., the commander-in-chief, Middle East (C-in-C. ME), informed the chiefs of staff that the operation had begun exactly on time and was being carried out in the spirit of the plan agreed on with the high commissioner. Jewish Agency headquarters in Jerusalem were taken over without resistance. Selective arrests were made in Tel Aviv and Haifa, and several buildings in which relevant documents might be found were seized. In Haifa, the army blew up the entrance to the headquarters of

Bank Hapoalim and of the Women's International Zionist Organization (WIZO).

In its next phase, the operation focused on Palmah units in the rural areas. As the roundup and identification of people in the kibbutzim continued, resistance grew though still remained largely passive. In Kibbutz Yagur, the troops used teargas to overcome passive resistance. In Ein Harod, one man was killed while attempting to escape and three were injured by a local truck that tried to block the road. There was resistance at the entrance to Tel Yosef, where a kibbutz member who attacked a British soldier was killed, along with the soldier, both by British fire. The searches were extended to two more kibbutzim, Afikim and Kfar Hittim. No resistance was reported. A few people were wounded at Givat Haim while engaging in passive resistance. In the south, the operation also targeted Kibbutz Na'an; in nearby Rehovot, meanwhile, the British dismantled roadblocks set up by the Haganah on the route into town from both north and south in an attempt to delay the transport of arrested Palmah members to the detention camp in Rafah. The roadblocks were put back in place, only to be removed again by the security forces. In Ramat Rachel, truncheons were used to break up a demonstration by women.

The country's borders were shut down for twenty-four hours. Telephone and telegraph communications (including those of the press) were blocked until the end of the operation, for almost two weeks. A preventive curfew was imposed on the Arabs in Jerusalem and in the Arab hinterland, particularly in Wadi 'Ara, the eastern section of Western Galilee, the Jordan Valley, the Beit She'an Valley, the Jordan Rift Valley, Samaria, and Judea. The large Arab cities in the north and center of the country—Acre, Nazareth, Jenin, Nablus, Ramallah, Ramle, Lod (Lydda), and Tiberias, a mixed city—were also placed under curfew. For their part, other mixed Jewish-Arab centers—Safed, Haifa, and Jaffa—were not placed under curfew, nor was Tel Aviv or the rural south. The majority of the first day's missions were completed by 10:30 a.m. To the satisfaction of Government House and army headquarters in the King David Hotel, resistance continued to be generally passive and weak. Quiet reigned in the big cities on the evening of June 29.[12]

Although telephones and the telegraphic service were disabled, the administration was able to issue public announcements by other means, particularly the radio and in press conferences. In the late morning, Cunningham spoke over the government radio station. Emphasizing that he and his government did not believe that the Palestine question would be resolved by force, he assured the public that the aim was to keep the operation focused, limited, and local in character. At the same time, he warned, the caution being shown by the security forces should not be taken as a sign of weakness. This approach, he explained, was rooted in the desire to implement the operation in full without being dragged into a larger action. (This may be the origin of the theory, then widespread in the Yishuv and repeated in Israeli historiography, to the effect that the British had prepared a large-scale plan code-named Broadside, of which Agatha was a part, but shied away from implementing it. The British material contains no evidence of such a plan. Broadside was actually a contingency plan drawn up after the assassination of Lord Moyne, the British minister of state in the Middle East, by members of Lehi in November 1944. The plan was shelved when Lehi and Etzel were targeted in the Saison.) Cunningham concluded his radio address by reminding his audience of the cardinal issue as he saw it: the political discussion of the country's future. His remarks made it clear that additional terrorism would rule out a political move. Both in his radio statement and in his reports to the colonial secretary, Cunningham painted a picture of a resolute but cautious operation whose ultimate purpose was to renew dialogue and reinforce the political process, not eradicate it. The restraint Cunningham showed was well calculated.[13]

As part of his publicity campaign, Cunningham had Chief Secretary John Shaw speak to the press. Shaw volunteered no details, noting only that the operation was not aimed at the broad law-abiding public but instead sought to contain a situation of emerging anarchy in which innocent people were being murdered. The wording used by the senior officials of the administration indicated clearly that their approach differed from that of the army. They were not waging a "war on the Jews" or emulating the methods used to suppress the Arab Revolt, which had included collective punishment. In the present case, the administration said it had no intention of harming the population as such, but only proving that the Yishuv leadership was an accomplice in the wave of terrorism and curbing its envoys in the Haganah-Palmah.[14]

Operation Agatha continued after June 29. The next day at first light, and on the following day, searches were conducted in more kibbutzim: Gvat, Ramat David, Degania Aleph and Degania Bet, Sarid, Betaniya (Alumot), Ayelet Hashahar, and Sdot Yam. These searches ended on July 1 in the evening. During the next ten days, documents were confiscated and subjected to preliminary sorting. At the same time, preparations were made for the orderly return to the Jewish Agency of the sites that had been seized.

On July 1, Cunningham informed the Colonial Office that two thousand of the detainees were connected to the Yishuv leadership. Everyone possessing influence or exercising authority and responsibility in connection with the revolt was arrested. Nevertheless, the abundant material that was seized—most of it in Hebrew—did not readily supply the proof Cunningham needed to back up his claim to the Colonial Office. The documents had to be sifted and, above all, translated. The high commissioner's defense of the large-scale arrests showed that he was disturbed by the difficulty of finding written proof of the Jewish Agency's complicity in terrorism—a key goal of Operation Agatha. On July 1, when the prime minister told the House of Commons that this was the operation's purpose, it was already clear that the seized material had not lived up to expectations. Cunningham told Hall that the police had solid information that the material linking the Jewish Agency to the Palmah and to the illegal immigration effort had been removed from a building raided by the security forces before their arrival.[15]

On July 2, Hall instructed Cunningham to withdraw from the Jewish Agency building and repair the damage done there. He also asked Cunningham to consider releasing most of the detainees against whom there were no specific charges. Hall urged the high commissioner to move quickly, because of the interest London was taking in the operation, reflecting his unease as the official responsible for backing up the prime minister's statement to the House of Commons. Cunningham immediately established a committee, headed by the deputy governor of the Jerusalem District, to estimate the amount of damage done at the Jewish Agency compound. The committee was given until July 9 to submit its report so that the British forces could evacuate the site on July 10 and the high commissioner could give the necessary budget for its renovations. The Jewish Agency was invited to send a representative to help decide about the repairs but declined, explaining that its presence had not been requested during the search itself.[16]

The searches were still continuing on July 3. The chance discovery of a large arms cache in Kibbutz Yagur that same day extended the operation, even though this had not been one of its aims. As for deciding whom to release, that would depend on the information retrieved from the large number of documents, on which much work remained to be done.[17]

The question of when to terminate Operation Agatha was more than an operative issue. Government House knew that the way the operation ended would affect relations with the Yishuv and its leadership, and thereby also the political solution. Certainly, the end would not come before the evacuation, both concrete and symbolic, of Jewish Agency headquarters in Jerusalem. On July 8, Cunningham reported that both the searches and the repair of the damage done to the compound had been concluded. On July 9, he announced that British forces would leave Kibbutz Yagur the following day and that prisoners whom there was no reason to hold—that is, those not suspected of involvement in anti-administration violence in recent months—were in the process of being released. Simultaneously, the security forces pursued their intelligence efforts to find and arrest wanted leaders not yet taken into custody but known to be in the country.[18]

Cunningham was perturbed that two of the principal proponents of the Jewish Agency's violent activism had not been arrested: David Ben-Gurion, the chairman of the body's executive, and Moshe Sneh, the head of Haganah National Headquarters. These men were prime targets, both in terms of antiterrorism and the political aspect. Any doubts Cunningham may have harbored about the Jewish Agency's ties with the Haganah were dispelled by British internal security service MI5, which furnished him with proof that Ben-Gurion and Shertok, the head of the Jewish Agency's Political Department, represented the supreme authority in the Haganah. Shertok was one of the first to be arrested; Ben-Gurion disappeared. Cunningham and his aides learned, probably from MI5, which had Ben-Gurion under surveillance, that he was scheduled to return to the country on the day a warrant for his arrest was issued, June 29. However, Ben-Gurion did not arrive in Palestine that day. After the senior leadership was detained, a worried Cunningham cabled London: "I understand that Ben Gurion, who was to have arrived here today, is staying in Paris until 1 July when it was his intention to return to London. If anything can be done to detain him or limit his activities, I should be most grateful if you would take action."[19]

Ben-Gurion did not return either to Tel Aviv or to London—if he had gone to the British capital, he most likely would have been arrested.

On June 29, no one in either the civilian or military branch of the administration knew where Ben-Gurion was. Some sensed he had managed to enter the country secretly. On July 2, his home in Tel Aviv was searched, but in vain. To Cunningham's chagrin, Ben-Gurion remained safely in Paris. The high commissioner was unaware that London did not need his evidence in order to arrest Ben-Gurion. According to Shabtai Teveth,

Ben-Gurion's biographer, on June 19 Ben-Gurion himself, in a conversation with Hall, had disclosed his ties to the Haganah. The next day—the same day on which the cabinet decided to take action against the Jewish Agency—Hall asked him about his plans. Ben-Gurion related that he had a ticket on a flight to Palestine via Malta on June 25. MI5 had planned to detain him in Malta if he were to attempt an escape after learning of his impending arrest in Palestine. The plan was shaky, because Ben-Gurion was due in Malta on June 25 but could not be arrested until June 29, as this would give away the coming operation. Nor is it clear why Cunningham and MI5 thought Ben-Gurion was supposed to arrive in Palestine on the twenty-ninth. In any event, chance apparently prevented his arrival before that date, and afterward it is clear why he stayed away. The same hand of fate brought Shertok to Palestine for a family visit ten days before Operation Agatha, and he was arrested.[20]

Equally puzzling is that Haganah chief Moshe Sneh, who was in Palestine on June 29, was not arrested. On July 9, the British, wishing to mitigate somewhat the harsh atmosphere created by the operation, suspended further searches for wanted individuals until the Yishuv's response to the measures taken so far became clear. This might well have been what allowed Sneh to flee the country. Teveth tries to show that Sneh was able to leave Palestine, rather than flee, on July 23, in a wide-ranging conspiracy that included Cunningham himself. His account hinges on the close relations between Weizmann and Cunningham. "Only Weizmann could have obtained this kind of tacit consent [to allow Sneh to get away] from the High Commissioner," Teveth writes. In the absence of hard evidence, Cunningham—as Teveth is aware—is the weak link in this story. Actually, Sneh's departure may have been related to an attempt to change the character of the Yishuv-Zionist leadership. The much-discussed possibility of releasing Shertok early, combined with Sneh's removal from the country, could have reduced the violence and strengthened the moderates. However, no evidence exists for a conspiracy of this sort. According to Sneh's biographer, Eli Shealtiel, he was able to leave thanks to felicitous advice from experts on secret flight and his own resourcefulness. In any event, Cunningham preferred a fugitive Sneh in Europe to a revered and active Sneh behind barbed-wire fences in Palestine. Contrary to Teveth's theory, the high commissioner did not know even on August 3 that Sneh had not been in the country for the past ten days. Sneh reappeared in public in Paris on August 4.[21]

For Cunningham, it was less the quantity of detainees than their quality that mattered. His aim was to arrest prominent leaders and prove their connection to terrorism. It was a far-from-simple task and yielded only partial success. Cunningham therefore set out to show that the Jewish Agency Executive collectively was responsible for the violence. His reactions during the operation show clearly—given the difficulty of using the confiscated documents as evidence—that he viewed the arrest of the leaders as paramount. The possibility that the arrests would facilitate the struggle against terrorism and, more broadly, further the political process was very much on his mind.

On June 29, there were 573 inmates, among them 16 women, in the detention camp at Latrun, west of Jerusalem. On the morning of June 30, the detention camp at Atlit held 1,375 men and 37 women, who were due to be sent to Rafah later. The arrests continued apace, netting another 1,300 people in the following two days. A report on the evening of July 1 stated that 2,659 men and 59 women were in detention. On July 9, Cunningham informed London that, after the first releases and the continuing arrests, 2,759 detainees were in custody. Of these, 478 were released that day. (On July 11, upon the conclusion of the operation, 644 more detainees were freed.) The examination process continued. The British interrogators were hampered by the refusal of some detainees to cooperate, including by declining to give their name or giving a fabricated one. More prisoners would be released in the next two or three days, Cunningham promised.[22]

On July 11 at 10 p.m., Cunningham officially announced the conclusion of Operation Agatha:

> The High Commissioner announces that military searches of settlements, as planned and commenced on 29th June, have now ceased and that troops have been withdrawn to their normal locations. The Jewish Agency, as already announced, has been vacated and handed back. It is to be hoped that there will be no further need for wide spread military action, but it must be stated that if, regrettably, there are any further outbreaks of violence, they will be dealt with utmost rigour.[23]

To avoid stirring expectations and creating pressure, the statement said nothing about the release of the detainees, which was already under way. At the same time, Cunningham did not refuse his minister's request to make this fact known in London, in order to calm the operation's opponents and ensure that the information would also reach the United States. The locations of the detention camps—Atlit, Latrun, and Rafah— were also made public. The administration's warning and threat, that the return of violence would generate similar measures, was now backed by concrete precedent. The high commissioner had proved he was capable of living up to the threat.[24]

Cunningham's reports to London highlighted the lower-than-expected scale of opposition and number of casualties. He attributed this to the element of surprise. On the first day of the operation, regional command in Cairo also attributed the absence of a reaction and minor resistance by the Yishuv to the total surprise and ensuing confusion within the Jewish community. The assumption had been that most of the casualties, if there were any, would occur on the first day of the operation. As it turned out, nowhere did the security forces come under fire. Only three Jews were killed on the first day, one by mistake, and a soldier (mentioned earlier) was killed by friendly fire. Of the wounded, only thirteen remained in the hospital. In each locale, the curfew was lifted when the search operation ended.[25]

The high commissioner also reported details not usually included in correspondence at this level of officialdom. On Sunday June 30, at 5 p.m., Cunningham related, two Public Works Department trucks taking Jewish workers home in Haifa's Hadar Hacarmel neighborhood were stopped by a mob. The trucks' military escorts tried to negotiate with the crowd and were answered with a volley of stones. A soldier opened fire, seriously wounding a woman and a child and lightly wounding another person. The high commissioner emphasized that there were no findings to corroborate allegations of atrocities or looting by His Majesty's forces. He also noted that when, during the searches in Tel Aviv, it became necessary to open a few safes, this was done in the presence of an officer to ensure no valuables were taken. Haganah sources, who sought to prove that the soldiers were "mostly enflamed and brimming over with anger, including some who were tipsy and drunk," were unable to produce convincing evidence to back this up and were compelled to add that many soldiers "displayed a humane attitude and did their duty against their will."[26]

The discovery of the arms cache in Kibbutz Yagur was both unplanned and embarrassing for both the British and the Yishuv. "The operation did not (repeat, not) include special searches for arms . . . ," Cunningham explained.[27] The security forces' catch in Yagur consisted of 325 rifles, 96 mortars with 6,257 shells, 10 Lewis machine guns with about 425,000 rounds, 5,017 hand grenades, automatic pistols, 10,000 bullets for light arms, and a quantity of explosives.[28]

Even before the operation ended, Cunningham tried to leverage the Jewish Agency's moderation in order to reach agreement on the fight against terrorism and a return to the partition concept. But then a threat emerged from unexpected quarters that the high commissioner would not easily be able to rebuff. On June 30, word spread that two leading American rabbis, Stephen Wise and Abba Hillel Silver, were on their way to Palestine. Cunningham informed Hall that their visit at this time was intolerable from his point of view. They should not be issued a visa, and if they entered without a visa he was determined to arrest them. In the end, they did not arrive. The high commissioner was fearful of outside intervention, particularly of the American Zionist variety, that would stir passions. If Shertok had been arrested, why would Wise and Silver be permissible? And anyway, the Palestine arena should be left clear for Weizmann.[29]

On the first day of the operation, Weizmann, at Cunningham's request, met with the high commissioner at his residence. The British Mandate chief secretary had announced publicly that morning that Weizmann was not on the list of candidates for arrest. The meeting was made public in a press communiqué. Weizmann arrived at Government House in the afternoon and was willingly received by Cunningham. The Zionist leader was effectively playing into his hands, offering Cunningham another opportunity to make his approach known publicly. The conversation itself was acrimonious. Nevertheless, despite his anger, Weizmann could not but tacitly agree (by not commenting, according to Cunningham's report) with the aims of Operation Agatha and with the high commissioner's observation that the Jewish Agency was collaborating with the Haganah behind his back. Yet Weizmann was concerned about an uncontrolled deterioration. He castigated the British for stirring not only the Yishuv against them but also the entire Jewish people. Cunningham replied that it was the Jewish Agency that had declared war on the British. However, as he wished Weizmann to leave with an achievement to his credit, he said he would call off the operation immediately if the Jewish Agency approached him with a plan to reduce its military force, place it under administration supervision, and fight the breakaway groups. Weizmann could of course make no such commitment. But he, too, wanted something to show for himself and focused his demand on the immediate release of the leadership.[30]

The timing of the meeting and the way it was made public were devastating for Weizmann. The wave of arrests had begun that day, and his arrival and departure from Government House as a free man, and moreover his failure to persuade the high commissioner to stop the operation or at least to release detainees, risked portraying him as a collaborator with a hostile regime. The situation hardly contributed to his ability to enter the temporary vacuum left by the arrested or escaped Zionist leaders. At the same time, the event, and Weizmann's diminishment, was also a setback for Cunningham's goals.

The two met again on July 14, three days after the end of Operation Agatha. Both men realized that they were now mutually dependent. Weizmann said he had informed his colleagues that if the Haganah or the Palmah carried out another action against the British, he would resign at once as the envoy of the Jewish Agency. Cunningham realized that this posed an equal threat to him: without the dominant position of Weizmann and the group of moderate leaders around him, executing his political plan, from Operation Agatha to partition, would be impossible. Aware of this, Weizmann urged the high commissioner to release the moderates (particularly Shertok and Remez) from Latrun to support his political activity in Europe, to which he would soon be returning. But Cunningham was now sufficiently confident to refuse this request. He did, however, urge Hall to try to arrange a meeting between Prime Minister Attlee and Weizmann, who was due in London on July 16. For the sake of balance, he suggested that Attlee also meet with an Arab representative, as the Arabs would not believe that the prime minister had met with the Zionist leader only to discuss the present situation and not long-range plans (of the sort both Cunningham and Weizmann wished for ardently). Attlee agreed immediately to see both Weizmann and an Arab envoy. Despite their very different frames of mind during the period of Operation Agatha, Cunningham and Weizmann were quite evidently of one mind on the broader issues. Weizmann emphasized his commitment to the Zionist-British alliance; Cunningham expressed understanding of and support for Weizmann's policy.[31]

Paradoxically, what Weizmann could say to the high commissioner he could not say to his public. In the heat of the revolt and the atmosphere of Black Sabbath, the Yishuv leadership did not make effective use of Weizmann's capabilities. His approach would later be accepted, but not him personally. It became clear to Cunningham that Weizmann could not or did not want to pick up the gauntlet, though he himself also contributed to the failure of the veteran Zionist leader. Weizmann announced publicly that his condition for meeting with Attlee was the release of the incarcerated Yishuv leaders. This infuriated Cunningham, who wrote to Hall that Weizmann's announcement enabled the Jews to depict themselves falsely as innocent victims and, as such, entitled to make demands of the government. He suggested that if Weizmann were to ask for a meeting with the prime minister, acquiescence should be presented as a favor and not accession to a request. "I would not resist the release of leaders against a substantial quid pro quo regarding illegal arms and armies and cooperation against Irgun and [the] Stern [gang]," Cunningham wrote. He was further upset to hear a report that the chief rabbi of Palestine, Isaac Herzog, who was then in London, had been promised by Attlee that the detained leaders would be released unconditionally. In an uncharacteristically acerbic note, Cunningham told Hall that this would amount to the failure of the operation.[32]

In Cunningham's view, the arrests constituted a bargaining card that must not be given up without a well-defined quid pro quo: a struggle against terrorism by the Jewish Agency and the agency's return to the political process. Cunningham also thought that London's readiness to release detainees ignored developments among the Arabs in Palestine. They had put on hold their preparations for a clash with the Jews in the wake of Operation Agatha. At the same time, the Arabs did not think the operation had gone far enough; they knew that the high commissioner had placed restrictions on the army. Cunningham believed it was important to persuade them that they were misreading the situation. He was concerned that the Arabs would think that their own stepping up of violence against the British authorities would induce the latter to take tougher action against the Jews in order to placate the Arabs. It followed that the unconditional release of the detainees would rob Britain and its envoys in Jerusalem of another crucial achievement of the operation: averting civil war in Palestine.[33]

It soon became apparent that the detainees' release was a major point of friction between the Yishuv and the administration, and between the latter and London. Cunningham refused to be the target of pressures on this subject. The ball, he believed, was now in the Jews' court. There would be no unconditional release. In the meantime, he placed Chief Secretary Shaw in charge of dealing with exceptional cases. On July 14, as we saw, Cunningham informed Weizmann of his conditions for freeing the detainees immediately. He added that it was pointless to threaten him with civil revolt (i.e., noncooperation with the administration in all areas). Cunningham and Weizmann both believed that a development of this kind—amounting to the intensification of the existing resistance instead of ending it—would be "madness," to use Cunningham's word, and that the main casualty would be the Yishuv itself.[34]

As the operation proceeded, Cunningham believed the Yishuv would react once the initial shock wore off. His fears were abated by the Yishuv's hysteria. On July 1, the members of the Jewish Agency Executive and other leaders who had not been arrested—the Zionist Executive, the National Council, mayors, and the leaders of Agudat Yisrael, an ultra-Orthodox movement—met in Jerusalem. Florid speeches cast the events as a deliberately planned attack on the Yishuv's very existence and its unity, and as a hopeless attempt to split the Yishuv from its detained leaders, who were being pressured to accept a policy that the Jewish public disdained. Cunningham quoted Voice of Israel radio, which declared that day, "The English Nazis have declared war on us. It should be clear to everybody that we shall retaliate. We shall fight the Palestine Titus."[35] Did this remark hurt the high commissioner or help him, offering proof of his toughness to the government and the army and, in turn, calming the public in Palestine? Whatever the effect, he believed his new resolute image could help advance his political program and the struggle against terrorism.[36]

Although Cunningham was concerned about Weizmann's failure to attend the meeting (because he was not feeling well), he could take comfort in the knowledge that some of the speeches had been moderate in tone and that the meeting's operative resolution referred to the intention of declaring civil noncooperation with the administration, not the continuation of terror acts, until the release of the senior leaders. Indeed, their absence, he noted with barely concealed satisfaction, was keenly felt at the meeting. "It is quiet right now," he summed up immediately after the end of Operation Agatha, "but tense."[37]

Cunningham was not especially perturbed about the noncooperation threat. "Of course I met him immediately," he wrote somewhat bemusedly, on the eve of his July 14 meeting with Weizmann, of the Yishuv's threat to break off ties with the administration if he did not see Weizmann immediately.[38] Unlike his desire to restore Weizmann to his former glory, in this case Cunningham saw things realistically. In July 1946, the Yishuv leadership, which was usually efficient and focused, was incapable of mounting an orderly response. Its usual advantage—the national authority of influential leaders—now played into the hands of the Mandate authorities. The Yishuv was paralyzed by the leadership's absence and reeling under the shock of Operation Agatha.[39]

The limited operation carried out from June 29 until July 11 was a direct result of the high commissioner's policy and of his principled and personal approach. This fact was critical to the fate of the Jewish Resistance Movement. It is not too much to say that Cunningham saved the Yishuv from itself. He distinguished clearly between terrorism per se, of the kind perpetrated by Etzel and Lehi, and the Jewish Agency's attempt to activate the Haganah symbolically as an army in order to pressure Britain over its policy as enshrined in the White Paper of May 1939. The Yishuv did not have to guess Cunningham's intentions. He made them abundantly clear in his announcements during the operation and in his aides' press conferences: he was not at war with the Yishuv; he wanted the leadership to abandon violence and renew its cooperation in the effort to eradicate the terrorism of the breakaway groups. The breakaway groups were not part of the Operation Agatha agenda, only a by-product. An operation against them by the Jewish Agency would be an achievement for the high commissioner and the administration toward their primary goal of renewing the political process.

Cunningham's reports to London were influenced by his desire to downplay the scale of the operation, while at the same time voicing his and the army's determination and efficiency. He projected control and restraint. The stunned surprise and the limited, generally passive response at the search sites, the overall paralysis, and the Arabs' nonintervention all contributed to the high commissioner's success in mounting an operation that was focused and limited, and also looked the part. This was essential, given the operation's harsh political implications, which amounted to a new low for Britain's relations with the Yishuv. But also, in the high commissioner's view, the operation had the potential to generate new and beneficial mutual relations between the two entities.

Operation Agatha, and the arrests in particular, proved effective. It is impossible not to link them to the waning of the Yishuv-wide revolt and to the renewal of the political process in August 1946. Cunningham stubbornly tied the final release of the detainees to political developments. Indeed, the last detainees were not freed until early November, ahead of a second attempt—the first having failed—to hold a Jewish-Arab conference in London. However, the arrests did not prevent the disaster that occurred at the King David Hotel on July 22, nor, at least at this stage, did it induce the Jewish Agency to send the Haganah to do battle with the breakaway groups once more.

NOTES

1. Cabinet meeting, June 20, 1946, NA CAB128/5.

2. Ibid.; Cunningham to Hall, June 18, 1946, MECA CP, B1, F1/109; Hall to Cunningham, June 29, 1946, NA C0537/1713.

3. Cabinet meeting, June 20, 1946.

4. Ibid.; Montgomery, *The Memoirs*, pp. 420–426, in which the author intermixes what he knew when he visited Palestine on June 14, 1946, and subsequent events of which he was apprised in his lightning visit on June 22. Those events included attacks by the Haganah and Lehi along with the abductions on June 17–18, compounded by Cunningham's ostensible hesitation to use the military. Montgomery did not meet with the high commissioner in his second visit, even though it had already been decided that the latter would have the last word. On the murder in Jerusalem, see also Slutzky, *History of the Haganah*, III, 2, p. 887.

5. Cabinet meeting, June 20, 1946.

6. Hall to Cunningham, June 18, 1946, MECA CP, B1, F1/102; Cabinet meeting, June 20, 1946.

7. "Respective Functions of High Commissioner and of the General Officer Commanding the Forces, Memorandum by Secretary of State for the Colonies (Ormsby Gore)," March 15, 1937, NA C0537/1731; Meeting of ministers, March 15, 1938, NA C0537/1731. For further discussion of the dispute between the high commissioner and the army during the period of the Arab Revolt over final authority in an emergency, see Eyal, *The First Intifada*.

8. "Commanders-in-Chief Middle East to Chiefs of Staff," June 25, 1946, NA C0537/1713; Montgomery to Dempsey, personal instructions, June 27, 1946, NA W0216/194.

9. Teveth, *Kinat David*, pp. 708–712, draws in part on the assessment of Moshe Sneh, the head of the Haganah National Command, that the operation failed; Avizohar, in the introduction to Ben-Gurion, *Toward the End of the Mandate*, pp. 15–17, relies on a similar assessment by Ben-Gurion.

10. Commander-in-Chief, Middle East Land Forces (Dempsey), to chiefs of staff, June 25, 1946; for security reasons, the cable announcing the date of the operation was sent separately, NA C0537/1713.

11. Cunningham to Hall, June 29, 1946, 9 a.m., NA C0537/1713; Commander-in-chief, Middle East Land Forces, to War Office, June 29, 1946, 9:20 a.m., and again at 10:50 a.m., NA C0537/1713; Cunningham to Hall, June 30, 1946, 3:15 p.m., NA C0537/1713. Under pressure from Weizmann, the British released Rabbi Fishman-Maimon for health reasons on July 12; the others were released on November 5: Weizmann to Shaw, June 30, 1946, Heller (ed.), *The Letters and Papers of Chaim Weizmann*, Vol. XXII, Series A, p. 163.

12. Commander-in-chief, Middle East Land Forces, to War Office, NA C0537/1713, 12:30 p.m. (updated to 10:30 a.m.), 4:30 p.m. (updated to 2 p.m.), 6:45 p.m. (updated to 4 p.m.), 9:55 p.m. (updated to 5:30 p.m.); Cunningham to Hall, June 20, 1946, 7:55 p.m., NA C0537/1713.

13. Mandatory press officer to Colonial Office, June 29, 1946 (4:25 p.m., 6:15 p.m.), NA C0537/1713; Cunningham to Hall, June 29, 1946, NA C0537/1713 (7:55 p.m.); Gelber, *Growing a Fleur-de-Lis*, vol. 2, pp. 580–581. For the Yishuv's response and the full story of Black Sabbath, see Efraim Dekel, *Shai: The Exploits of Hagana Intelligence*, New York and London 1959, pp. 132–151; Slutzky, *History of the Haganah*, III, 2, pp. 889, 891, 1262; Avizohar, introduction to Ben-Gurion, *Toward the End of the Mandate*, p. 4.

14. Cunningham to Hall, June 29, 1946, 3:05 p.m., NA C0537/1713; Montgomery, *The Memoirs*, p. 423.

15. Cunningham to Hall, July 1, 1946, July 2, 1946, NA C0537/1713; according to Slutzky, *History of the Haganah*, III, 2, p. 893, Yosef Ruchal (Avidar) ordered the burning of forty bags of documents that had been in a cache of the Haganah high command.

16. Commander-in-chief, Middle East Land Forces, to War Office, June 30, 1946, 7 a.m., NA C0537/1713; Cunningham to Hall, July 1, 1946, NA C0537/1713; Hall to Cunningham, July 2, 1946, NA C0537/1713.

17. Cunningham to Hall, July 3, 1946, July 7, 1946, July 8, 1946, NA C0537/1713.

18. Cunningham to Hall, July 3, 1946–July 9, 1946, NA C0537/1713.

19. Cunningham to Hall, June 29, 1946, 10:10 a.m., NA C0537/1713.

20. The high commissioner was in touch with Keller from MI5, ibid.; Interim report of commander-in-chief, Middle East Land Forces, on Operation Agatha, July 2, 1946, NA W0275/129; Teveth, *Kinat David*, pp. 699–706.

21. Cunningham to Hall, July 8, 9, 1946, NA C0537/1713; and also August 3, 1946, NA C0537/1708; and August 19, 1946, MECA CP, B1, F2/41, and September 19, 26, 1946, MECA CP, B1, F2/65, 104; Eli Shealtiel, *Always a Rebel: A Biography of Moshe Sneh, 1909–1948*, Tel Aviv 2000, pp. 260–262, 278–287 (Hebrew); Teveth, *Kinat David*, pp. 710–723. There is no mention of Sneh in Weizmann's meetings with Cunningham after Operation Agatha; see also Shabtai Teveth, "Puzzling Exercise (Dr. Moshe Sneh's Slipping Away, Flight, or Invitation to Paris, July–August 1946)," *Zmanim* 76 (fall 2001), pp. 71–89 (Hebrew).

22. Commander-in-chief, Middle East Land Forces, to War Office, June 29, 1946, 4 p.m., June 30, 1946, 7 a.m., NA C0537/1713; Cunningham to Hall, July 1, 1946, July 9, 1946, NA C0537/1713.

23. The statement appeared verbatim in a letter from Cunningham to Hall, July 11, 1946, NA C0537/1713.

24. Ibid.

25. Commander-in-chief, Middle East Land Forces, to War Office, June 30, 1946, 12:15 a.m., NA CO537/1713; Cunningham originally reported three killed, and then, in contrast to the army, accepted the Yishuv figure: four dead. Slutzky, *History of the Haganah*, III, 2, pp. 892–893, states that one person from Kibbutz Tel Yosef was killed along with two members of Kibbutz Nir David who came to the aid of Tel Yosef and Ein Harod—not one, as army sources said. As Slutzky cites names, this account appears reliable. The British soldier who was killed was not mentioned in the Haganah sources.

26. Cunningham to Hall, July 1, 1946, NA CO537/1713; quotations from Slutzky, *History of the Haganah*, III, 2, pp. 892–893.

27. Cunningham to Hall, August 3, 1946, NA CO537/1713; August 3, 1946, NA CO537/1708.

28. Cunningham to Hall, June 30, 1946, July 1, 1946, NA CO537/1713.

29. Cunningham to Hall, July 1, 1946, NA CO537/1713.

30. Cunningham to Hall, June 29, 1946, NA CO537/1713; Rose, *Chaim Weizmann*, p. 412, formed the impression that "something had snapped in Weizmann's attitude toward Britain."

31. Cunningham to Hall, June 14, 1946, NA CO537/1713; "Minute by the Prime Minister on Cunningham's Telegram of 15th July about the Situation in Palestine," July 16, 1946, NA CO537/1713; Hall to Cunningham, July 17, 1946, and Cunningham to Hall, July 18, 1946, NA CO537/1713.

32. Cunningham to Hall, July 8, 1946, July 13, 1946, July 18, 1946, NA CO537/1713.

33. Ibid.

34. Cunningham to Hall, July 8, 1946, July 9, 1946, July 14, 1946, NA CO537/1713.

35. Cunningham to Hall, July 1, 1946, NA CO537/1713.

36. Sharett, *Imprisoned with Paper and Pencil*, pp. 16–17.

37. Cunningham to Hall, July 1, 1946.

38. Cunningham to Hall, July 14, 1946.

39. Sharett, *Imprisoned with Paper and Pencil*, p. 17. The Jewish Agency imputed the blame for the failure of the noncooperation plan to Weizmann (who wanted to give priority to the release of the detainees), to a financial shortfall, and to the King David Hotel disaster on July 22. Meeting of the Jewish Agency Executive, Paris, August 2, 1946, Ben-Gurion, *Toward the End of the Mandate*, pp. 103–106.

4 A State First, Immigration Later

Operation Agatha ended; the troops returned to their barracks. Cunningham's patience and persistence seemed to have borne fruit in both Britain and Palestine. The colonial secretary informed him with cautious satisfaction about a shift in the government's thinking. The ministers now understood that the single-state idea was not viable, and given the certain objection by the chiefs of staff (Hall did not dare write that the Foreign Office, too, held the partition idea in low regard) it had been decided that the British delegation to the newly created Anglo-American committee of experts—the Morrison-Grady Committee—would submit the provincial autonomy concept for consideration. That plan, derived from ideas put forward by Hall himself in summer 1945, would serve as an alternative to the binational idea formulated by the Anglo-American Committee of Inquiry. American support would be sought for the plan.

Cunningham probably smiled sadly at his minister's convoluted efforts to explain why the cabinet saw an advantage in the provincial autonomy idea: it would show both sides that federative cooperation was preferable to full partition. The high commissioner could find some consolation in the report that the autonomy plan would be an interim stage on the way to partition. The cabinet had begun to grasp what the Peel Commission had understood ten years earlier: that the only tenable solution was one in which each side managed its own affairs. Hall also reminded Cunningham about the proposed separate political and geographic arrangement for Jerusalem, in the spirit of 1937, which would leave the Mandatory power with a foothold in Palestine.[1]

Cunningham replied that after eight months in Palestine and after having acquainted himself thoroughly with the problem, he was certain a binational state could not work. Without partition, there would be neither peace nor stability. This, he suspected, was precisely what some in the cabinet wanted. He asked Hall to pass on his personal opinion that partition should be introduced without interim stages, as they would only exacerbate the situation.[2]

His efforts seemed to be bearing fruit. After Operation Agatha, the Jewish Agency showed clear signs of readiness to call off the revolt and return to political discussions. Like Cunningham, Attlee too believed that an unflinching policy against terrorism would help bring the moderates to the negotiating table. Cunningham, then, received quiet backing not only from the politically weak Hall but from the prime minister himself. His problem lay with the Foreign Office and the army.[3]

On July 8, just before the conclusion of Operation Agatha, Cunningham, concerned that some in London might undermine the results of the operation, proposed a short home visit. London asked why he was so eager to come to Britain when a new joint committee was about to arrive in Palestine. To this, the high commissioner, heady and confident thanks to Operation Agatha, replied that he was aware of the committee's arrival and of the need to accompany it, and that his proposed visit would accomplish two ends with this in mind. He would be able to update the minister about the current situation—namely, the apparent success of Operation Agatha both politically and in terms of security—and he would hold talks on the "final solution" [sic] about to be proposed by the joint committee or the government. Feeling that he could promote the partition idea, he requested that a special plane be put at his disposal for a short excursion to London.[4]

On July 17, he was informed that a plane would be available on Friday July 19 in the morning, enabling him to be in London that afternoon. Nevertheless, he felt that his visit had not been approved unreservedly. He took exception to the draft communiqué of the Colonial Office to announce his visit, specifically to the sentence stating that in London the results of the recent operation would be discussed. That, he thought, might be construed to mean that the operation had failed and that he had been summoned for a clarification. Cunningham wanted the announcement to mention the long-term political solution, whose resuscitation had been one of the operation's goals. London, for its part, wanted a compromise and flattered Cunningham by putting him up at a central hotel and holding an official reception for him. As for the communiqué, although it would not mention a long-term political solution, it would state that the presence of Grady's delegation of American experts in London would be exploited for consultations about a political solution.[5]

Once more, his experienced superiors in London had spared him the embarrassment of making insubstantial declarations. After being rebuffed, he himself realized the potential danger of a statement indicating that he would return from London with a solution in his pocket. Cunningham was aware of the expectations for an immediate political solution that he himself had created in connection with Operation Agatha. At the same time, exploiting the momentum was crucial. The combination of the shock of the operation and the feeling that Jerusalem and London could plan their coming moves—perhaps for the first time since the suppression of the Arab Revolt—might have generated unwarranted expectations but equally could lead to the acceptance of a political solution originating in London (with Washington's support). It was a propitious moment— with the emphasis on *moment*—and the only one there would be during Cunningham's tenure in Palestine. He did not wish to suppress either the Jews or the Arabs, only to bring both sides to the negotiating table to work out a political agreement. He had successfully come through his true baptism of fire, in every sense, and had also, he believed, passed the test of his government and of the Jews and Arabs. As such, he was determined about pursuing a political solution based on partition. Whether the problem lay with policy, as seen in the clear failure of the Anglo-American Committee, or with politics, namely, the impasse reached by the decision-makers in London, he was confident of his ability and of his image after proving he could wield force when needed and, no less critical, also contain it.[6]

The propitious moment was indeed short-lived. On July 22, forty-eight hours after Cunningham arrived in London to reap the fruits of Operation Agatha, an unprecedented terrorist attack was perpetrated on the Chief Secretariat and army headquarters in the King David Hotel in the heart of Jerusalem.

In the summer of 1946, Britain found itself caught in the bind of being unable to accept the recommendations of the Anglo-American Committee but also desiring powerfully to hold on to Palestine with American backing, at least political and economic. The problem lay in President Truman's support for the entry of 100,000 Jewish refugees into Palestine and his apparent inclination toward a partition solution. Britain's withdrawal from Palestine actually began that summer, in the consciousness of the decision-makers. Still, perhaps by force of imperialist routine, under which the ruler bore responsibility as long as it ruled, London and Jerusalem continued the search for an agreed Jewish-Arab political path. The solution would also have to account for Britain's interests given the serious economic and imperial crisis that followed the war and the advent of the Cold War. Policy was only slightly affected by the massive terrorist attack in Jerusalem on July 22, 1946. Two days later, the Morrison-Grady Committee submitted a report to the cabinet recommending provincial autonomy. The cabinet approved the report. British policy was more beholden to relations with the United States than to the unfolding events in Palestine.[7]

The man on the spot amid this tangled and discouraging situation was the high commissioner, Sir Alan Cunningham. Although he liked to think he and the government occupied the same wavelength, it emerged that even after Operation Agatha they were not. The British government sought an agreement with the Americans and not with the Jews or with the Arabs or between the two sides, whereas the high commissioner dealt with the rival sides in Palestine. He was promised that the joint Anglo-American decisions would be made public ahead of a Jewish-Arab conference that Britain would convene to calm the situation. Cunningham was far from certain that everyone in London realized that an agreement with the United States on Palestine would be pointless without first thoroughly clarifying the issues surrounding a Jewish-Arab agreement.[8]

Toward the end of July, Cunningham came increasingly to feel that London did not grasp what was going on in Palestine and did not understand his approach. In his reports to the Colonial Office, he emphasized that he was not alone in his thinking and that his assessments were reached in concurrence with the senior echelon of the administration. Unable to leave Palestine again after the King David bombing in order to lobby for partition, he announced that he was sending the chief secretary, John Shaw, to London immediately.[9]

Hall, somewhat shaken by the announcement of Shaw's impending visit, dashed off an unedited reply asking Cunningham not to make unnecessary waves. This may well have reflected Hall's deteriorating political status and his inability to show concretely that he saw eye to eye with his envoy in Jerusalem. Certainly, it reflected his and Cunningham's mutual concern about a possible eruption of violence by both the Jews and the Arabs, and a consequent loss of control by the Mandatory authorities. Hall informed Cunningham that he would be accompanying Attlee and Bevin to Paris for talks with the Americans. On the Palestine question, the British sought the Americans' agreement to the wording of a forthcoming government statement in the House of Commons. It would be made clear that the 100,000 Jewish refugees would be settled exclusively in the proposed Jewish province and that no plan, including partition, would be implemented unilaterally. Hall also reminded the high commissioner that much still depended on the Americans' reaction to the provincial autonomy plan. Cunningham appreciated the minister's efforts; he knew he had an ally in the Colonial Office but knew equally well that his influence was limited.[10]

Cunningham welcomed the thrust of the proposal submitted by the Anglo-American committee of experts, but not its likely substance: provincial autonomy under British auspices and American funding. British-American agreement was all very well, but it bore no connection to the negative take on the plan by the local inhabitants, particularly the Jews. London, though, refused to accept the idea of partition into two states. This attitude seemed reasonable from the perspective of the Foreign Office, which cultivated British and Western interests in the Arab world. However, from the viewpoint of observers in Jerusalem, partition loomed more urgently than ever. Still, at the end of July 1946, with terrorist acts having powerful short-term effects on the local Mandate administration policy, London and Jerusalem agreed, if only in principle, on the overriding necessity of a political solution, if not on its form.

Cunningham believed that the Arabs, too, could be persuaded to accept partition. He noted that at an Arab League meeting held in Alexandria in late July 1946, only faint echoes could be heard of the Arab Higher Committee's uncompromising stance. The Arab states tended toward a federative solution, though only unofficially. Their principal desire was to end the Yishuv's ongoing threat to the Arab community. That, in Cunningham's view, was another good reason to take action in this direction in cooperation with the Zionists.[11] As for the provincial autonomy plan, the high commissioner, in common with the Jewish Agency and the Arab Higher Committee, was an opponent because the plan demanded Jewish-Arab cooperation, an unthinkable proposition. He expected the Arabs to accept partition tacitly, and no more, and accordingly occupied himself less with them.[12]

In the days after the King David Hotel incident, Cunningham desperately grasped for even the flimsiest straw, anything that would allow him to continue pursuing a political policy to prevent an additional, even larger disaster. The Zionists, he wrote, were surprised by the announcement of the provincial autonomy plan. Their responses included denial, expressions of no-confidence in the British government, and pessimism about the prospects for the plan's implementation. The national institutions instructed the press not to react to the announcement: the situation was sensitive and the newspapers should wait for the authorized Zionist bodies to articulate a position. Even this small indication of a departure from an unequivocal rejection of British policy was enough to hearten Cunningham.[13]

Never had the situation of the Yishuv resembled that of the Arab community more closely than in August 1946. No obvious person was in charge after the recent events: the violent struggle waged since the previous autumn, Operation Agatha, the King David Hotel bombing, and, finally, the decision by the Jewish Agency Council in Paris at the beginning of August to end the violent insurgency. This sense of rudderlessness was unusual in the organized Jewish community and, more particularly, in the Zionist movement. Cunningham's initial success lay in suppressing the revolt. He complained that, despite the roiling political situation, the senior members of the leadership—those not incarcerated at Latrun—had left the country to attend the Jewish Agency Council meeting in Paris, leaving behind only junior figures. Cunningham's feigned astonishment was also seen in his supposed surprise that the council was not meeting in London, as Weizmann had requested. Cunningham had little interest in pointing out the simple fact that some of the leaders, notably Ben-Gurion, would be arrested if they set foot in London. Paris was chosen as a compromise between London and New York. With unconcealed anger, the high commissioner noted that he was left with Moshe Sneh (he did not know Sneh had departed the country on July 23) and Abba Hushi, second-tier leaders. They, he claimed, were responsible for continuing to manage the armed resistance from the underground.[14]

In fact, Cunningham's understanding of the situation ran deeper. He knew well that the Zionist ship was rudderless because some of the senior crew had fled and others were in detention. There were also those who were torn between the need to respond to the militant atmosphere on the Yishuv street and the need to pursue a moderate policy that would advance the cardinal goals of the Zionist movement: immigration and establishing a state. Still, things were not all that bad, Cunningham wrote to Hall. The situation might make it possible for the moderate right in the Yishuv, along with the business class and the practitioners of the liberal professions (he mistakenly wrote of a new party of immigration but meant the quiet "civic" majority), to call for an alternative approach to the disastrous course being pursued by the present leadership. The high commissioner drew encouragement from the approach taken by *Ha'aretz*, the moderate Zionist newspaper that served as the mouthpiece for these middle-class groups.

However, Cunningham did not allow his hopes to cloud his assessments of the situation. Even with the Zionist movement at a nadir, no one could match the influence wielded by Ben-Gurion. After Operation Agatha and the King David Hotel bombing, Cunningham was more realistic about Weizmann's ability to act as the standard-bearer for moderation in the Zionist movement. Ben-Gurion and his circle might have difficulty making decisions and implementing them, he wrote, but they could prevent others from acting. He could not, he explained with frustration, fight the Zionist leadership on the grounds that it was socialist, as such an approach obviously would not go over well with the present government in London—even if the Yishuv version was very different from British Labour. Mapai was a socialist party that held unchallenged sway among the Yishuv, the Jewish Agency, the National Council, and the Histadrut federation of labor. The high commissioner's conclusion was pessimistic: with leaders like Ben-Gurion and Sneh, almost every one of the proposed political solutions under discussion between Britain and the United States would be rejected. Cunningham was worried at the vociferous backing the Yishuv leadership was getting from American Zionists like Abba Hillel Silver. In these conditions, he summed up apprehensively, the moderates in the Yishuv and in the Zionist movement would have no chance until the militant Zionist leadership was eliminated.[15]

On September 25, 1946, 558 detainees from Operation Agatha remained in custody (of 1,535 who had been arrested for the long term, and not including those who had been detained, questioned, and released immediately). Of them, 135, who were being held at Latrun, were categorized as leaders: 6 members of the Jewish Agency Executive and 129 from the Palmah or the breakaway organizations. The remaining 423, most of whom were incarcerated at Rafah, were from the Haganah (mainly from the Palmah), along with a few from Etzel and Lehi.[16] Cunningham's concern focused on the Latrun detainees. As we have seen, he differentiated between the Jewish Agency and Haganah (including the Palmah) and the breakaway organizations. Whether or not the first group would be freed was a political issue that would affect the prospects for the political solution sought by his administration. Cunningham maintained that this group's release must be considered only within the political context. As for the breakaway leaders, their release would become a policy question after a political agreement was achieved. In the meantime, it remained purely an issue of legality and security.[17]

Cunningham's consternation was acute. He had no practical proposals for getting the Zionist leadership to go to London for direct talks with the government. The only form of pressure remaining to him was the freeing of the Operation Agatha detainees. In August–September 1946, Cunningham knew it would be necessary to release them if he wanted the Yishuv delegation to attend the planned conference in London. He was able to promise the Jewish Agency that moderates like Eliezer Kaplan could return to Palestine without being arrested. Nevertheless, he seemed unable to detach himself from a formula he had already put forward—most recently on the eve of Operation Agatha—and now proposed again: to exert pressure on moderate leaders such as Weizmann, Stephen Wise, and Nahum Goldmann in order to eliminate the lethal influence of the activist leaders, and to be more aggressive in controlling the affairs of the Yishuv.[18]

———————————

From the perspective of Palestine, a key event of summer 1946 was the parliamentary debate spanning late July and early August that signaled the onset of a new and more independent effort by the government on the Palestine question, following the crisis of the report of the Anglo-American Committee and of the committee of experts (Morrison-Grady). The peak event was supposed to be a tripartite conference—Jewish-Arab-British—to be held in London in September and October. Driven by American pressure and a desire to see the Jewish Agency leaders at the conference, London asked the high commissioner for his opinion about releasing the detainees.

Cunningham wrote to Hall that if he was being forced to address this question in its own right, without consideration of what the Jewish Agency could offer in return, the colonial secretary should remember that the Arabs were already complaining of the administration's softness. Only recently, the release from custody of a relatively senior Revisionist leader, Ze'ev (Wolfgang) Von Wiesel, for health reasons, had gone down poorly with the Arab community. It will be impossible to release Jewish detainees at this time without getting something from the Jewish Agency, measure for measure, Cunningham explained. A Jewish Agency quid pro quo should entail, for example, a scaling down of the Jewish armed forces and British supervision of the remaining forces, cooperation in the struggle against Jewish terrorism, and a curbing of illegal immigration. In the present circumstances (September 1946), it was unreasonable for the Jewish Agency not to yield on any of these issues.[19]

Nevertheless, Cunningham addressed the question of the Jewish Agency delegation. It must represent the Jewish majority in Palestine and be capable of living up to its promises, he wrote. The leadership that was presently outside the country had not made a genuine effort to empower the moderates who remained in Palestine, owing to the ongoing policy dispute between the activist and moderate factions. In fact, the high commissioner himself could have played a part here, as some of the moderates were in British custody (notably Shertok and Remez, the chairman of the National Council). Cunningham also wanted the representatives of the moderate right (the "civic sector") to attend the London conference, as well as Yitzhak Ben-Zvi, the president of the National Council. They did not support illegal immigration and certainly did not condone violence, he thought. Cunningham was acting on the basis of a cabinet decision from early July to strengthen Weizmann and his supporters. He drew up what he considered a proper list of senior figures who had not been arrested: Yitzhak Ben-Zvi, Rabbi Isaac Herzog, Golda Meyerson, Rabbi Y. M. Levin, Werner Senator, Felix Rosenblit, Israel Rokach, and Yosef Sprinzak. Also invited were Jewish organizations in Britain. It was a clumsy attempt to sidestep the Jewish Agency.[20]

The appearance of Golda Meyerson's name on the list was especially interesting. Cunningham considered her an effective leader in terms of the Yishuv's interests.[21] Did he not know that she was part of Ben-Gurion's circle? Or was that precisely why she was invited? Even though she was in the country during Operation Agatha and made no effort to hide, she was not arrested. This had nothing to do with gender—dozens of other women were taken into custody. Nor was it because of her command of English, which facilitated conversation with her. In any event, her political status soared after Operation Agatha, when she became the acting director of the Jewish Agency's Political Department. Toward the end of the Mandate period, Meyerson became the Jewish Agency's main representative in contacts with the high commissioner. She would later recall him as "very kind and decent. . . . No matter how tense or unruly the situation in Eretz Yisrael was, we were always able, he and I, to talk as friends."[22] He returned the compliment. Ten years after leaving Palestine, he summed up, "I liked her, she was smart."[23]

Even though he knew London would offer a more conducive atmosphere for a conference, Cunningham thought it should be held under his auspices in Jerusalem. It was essential, he wrote in this connection, to deport Ben-Gurion and Moshe Sneh, at least until a political agreement was reached, and to arrest them. Two birds with one stone—distancing the two and co-opting the moderates from the Yishuv and from the American

Zionist leadership—was the condition for the conference's success, in his view. However, the Zionists and the British Jews declined the invitation. The attempt by Cunningham and by his superiors in London to go over the head of the Jewish Agency, or at least to ignore it, had failed.[24]

Toward the middle of October, as unofficial talks were under way in London with Weizmann, Kaplan, and Rabbi Fishman-Maimon, Cunningham discerned a hardening of their approach over the conditions for participation in the future conference. He reported to London that a series of developments—rumors about an exchange of messages between Truman and Attlee over the Palestine question, the talks being held by senior Jewish Agency officials at the Colonial Office in London, and their contacts with key figures in London and Washington—had created the impression that the political initiative was passing into the agency's hands. It was no accident, the high commissioner noted worriedly, that the Jews were adding more conditions for attending the conference and that the established Zionist press rejected the idea of waging a war on terrorism in return for holding the conference. Cunningham's observations echoed the effect of Nahum Goldmann's mission to the United States in August 1946, following which the Americans were persuaded to oppose provincial autonomy and accept partition. In London, this undoubted Zionist success bolstered the myth of Jewish influence in the United States.[25]

In the autumn of 1946, unproductive official talks were held in London with the Arabs and unofficial talks with the Zionists. We need not dwell here on the many reasons—among them Cunningham's policy of not releasing detainees—for the Jewish Agency's failure to attend the planned conference (which was the cause of its cancelation). Still, the preparations for the meeting were like oil on the rusty wheels of the political process. Toward the end of September 1946, with the prospects for convening the conference fading and the two sides toughening their approaches, Cunningham assured Hall that despite the problems all the departments and districts of the civil administration were operating fully, adding that this was a notable achievement. Nevertheless, the looming political failure made him anxious that he was not living up to his superiors' expectations. He had good reason to worry. Palestine was one of the reasons for Attlee's removal of Hall in October in favor of his deputy, Arthur Creech-Jones.[26]

In mid-August, on the eve of the planned London conference, Cunningham had been optimistic about the Palestine Arabs' reaction to the new Anglo-American proposals. He believed they would be willing to accept part of the country, as long as they were allowed to manage their own

affairs. However, the anti-British past of Jamal al-Husseini did not promise genuine cooperation.[27] Cunningham made no secret of his feelings
about al-Husseini. In July 1946, London had been trying to decide which
Arab leader might be a useful counterpart to Weizmann. The Colonial Office thought that Musa al-Alami, who was then in London, could fit the
bill. Although Alami did not represent anyone, Cunningham thought he
should meet with him, if only to avoid having to meet with al-Husseini.
The high commissioner had more than once told Hall angrily of his scorn
for al-Husseini's qualities as a leader and about his meager public support. After all, it was the British who had released him from his exile in
Rhodesia after the war with a view to creating a local Arab leadership in
Palestine.

Nevertheless, toward the end of August, a meeting between Jamal al-
Husseini and the high commissioner took place in Government House.
Cunningham suggested that the Palestine Arabs should drop the idea of
making the grand mufti, Haj Amin al-Husseini, a member of their delegation to the London conference. The mufti had been Britain's enemy
since the war, he said, and Cunningham's instructions on this subject
were clear. He added that London was concerned about the mufti's move
from France to Egypt and that his stay there was conditional on his shunning political activity. Al-Husseini fidgeted palpably in his reply. He tried
to explain that during the period of the pro-Nazi revolt in Iraq, in 1941, his
cousin Haj Amin had wished to avert an intra-Arab conflict and that he
was forced to go to Germany because there was no other place on earth in
which he could set foot. If the Palestinians insisted, Cunningham said in
response, the whole delegation would be ejected. And in any event, the in-
vitations were being issued by the government of Britain, not by the Arab
Higher Committee.[28]

Cunningham's aim was to weaken the extremists among the Palestinians too. But his and London's wish for their delegation to include also
merchants, trade unionists, and mayors, and not only members of the
AHC, was rejected. Miffed, al-Husseini spoke a basic truth, perhaps the
most honest comment in the conversation: in any event, he said, the AHC
has no expectations from the London conference.[29]

On another occasion, Cunningham urged Jamal al-Husseini to broaden
the base of the al-Husseini-controlled AHC outside the country's borders—in other words, to have it encompass the Arab League. Al-Husseini
demurred. In his frustration, Cunningham later revealed his opinion of
the Palestine Arabs, informing Hall and the Foreign Office envoys in the

Arab capitals that it was all the same to him if the Palestinians did not attend the London conference—their presence was only needed for psychological reasons. Faithful to the British heritage, he added that what truly mattered was the approach of the Arab states.[30]

Jamal al-Husseini continued to insist that the mufti be invited to the London conference and that the Palestine Arabs had the right to choose their own representatives. In short order, the mufti was transformed from a means to an end. The rehabilitation of the Palestine Arabs' leadership was examined in terms of his status. Its members demanded that he be allowed to enter the country, arguing that he was their chosen leader and was not as extreme as the British made out. However, London as well as Cunningham continued to see the mufti as an enemy whose presence in Palestine would certainly spell the end to the already flimsy prospect for a political settlement. As it was, the high commissioner was concerned about the mufti's deep involvement in managing the affairs of the Palestine Arabs from Cairo.[31]

Cunningham thought that the Palestine Arabs might opt either for a political settlement or for violence. Explaining to London why a political agreement was urgently needed, he noted that the Palestinians, too, were approaching the point at which they might take up arms in their defense on the grounds that the administration was failing to protect them. They too were victims of Jewish terrorism (by Etzel and Lehi), and reports about their efforts to arm themselves suggested that a clash was inevitable. The extremists, in the form of ultranationalist religious or semireligious organizations, were making deep inroads in the Palestine Arab community, Cunningham feared. The trend toward extremism had intensified since the end of the war. The extremists, who did not balk at inciting murder and mayhem, were, he believed, capable of setting the country ablaze in an attempt to emulate extremist Nazi and fascist movements and their like among the Jews in Palestine. From the perspective of Government House, the nationalism of the Jews and of the Palestine Arabs was more alike than both sides tended to think.[32]

In Cunningham's view, Jamal al-Husseini and his faction were incapable of organizing an all-Palestine political coalition that would take a more complex approach and one more desirable to Britain. Like his predecessors in the 1930s and during the Second World War, Cunningham placed his faith in the Arab states. His unequivocal recommendation to the colonial secretary not to consider forging ties with the mufti reflected his efforts to quell the extremists on both sides—but was also his way of expressing utter contempt for the Palestine Arabs' political desires. He considered them a nuisance to be dispensed with.[33]

———————

After a few months in Jerusalem during which he crystallized his policy doctrine, Cunningham knew that for the Zionists a key obstacle toward accepting partition lay in the equation that immigration must come first and a state afterward. At the beginning of 1946, the Jewish Agency was still captive to its commitment in the Biltmore Program, adopted by the American Zionists at their conference in May 1942 and afterward ratified by the Zionist Executive. Its main points were the transfer of immigration from the responsibility of the Mandate government to that of the Jewish Agency and a demand for future sovereignty throughout Mandatory Palestine. The program could be amended only by the institutions of the Zionist movement in a formal resolution. Declaratively, then, not only Britain was against partition at this time; so was the Jewish Agency.[34]

Analyzing the policy of the Jewish Agency vis-à-vis the work of the Anglo-American Committee of Inquiry, the historian Joseph Heller maintains that in the winter of 1945–1946 the Biltmore Program was the cement that prevented internal political disunion, not a realistic policy plan. The majority in favor of the program was too blatant to risk forgoing it. Accordingly, the Jewish Agency continued to declare its commitment to the program. Secretly, however, the Zionist leaders—Weizmann, Ben-Gurion, and Shertok—apprised the pro-Zionist members of the Anglo-American Committee that in practice they supported partition. They even presented a map. At the same time, the Jewish Agency continued to insist, at least officially, that only a Jewish majority would bring about a Jewish state. Summing up, Heller writes:

> [Ben-Gurion] urged the Jewish Agency to advocate the Biltmore line to the [Anglo-American] committee. If the question should arise of when a Jewish state will be established, the answer is that this will occur when a Jewish majority is created in the Land of Israel. . . . He would agree to a partition proposal only if the British government were to propose it as an alternative to the White Paper.[35]

On February 24, 1946, Ben-Gurion articulated the traditional Zionist formula in a meeting of the Zionist Inner Executive: a Jewish majority, meaning immigration, which would result in the state's establishment. In contrast, in a memorandum to Churchill in May 1945 and in the London conference that year, Ben-Gurion supported the declaration of a state irrespective of whether a Jewish majority existed. It would appear that since Churchill's appointment of a cabinet committee, in 1943, to review the policy of the 1939 White Paper, Weizmann, Ben-Gurion, and Shertok had reverted to support for the partition idea—which they had not fundamentally rejected even earlier. This meant a state first and immigration afterward, and not vice versa, as official Zionist policy held.[36]

Moreover, the high commissioner was obliged to consider the Jewish Agency's reaction to the talks between the administration and Transjordan. The agency responded with surprise and disappointment to Bevin's announcement in the United Nations, in January 1946, that his government was in very advanced negotiations with Transjordan toward its recognition as an independent state (with recognition taking place at the end of May). The Jewish Agency wanted to know why a committee was inquiring into the future of Palestine while simultaneously decisions were made about its eastern section only. This protest, though, was accompanied by a statement of the agency's willingness to conduct negotiations on the future of the country. Thus, by February 1946 Cunningham grasped the Jewish Agency's orientation. Its readiness to present its case to the Anglo-American Committee reflected a desire to achieve a political solution ahead of the Mandate's possible termination. It followed that he must pressure the agency to announce officially that it was reversing its order of priorities and advocating a state ahead of immigration.[37]

From this point of view, Operation Agatha was not productive. Not immediately anyway. At the beginning of August, on the eve of the Jewish Agency's policy shift, Cunningham believed that the Jews would not openly support partition even if they accepted the idea. They would cling to every pretext to promote their goal: first to become a majority and then to become as populous a country as possible. He was wrong. As noted, within a few days the Jewish Agency reverted officially to support for partition.[38]

Toward the end of 1946, the political process assumed greater momentum. An atmosphere of political and economic crisis hung over London. Interest in overseas developments shifted from east to west, to the United States. As a result, the importance of the Colonial Office—and to a lesser degree of the War Office (i.e., the army)—declined precipitously. The affairs of the fading empire were managed largely by the Foreign Office, in coordination with the prime minister. In India, as in Burma, Greece, Egypt, and Palestine, the British made their final political moves before deciding to leave in each case.

Creech-Jones, the new colonial secretary, had been Bevin's man since serving under him in the trade union movement. He too favored partition and took a mostly positive approach to the Zionist movement. The new appointment was beneficial, at least in the short term, for London's relations with the Zionists. The London-based talks in September 1946 between Britain and the Arabs produced nothing but the awareness that any prospect of a political solution that would be auspicious for British interests might lie with the Arab League but not with the Palestine Arabs. The latter were in any case represented only behind the scenes at the conference. London made one last effort on the Palestine question by means of a policy that was closer to partition than anything before. President Truman's pro-Zionist declaration in his annual greetings to American Jewry, on the eve of Yom Kippur in September 1946, prompted the British government to examine the possibility of cooperating to a degree with the Zionists, who were seen to wield great influence in Washington. It was in this atmosphere that the Yishuv leaders detained at Latrun were released at the beginning of November. Without either side—the British or the Zionists—admitting it, they both began to consider enlisting each other's aid to find a solution that would be mutually satisfactory and leave the Arab League no choice but to cooperate.[39]

The improved relations between Britain and the Zionists in the autumn of 1946 produced a series of British goodwill gestures: the recall of the GOC Palestine, Lieutenant General Barker, who was on bad terms with the Yishuv leadership; the inclusion of the refugees in the Cyprus camps in the monthly immigration quota; and the release of the leaders from Latrun. For its part, the Jewish Agency, as noted, forsook the violent resistance campaign beginning in August 1946 and returned to the partition concept, while making loud noises to disguise the new-old policy sanctioning a state first.

Despite the Jewish Agency's continuing refusal to attend the London conference unless the agency's legal status was restored to what it had been before June 29, the detainees were freed, and it was allowed to choose its delegates, greater substance inhered in the platform drawn up by Ben-Gurion in September 1946 for Mapai ahead of the Zionist congress scheduled for December. Immigration was formally the first priority, and the establishment of a state was in fourth place. But in the operative section, the first two clauses dealt with the means for establishing a state, with immigration in third place. From August 1946, then, the Jewish Agency effectively reverted to the policy it had espoused during the period of the partition plan put forward by the Peel Commission of 1937: first a state. Cunningham played a part in bringing about this historic reordering.[40]

The disappearance of the Latrun "bargaining card" after the release of the Yishuv leaders was a significant development for Cunningham and for his status in the political discourse toward the end of 1946. Already in a conversation with Shertok, some two weeks after the latter's release, Cunningham was compelled to say what he would never have thought to say in July–August. He denied the rumors that he intended to replace the Zionist movement's leadership. This declaration spelled the end of the failed attempt to bring the moderates to power. Shertok, for his part, did not conceal that events in London were of greater interest to him than those in Government House.[41]

Cunningham's contribution to the revision of the Zionist agenda is evident in his firm policy toward the insurgency, his lobbying for partition, and his approach to the issue of Jewish immigration. He did not deny the centrality of immigration but argued that precisely because of its primacy it must be the result of a political solution in the form of partition, not the solution itself. Cunningham maintained that the establishment of a Jewish state in part of Palestine would solve the immigration question. Restricting Jewish immigration, he knew, was a sine qua non for persuading the Arabs to accept partition. As such, he opposed the Anglo-American Committee's recommendation to allow 100,000 Jewish refugees into the country immediately. That would only make immigration the burning issue of Jewish-Arab relations. On this point, Cunningham saw eye to eye with the government. London sought at all costs to prevent illegal Jewish immigration, which was apt to bring down its rule in Palestine, undermine its relations with the Arab world and its status in the region, and have implications for the embryonic Cold War. It was not by chance that Britain and America were so sharply divided over the immigration issue. Unlike the question of the political solution or the attitude toward violence and terrorism, the high commissioner could wield little influence on immigration policy. He complained much about this but did little, believing that the problem would be resolved as part of the comprehensive political solution.[42]

To understand Cunningham's approach to the issue of illegal Jewish immigration, we must return to the period of his arrival in Palestine. The new high commissioner was unfamiliar with this subject when he took up residence in Government House in November 1945, and his approach was shaped by a number of factors. Like many in Britain overall, and in the military in particular, he had a clean conscience regarding the fate of the Jews in the Holocaust. Even though he had not been one of the liberators of the camps in Europe, he believed that his service in the Western Desert had helped prevent the Nazis from reaching Palestine, averting horrific consequences for the same Jewish community now under his authority. The highly charged encounter with the survivors also influenced him in other areas. He learned that immigration (aliya, "ascending," in the Zionist argot, which he picked up quickly) was the apple of the Yishuv's eye and of the Zionist movement: it took precedence over all else. He also grasped that the Arabs viewed free Jewish immigration as a danger that could turn them into a minority and actualize a Jewish state. From this point of view, he thought, there was no difference between the two sides. Both viewed a Jewish state as being conditional on Jewish immigration. Immigration, then, was palpably the raw nerve of the conflict. At the same time, the deliberations about the work of the Anglo-American Committee showed Cunningham that the question of Jewish immigration was also a cardinal political issue in the British-American clash over Palestine, and made clear that his government's policy was subject to clear quota rules laid down by the White Paper of 1939.[43]

On November 22, 1945, the day after he took up residence in Government House, a group of illegal immigrants was detained while trying to enter Palestine by sea for the first time since the end of the war. The next day, in a meeting with Ben-Gurion and other Jewish Agency and Yishuv leaders, the newly installed high commissioner first heard their position on the issue of free immigration and the restrictions imposed since 1939. On November 26, the senior officials of the administration met to discuss the subject; also present was the GOC Middle East, General Paget. Cunningham explained to him that the Mandatory police force lacked the necessary equipment and manpower to deal with the subject within the territorial waters of Palestine. He requested that the navy take charge of this problem. It was clear from his remarks that he wished to soften the implementation of the government's aggressive policy against illegal immigration. He shared the view of his senior officials, who on the eve of his arrival had not accepted the Colonial Office's suggestion to deport the illegal immigrants to Cyprus and thence to Europe. He also agreed with the view expressed by the regional commander: to make public the policy consolidated on the eve of Cunningham's arrival, by which illegal immigrants who were caught would not be deported but would be considered part of the quota in effect since 1939.[44]

The large-scale attempts to smuggle Jews into the country illegally meant that the quota was filled quickly. On January 7, 1946, Cunningham informed Hall that that month's quota had been met—nearly a quarter of the immigrants were "illegals"—and no further immigration permits would be issued. However, on January 30, in response to American pressure and the work of the joint committee, the British government decided to renew the immigrant quota stipulated in the 1939 White Paper: 1,500 a month. Cunningham immediately announced this plan, even before receiving the official confirmation from the colonial secretary (which arrived later that day—Cunningham apologized for not having waited). His aim was to prevent a three-hour strike called by the Jewish Agency Executive for the afternoon of January 31. He still believed that he could pacify the Yishuv with small concessions on the quota. According to his calculations based on the White Paper quota, after deducting the illegals and a small quota for Arabs, 2,100 legal immigration permits for Jews could be issued retroactively to cover the period of December 15, 1945, until March 14, 1946.[45]

As with the other policy issues, the Anglo-American Committee, which for Cunningham was a concentrated and efficient laboratory for experimentation and learning, helped him get a better grasp of Jewish immigration. While Truman's demand to allow 100,000 refugees into Palestine immediately was being debated, the new high commissioner discovered that no number would satisfy the Zionists. They were focused less on numbers and more on the principle: free immigration. This posed a danger, if the Zionists were aiming at numbers that would create a Jewish majority in Palestine. This awareness helped him formulate his support for partition, which would give the Zionists what they wanted in terms of free immigration.[46]

At the height of the quota crisis, Hall solicited Cunningham's opinion on a delicate matter that, if incorrectly handled, might have harmed Britain both politically and in its public image. London had learned about a Jewish Agency request for the Mandatory authorities to allow it to issue 50,000 Palestine identity cards for Jewish refugees in occupied Germany, primarily in the American zone, where most of them were located. The government was concerned that once the documents were distributed it would be impossible to prevent the refugees from reaching Palestine.

This was the new high commissioner's first test of how to please one side without infuriating the other, and vice versa. With his own prestige on the line—sooner than he had expected—his response was suitably cautious and complex. He recommended not rejecting the request, as it was legitimate for an officially recognized body (under the terms of the Mandate) to deal with candidates for immigration (who would immigrate, not how many—the latter of which was up to the British government). Accordingly, the ID card should state in bold red that its bearer was not allowed entry to Palestine, now or in the future—showing the printing of the cards to be for purposes of morale and propaganda. His recommendation was approved, and Cunningham informed the Jewish Agency, explaining the restriction. He knew that the agency could get the documents to Germany—forged, or worded as it wished—even without his authorization. He cautioned London accordingly and suggested that the authorities in Germany look into the matter, as the papers might already be there.[47]

In the summer of 1947, Cunningham, summing up his approach, referred to three aspects of the illegal immigration question. First was the formalistic aspect, namely, that illegal immigration violated the laws of Mandatory Palestine and of the refugees' countries of departure. The second aspect involved propaganda: in Cunningham's view, it was right to explain that no country had agreed to admit Jewish refugees, whereas the British administration had increased the quota for humanitarian reasons. Third, and substantively, every Jew who entered stirred discontent among the Arabs against the Yishuv and against the administration for permitting immigration and defending it judicially and militarily.[48]

Cunningham did not deny either the Jews' right in principle to settle in Palestine or their right to a state. At the beginning of January 1946, he reported that the Jewish Agency wished to send 50,000 pins to the displaced persons camps in Germany bearing the inscription, "If I forget thee, O Jerusalem, let my right hand forget its cunning." He realized that this was a propaganda ploy, intended to impress the Anglo-American Committee in its visit to the camps (on a dual mission: to examine the question of the Jews and the question of Palestine, and the connection between them) with the large number of those seeking to immigrate to Palestine. At the same time, the pins bore a symbolic educational purpose: to persuade refugees who were bound for destinations other than Palestine to change their mind. Cunningham recommended that London not be unduly impressed by this tactic, which was in itself legitimate, and not view the pins as constituting formal British approval for Jews to immigrate to Palestine. He saw no reason not to allow the shipment of the pins to Germany. The Colonial Office's response was positive.[49]

Unlike Foreign Secretary Bevin, Cunningham accepted without question the Jewish Agency's working assumption that the refugee problem would be solved only in Palestine. Like the agency, the high commissioner considered illegal immigration to be a political instrument, but one that he believed would lead to the establishment of a Jewish state in only part of Palestine. In other words, the high commissioner accepted the Jewish Agency's approach morally but his government's approach operatively. Unrestricted immigration would be a serious obstacle on the road to the desirable political solution of partition.[50]

Until the autumn of 1946, then, Cunningham tried to promote the idea of a state first and immigration afterward. Though grasping the overriding importance of immigration for the Jews, he believed that shifting the order of priorities would benefit all the sides in the Palestine triangle. He rejected the Foreign Office's conception that if partition were to ensure a cessation of Jewish immigration the moderate Arabs might accept it. Immigration, he understood, was the existential goal of the Zionist movement; indeed, even the establishment of a state would be postponed for the sake of immigration. For his part, the embassy official in Cairo who raised the idea of partition in return for a stop to immigration also understood how unrealistic it was from the perspective of the other side: it was hard to find an Arab who believed that the Jews would give up immigration for any condition.[51]

Of the secondary problems that engaged Cunningham in connection with illegal Jewish immigration, a key issue was the British government's decision in August 1946 to use the island of Cyprus as a deportation/detention/waiting/transit site for Palestine-bound Jewish refugees. This decision involved the Mandatory administration more than any other British move against illegal immigration outside the borders of Palestine. Geography was paramount here. Cyprus could be the first stop on the way back to Europe or the last on the way to Palestine. Even if this was not the original intention of the British government, the situation played into the hands of both the Zionists and the high commissioner.

It was not Cunningham's idea to send illegal immigrants to Cyprus—the notion was first broached in the Colonial Office toward the end of 1945—but his opinion was crucial in the cabinet decision of August 7, 1946. Dead-set against illegal immigration outright, he supported almost any proposal to block it, whether sending the refugee immigrants back to Europe or to Africa, or obstructing them at the embarkation ports. However, true to his response to the immigration question overall, he initiated nothing but was swept forward on others' ideas, some of them contradictory. The context was critical for him: to block immigration to ensure that it would not prevent partition. One consequence of the King David Hotel bombing was a punitive element that entered Cunningham's rationale in his recommendations to the government about the use of Cyprus.[52]

Cunningham's attitude toward the Cyprus camps thus derived from his take on the political question. The methods employed in the struggle against illegal immigration were determined by the needs of the time and his estimation of his ability to deal with the problem. Thus, after Operation Agatha he recommended more moderate methods, whereas after the King David Hotel incident he urged a complete halt to immigration pending a political solution. In any event, because he viewed illegal immigration as a key political tool of the Jewish Agency, he wanted the efforts against it to be plain to all. It was all the same if this entailed deducting the illegal immigrants from the quota of legal immigration, returning the ships to their port of departure, or deporting the would-be immigrants to Cyprus.[53]

The episode of the Cyprus camps has been researched thoroughly from the perspective of the British government, the Zionist movement and the Yishuv, and the occupants of the camps themselves. The Cyprus option first arose in the immigration context about a week before Cunningham's arrival in Jerusalem. The Colonial Office suggested deporting the illegal immigrants to the island as a first stage on the way back to their countries of embarkation. The administration, just then between two high commissioners, did not want to make dramatic decisions, in part for fear of reactions with consequences such as when the Haganah accidentally sank the *Patria* in November 1940. In any case, there were relatively few illegal immigrants.[54]

In 1946, with the Colonial Office having retracted the Cyprus idea late the year before, the army took the lead in urging that would-be immigrants be deported to Cyprus and afterward to Europe. This proposal gained the occasional backing of the Colonial Office and of Cunningham himself, each for their own reasons. The main alternative destinations were Libya and Cuba. The former had the drawback of being a largely Muslim and Arab country, the latter of its great distance. Sending ships back to their ports of embarkation in Europe entailed large-scale technical, economic, political, and propaganda difficulties, as the affair of the *Exodus* would show a year later, and it was uncertain that the governments concerned would cooperate. The possibility of sending back potential immigrants to the British occupation zone in Germany was not raised at this time, and later proved counterproductive for British interests. Cyprus remained the default option. The island possessed several distinct advantages, in particular its proximity to Palestine: a day and a half by ship from Haifa (at that time). Indeed, there was no adjacent territory to Palestine that did not possess an Arab or Muslim majority and had effective British rule.[55]

Cyprus was thus a convenient solution for the Mandatory administration, at least initially. In particular, housing for the refugees presented a real and acute problem. The Atlit facility had a limited capacity and was soon filled. The detention camps at Rafah were acknowledged as unfit for the refugee population, especially the women and children. In essence, the problem was technical and budgetary and could have been solved inside Palestine. The Cyprus project, too, cost money, and probably more than the Palestine option. Its implementation must therefore be viewed in political terms. What response would the plan elicit in the United States, in Palestine, and in Cyprus itself? The high commissioner's approach had a place, albeit not an exclusive one, in London's consideration of this question.[56]

The dominance of the Anglo-American channel kept the Cyprus option on the back burner as long as London believed this channel might lead to a resolution of the Palestine question. The failure of the second joint Anglo-American attempt to devise a solution—in the form of the provincial autonomy plan of early August 1946—was a major factor in the decision that was finally made in favor of Cyprus. London, disappointed with Truman's policy, overcame its concern over Washington's reaction to its Palestine policy, while at the same time the Mandatory authorities, buoyed by the results of Operation Agatha, no longer flinched at possible Yishuv violence. In this atmosphere, with the added motivation of punishing the Yishuv after the King David Hotel bombing, there was no reason not to proceed with the Cyprus option.

As mentioned, Cunningham's input also contributed to the Cyprus decision. A comprehensive situation appraisal of immigration that he had his staff prepare in late July found that the Arabs were in a foul mood following the King David Hotel incident and would respond more sharply than usual to continued Jewish immigration. If since the war's end they had shown a modicum of equanimity regarding the constant but relatively small influx of Jews, a possible outburst now loomed. At the same time, Cunningham had to cope with the Jews' inevitable reaction to the interception of their immigrant ships. Accordingly, he recommended that the illegal ships be sent back to their ports of departure, with the exception of those arriving from the Balkans and Russian-occupied territories—which should be sent on to Tripoli, in Libya, or to Cyprus. This was the sensible policy from his perspective, given the serious security situation generated by the recent Jewish violence and the ongoing need to contain the unrest or eradicate its sources. Military intelligence believed that the organizers of illegal immigration were giving priority to former partisan fighters who would use their experience against the British Army. According to the information contained in a document confiscated at Kibbutz Yagur, and as far as was known, most of the partisans joined the breakaway organizations.[57]

At the end of July, Cunningham, contrary to his basic approach, cautioned the government that given the state of mind of the Arabs—who were burying their dead after the King David Hotel attack and saw no firm response by the administration—it would be a mistake to precede the presentation of the government's political plan in the House of Commons in a few days' time with a declaration of intent to settle the refugee issue within the framework of a comprehensive political solution. Any such declaration would hasten a new Arab eruption. In Cunningham's view, during July 1946—even before the King David Hotel massacre and more intensely afterward—the Arab leadership had heightened its opposition to Jewish immigration. Thus, the Arabs took the rumors about the arrival of illegal ships on July 29 and 31 as the continuation of the King David Hotel provocation and intended to resist them with firearms. Only their poor military and organizational ability, together with the hope of additional British action, had prevented them from acting, the high commissioner believed.

He wanted it made clear to the Zionist leaders in London that the illegal immigration was endangering both a political solution and the future absorption of the 100,000 refugees. For the British authorities, therefore, priority must be given to dealing with the ships at their ports of departure or even with the agencies that ran the vessels. Cunningham also seized on the formality that he would not be able to allow immigrants without a visa to enter the country, as had been the practice until now. In this case, he and the military joined forces to urge dramatic action on the immigration issue.[58]

London acceded this time, and fast. The logic of the high commissioner and the army was taken as sound. The British were no longer hamstrung, following the fallout with Washington over the provincial autonomy idea. The decision was made on August 7; Cunningham requested that it not be publicized immediately. On August 13, the government announced the opening of the camps in Cyprus. That very day, the first two ships were sent to the island—the *Empire Heywood* and the *Empire Rival*, carrying a total of 1,285 refugees who had reached Palestine aboard the *Yagur* and the *Henrietta Szold*. Five days later, a second group of illegal immigrants was transported to Cyprus. All told, 51,530 refugees passed through the Cyprus camps before they were shut down in February 1949. All of them eventually reached Palestine, the vast majority before the end of the Mandate.[59]

Moshe Shertok was incarcerated in Latrun from the end of June until the beginning of November 1946. He worked hard in the facility, according to his own testimony. At the same time, during this period he was able to view developments as a side observer. He seems to have been disappointed in the Yishuv's lukewarm response to the creation of the Cyprus detention camps. "I am sorry that there was no more than this—in the number of those who broke out—even at the price of more victims." Nahum Bogner, the author of a study on the subject, notes "the unease felt by those involved in illegal immigration activity at the Yishuv's nonresponse to the immigrants' deportation."[60]

Cunningham, too, was surprised by the Yishuv's minor reaction—he had apparently expected more. From his point of view, the Jewish Agency had fulfilled its obligation and little more. Apart from a few demonstrations and threats of refusal to cooperate about civilian matters, the high commissioner saw a halfhearted response to an issue that in another period could have spawned a "modern Bar Kochba," as he put it.[61]

Nonetheless, on August 13, 1946, the first day of the deportations to Cyprus, the administration was concerned about the Yishuv's possible reaction (as a lesson from the events of "Wingate Night" in Tel Aviv on March 25–26)[62] and imposed a general curfew on Haifa. The port was declared a closed military zone. Voice of Israel radio called on the city's residents to ignore the curfew and storm the port. Several hundred people did so and the police were forced to open fire. One demonstrator (a woman) was killed and nine were wounded, two seriously—both later died of their wounds—in riots that erupted in several places in the city. Tel Aviv and Jerusalem made do with protest gatherings—far less intense than what the authorities had feared. The second deportation, on August 18, triggered no significant events other than symbolic attempts to sabotage the ship carrying the illegal immigrants and resistance by the immigrants themselves, which was quelled by teargas. The start of the Cyprus project did not elicit an exceptional Yishuv response, Cunningham wrote with satisfaction in his report for August 1946. There had been assemblies, media grumbling, some early shutdowns of places of work in protest, but no major events, certainly no violence. In contrast to the Yishuv's wide-ranging resistance to Britain's immigration policy, the deportations to Cyprus had by and large passed quietly.[63]

On December 6, 1946, amid another wave of terror, Cunningham wrote a secret personal report to Colonial Secretary Creech-Jones about an episode that he thought could explain the Jewish national institutions' undeclared approach to the Cyprus camps. At the time, the senior Jewish Agency leadership was in Basel, Switzerland, to attend the Zionist congress. In light of the renewed terrorism by Etzel and Lehi, the high commissioner met several times with the president of the National Council, Yitzhak Ben-Zvi, the most senior leader remaining in the country. In one of the meetings, which was also attended by representatives of the non-socialist "civic circles," as they were known, among them Tel Aviv mayor Israel Rokach, the delegation—to which the breakaways had promised to cease their activity by the end of the Zionist congress and the London talks—tried to negotiate with Cunningham about the illegal immigration activity. According to Cunningham's report, his interlocutors claimed that only one ship was on the way and implored him to allow it to dock in Haifa. Upon hearing Cunningham's refusal, Ben-Zvi said that in order to reduce the tension and not give the terrorists a reason to break their promise of a ceasefire, the navy should force the ship to change course for Cyprus. Cunningham did not conceal his satisfaction at this remark. He replied that although it was impossible to force a ship on the high seas to deviate from its course, if the immigrants could be persuaded to go to Cyprus the British would give them all possible aid. The delegation agreed; at its members' request, the high commissioner kept the conversation secret.[64]

Cunningham took the tepid Zionist reaction to the Cyprus deportations as a positive political signal. First, some in the Yishuv plainly understood the advantages of Cyprus, particularly given the determined stance of the high commissioner and the government on the question of illegal immigration and considering that the Yishuv-Zionist leadership had reverted to support for the idea of partition and negotiations with the British government. In this connection, the Yishuv could allow itself to agree tacitly to the existence of a pool of immigrants in Cyprus. Second, even if Cyprus was a no-choice option, Cunningham felt that, practically, it was also right to bring the refugees there on an interim basis and afterward to the Jewish state, which would be established within the partition framework and in accordance with his conception: a state first, immigration afterward.[65]

Cunningham thus drew a link between the Jewish Agency's return to the partition idea in summer 1946 and its restrained response to the deportation of illegal immigrants to Cyprus. No one in the agency would admit to this connection, of course, but his analysis was not without foundation. The Yishuv seemed to grasp that "Cyprus was the eve of the Land of Israel."[66] By November 1946, it was already clear that Cyprus, like Atlit earlier, was the reservoir from which the monthly quota would be filled after the "illegals" were deducted. Thus, refugees were taken to Palestine from Cyprus every month. The high commissioner, loyal to his "first a state" approach and worried about the Arabs' reaction, initially objected to these transports but was soon persuaded. He agreed with the colonial secretary that this would strengthen the Zionist moderates just before the Basel meeting and ahead of the possible resumption of talks between the British government and the Jewish Agency.[67]

Zionist-oriented studies of the Cyprus episode shed little light on its role in the Jewish Agency's renewed espousal of partition. Circumstantially, it appears that deportation to the nearby island, rather than Europe, had a moderating effect on the Jewish Agency's response. That, in any event, was the conclusion reached by Cunningham, who wanted to leverage Cyprus to advance the political solution. To that end, he was even willing to tolerate the financial difficulties of funding the camps and cope with the criticism in the Yishuv and the United States.

In a vicissitude of history, Cyprus underwent a face-lift with the monthly transports to Palestine: instead of a transit camp for refugees on the way back to Europe, it became the "waiting room" for entering the Land of Israel. A year later, when Britain departed from its policy of sending illegal immigrants to Cyprus, it did so knowing that this would stir strong Zionist opposition. In July 1947, the colonial secretary was worried about how the *Exodus* deportees and the Yishuv would react when they discovered that the destination of the deportation ships was far from Cyprus. He assumed, based on the experience of the previous months, that there would be no serious opposition to Cyprus itself. Moreover, at the height of the *Exodus* crisis Creech-Jones informed Cunningham in a personal cable that the government had decided that, whatever the outcome of the crisis, these Jews would not be allowed to reach either Palestine or Cyprus. The latter, then, was perceived as a default destination to which the Jewish Agency would not object.[68]

In one sense, the Cyprus solution heralded the start of Britain's physical departure from Palestine. Not only the Jewish Agency and the refugees had to accept Cyprus as a compromise on the way east. From a western perspective—both geographically and historically, albeit with different state, political, and moral implications—Britain, too, compromised by sending the refugees to Cyprus.

NOTES

1. Hall to Cunningham, June 13, 1946, MECA CP, BI, F1/147.

2. Cunningham to Hall, July 15, 1946, MECA CP, BI, F1/149.

3. Cunningham to Hall, September 29, 1946, MECA CP, BI, F2/103; Louis, *The British Empire*, pp. 446–447; Avizohar, introduction to Ben-Gurion, *Toward the End of the Mandate*, pp. 16–17.

4. Hall to Cunningham, July 8, 1946, July 13, 1946, NA C0537/1713.

5. Hall to Cunningham, July 17, 1946, July 18, 1946, NA C0537/1713; Cunningham to Hall, July 17, 1946, NA C0537/1713.

6. Hall to Cunningham, July 13, 1946, July 18, 1946, NA C0537/1713.

7. Cabinet meeting, July 24, 1946, NA CAB129/9.

8. Hall to Cunningham, July 24, 1946, MECA CP, B1, F1/166; Cunningham to Hall, July 27, 1946, MECA CP, B1, F1/178; August 1, 1946, MECA CP, B1, F2/4; August 3, 1946, MECA CP, B1, F1/10.

9. Cunningham to Hall, July 27, 1946, MECA CP, B1, F1/178, and also August 3, 1946, MECA CP, B1, F2/10.

10. Hall to Cunningham, July 28, 1946, MECA CP, B1, F1/179; Cunningham to Hall, July 29, 1946, MECA CP, B1, F1/181.

11. Cunningham to Hall, July 29, 1946, MECA CP, B1, F1/181.

12. Ibid.; and also Cunningham to Hall, August 3, 1946, September 3, 1946, September 29, 1946, NA C0537/1708.

13. Cunningham to Hall, August 3, 1946, NA C0537/1708. On August 5, the Jewish Agency Executive rejected the provincial autonomy plan and declared its unwillingness to hold talks with the government if it could not choose its own representative. Jewish Agency Executive meeting, Ben-Gurion, *Toward the End of the Mandate*, p. 119.

14. Hall to Cunningham, July 28, 1946, MECA CP, B1, F1/179; Cunningham to Hall, July 29, 1946, MECA CP B1, F1/181; and also August 3, 1946, NA C0537/1708.

15. Cunningham to Hall, August 19, 1946, MECA CP, B1, F2/41; and also September 19, 1946, MECA CP, B1, F2/104.

16. Cunningham to Hall, September 26, 1946, MECA CP, B1, F2/65.

17. Ibid.

18. Cunningham to Hall, August 19, 1946, MECA CP, B1, F2/41; and September 19, 1946, MECA CP, B1, F2/104; Ze'ev Sherf to Moshe Shertok, August 14, 1946, CZA, S25/10016.

19. Cunningham to Hall, August 19, 1946, MECA CP, B1, F2/41.

20. Hall to Cunningham, September 4, 1946, NA F0371/52642; Cunningham to Hall, September 15, 1946, NA F0371/52644.

21. Cunningham to Hall, October 10, 1946, NA C0537/1712.

22. Meron Medzini, *The Proud Jewess: Golda Meir and the Vision of Israel*, Jerusalem 1990, p. 116 (Hebrew); Golda Meir, *My Life*, London 1976, p. 167.

23. Rosenthal, "Revelations of the Last High Commissioner."

24. Cunningham to Hall, September 26, 1946, MECA CP, B1, F2/65.

25. Cunningham to Hall, October 14, 1946, MECA CP, B1, F2/184; Avizohar, introduction to Ben-Gurion, *Toward the End of the Mandate*, pp. 26–30; *The Autobiography of Nahum Goldmann*, New York 1969, pp. 230–241.

26. Cunningham to Hall, September 27, 1946, MECA CP, B1, F2/67.

27. Jamal al-Husseini (1893–1982), the chairman of the Arab Higher Committee (1946–1948), was born in Jerusalem. He was secretary of the Palestinian Arab Action Committee (1921–1934) and of the Supreme Muslim Council. He served as president of the Palestine Arab Party, which was founded in 1935. Beginning in 1936, he was his party's representative on the Arab Higher Committee. In 1937, he fled Palestine during the Arab Revolt, and was captured by the British in Iran during the Second World War and exiled to Rhodesia. Released in 1945, he returned to Palestine the following year and represented the Palestine Arabs at the United Nations in 1947–1948. Hall to Cunningham, July 17, 1946, and Cunningham to Hall, July 18, 1946, NA C0537/1713.

28. Cunningham to Hall and to Britain's envoys in the Arab capitals, August 26, 1946, MECA CP, B1, F2/65.

29. Ibid.

30. Ibid.

31. Cunningham to Hall, October 14, 1946, MECA CP, B1, F2/184.

32. "High Commissioner for Palestine, Note on Potential Arab Political Violence in Palestine (April 1946)," NA C0537/2416.

33. Cunningham to Hall and to Britain's envoys in the Arab capitals, August 26, 1946, MECA CP B1, F2/56.

34. Joseph Heller, "From Black Sabbath to Partition: Summer 1946 as a Turning Point in the History of Zionist Policy," *Zion*, 43 (1978), pp. 314–361 (Hebrew).

35. Joseph Heller, "Zionist Policy in the International Arena in the Wake of the Second World War—The Case of the Anglo-American Committee of Inquiry, 1945-1946," *Shalem* 3 (1981), pp. 236-237, 243-244, 248 (Hebrew).

36. On the turning point following the establishment of the 1943 cabinet committee—which, to the Zionist movement's misfortune was disbanded after the assassination of Lord Moyne, the British minister of state in the Middle East, by Lehi in November 1944—see Heller, "Zionist Policy in the International Arena," note 65; in the same piece, see pp. 245, 248, p. 250, and note 70.

37. Joseph Linton (the political secretary of the Zionist Office in London) to Colonial Office, January 16, 1946, CZA, S25/3505; Cunningham to Hall, February 19, 1946, MECA, CP, B1, F1/30.

38. Cunningham to Hall, August 3, 1946, NA C0537/1708. Cunningham later retracted this accusation and maintained that the Jewish Agency's agreement to partition was genuine, not a tactic. Cunningham's summation at Chatham House, July 22, 1948, RIIFA, 8/258.

39. The talks with the Arabs concluded on October 2. Between the first and the eighteenth of the month, the Foreign Office and the Colonial Office conducted talks with a delegation headed by Weizmann and Kaplan, with the quiet backing of the Jewish Agency, ahead of a planned Jewish-Arab conference in early 1947. High commissioner to Colonial Office, monthly report, December 5, 1946, NA C0537/1708; Gershon Agronsky (editor of the *Palestine Post*), "Notes on London Visit, September 4th to October 23rd, 46," MECA CP, B4, F4/43.

40. Ben-Gurion called this approach "not Masada, not Vichy"; Weizmann termed it "hot frost." Ben-Gurion, *Toward the End of the Mandate*, pp. 17, 153-155; Teveth, *Kinat David*, pp. 775-778; Ben-Gurion to Golda Meyerson, September 27, 1946, *Toward the End of the Mandate*, pp. 181-182; Ben-Gurion, "Main Points for Platform," September 28, 1946, *Toward the End of the Mandate*, p. 183.

41. Cunningham talk with Shertok, Government House, November 19, 1946, Sharett, *Imprisoned with Paper and Pencil*, p. 431.

42. Cunningham's objection to the entry of 100,000 refugees was expressed in his conversation with Henry Montor, a senior official of the United Jewish Appeal in the United States. Sherf to Shertok, August 14, 1946, CZA, S25.10016; Cunningham summed up his approach on the immigration issue in his testimony to members of the UNSCOP delegation, "Notes on the Address Given by the High Commissioner of Palestine to the Chairman and Delegates of UNSCOP at an Informal Meeting at Government House on Thursday, 17th July 1947," CZA, A366.

43. Cunningham to Hall, November 23, 1945, NA C0537/45407; Bernard Wasserstein, *Britain and the Jews of Europe, 1939-1945*, London and Oxford 1979, shows quite

convincingly that the Jews had an account to settle with Britain over its refugee policy. The extensive research literature on illegal Jewish immigration (*ha'apalah*) and its by-products make unnecessary a discussion here of its background and history; see especially the inter-university project on the subject and its series of publications; *The Ha'apalah Library*, Tel Aviv University (Hebrew). On the connection drawn by Cunningham between his service in the Western Desert and the fate of Palestine, see his summarizing remarks at Chatham House, July 22, 1947. On Jewish immigration as an element of the British-American dispute at the time, see Martin Jones, *Failure in Palestine: British and United States Policy after the Second World War*, London and New York 1986. On Britain's decision to persist with the White Paper policy on immigration, see Aryeh Kochavi, *Displaced Persons and International Politics: Britain and the Jewish DPs after the Second World War*, Tel Aviv 1992, p. 42 (Hebrew).

44. A group of twenty illegal immigrants along with the crew were seized aboard the *Berl Katznelson*, which had arrived from Greece and had managed to put about 190 immigrants ashore; see Kochavi, *Displaced Persons*, p. 44. Cunningham to Hall, November 23, 1945, NA C0537/45407; "Minutes of the Twenty-third Meeting of the Executive Council Held at the Secretariat, Jerusalem, on 26th November 45, Confirmed by Cunningham, November 29, 1945," MECA, CP, B4, F/3/12; Shaw (acting high commissioner) to Gater (Colonial Office), November 16, 1945, NA C0537 F0371/45407; Cunningham to Hall, November 23, 1945, NA C0537 F0371/45407.

45. Cunningham to Hall, January 7, 1946, January 31, 1946, NA C0537/1703; March 24, 1946, NA C0537/1703.

46. Cunningham to Hall, January 31, 1946, NA C0537/1703; and also February 13, 1946, NA C0537/1703.

47. Hall to Cunningham, January 30, 1946, NA C0537/1706; Cunningham to Hall, February 5, 1946, NA C0537/1706. The Jewish Agency understood the restrictions well; the text on the proposed document was therefore as follows: "Registered for immigration to Palestine at . . . by Palestine office." The ID cards were part of an internal propaganda campaign intended to persuade the DPs to immigrate to Palestine and not to the United States, particularly on the eve of the joint committee's visit to the camps. Irit Keynan, *The Hunger Has Not Abated*, Tel Aviv 1996, pp. 182–186 (Hebrew).

48. "Notes on the Address Given by the High Commissioner," CZA, A366.

49. Cunningham to Hall, February 5, 1946, NA C0537/1706; Trafford Smith (Colonial Office) to [First name unavailable] Gottlib (Chief Secretariat), February 14, 1946, NA C0537/1706.

50. Cunningham to Hall, July 27, 1946, MECA CP, B1, F1/174,178.

51. Louis, *The British Empire*, p. 451.

52. Cunningham to Hall, July 25, 1946, MECA CP, B1, F1/179; Cabinet meeting, August 7, 1946, NA CB128/6.

53. Cunningham to Hall, July 24, 1946, MECA CP, B1, F1/169.

54. Wasserstein, *Britain and the Jews of Europe*, and Ronald W. Zweig, *Britain and Palestine during the Second World War*, London 1986, deal with Britain's attitude toward the Jewish refugees during the Second World War; Kochavi, *Displaced Persons*, addresses the British aspect after the war; Nahum Bogner, *The Deportation Island: Jewish Illegal Immigrant Camps on Cyprus, 1946–1948*, Tel Aviv 1991 (Hebrew), considers the perspective of the Yishuv and the camp occupants; and the same perspective is found in David Schaary, *The Cyprus Detention Camps for Jewish "Illegal" Immigrants to Palestine, 1946–1949*, Jerusalem 1981 (Hebrew).

55. Aviva Halamish, *Exodus—The Real Story*, Tel Aviv 1990, pp. 159–172 (Hebrew).

56. Shertok conversation with Cunningham, November 19, 1946, Sharett, *Imprisoned with Paper and Pencil*, p. 433.

57. Hall to Cunningham, July 26, 1946, MECA CP, B1, F1/181; Kochavi, *Displaced Persons*, pp. 49–50; [First name unavailable] Scott for high commissioner to colonial secretary, July 25, 1946, MECA CP, B1, F1/174. The only evidence for this extreme generalization about a connection between the immigrants and the breakaways was that some of the Lehi activists who were arrested in a June 18 raid on the railway workshops did not speak Hebrew.

58. Cunningham to Hall, August 3, 1946, NA C0537/1708; [First name unavailable] Newton for high commissioner to colonial secretary, July 28, 1946, MECA CP, B1, F1/180.

59. Cunningham to Hall, August 3, 1946; Bogner, *Deportation Island*, p. 219.

60. Sharett, *Imprisoned with Paper and Pencil*, August 13, 1946, p. 164; Bogner, *Deportation Island*, pp. 43–46; Schaary, *Cyprus Detention Camps*, p. 89.

61. Cunningham to Hall, monthly report, September 3, 1946, NA C0537/1708.

62. See chapter 2.

63. Ibid.; Bogner, *Deportation Island*, p. 44; the attempted sabotage of the ships, discussed extensively by Slutzky, *History of the Haganah*, III, 2, pp. 903–904, is barely mentioned in passing by Cunningham and his aides. See monthly reports for September–November 1946, all of them at NA C0537/1708.

64. Cunningham to Creech-Jones, "personal and secret," December 6, 1946, NA C0537/1712; as far as is known, no ship with refugees arrived in Cyprus in this period.

65. Cunningham to Hall, September 3, 1946, NA C0537/1708.

66. Bogner, *Deportation Island*, p. 323. This phrase, of unclear origin, encapsulates Bogner's Zionist-centric study. The conclusion that Cyprus was the last stop on the road to the Land of Israel comes up repeatedly in his book. However, his perspective, namely, that of the deportees, prevents him from seeing the positive aspect of the Cyprus episode from the Zionist position.

67. Cunningham to Creech-Jones, monthly report, December 5, 1946, NA C0537/ 1708; Bogner, *Deportation Island*, pp. 63–69; Grinwood for high commissioner to governor of Cyprus, July 23, 1946, MECA CP, B2, F1/157.

68. Creech-Jones to Cunningham, July 17, 1947, MECA CP, B2, F1/176; also "personal and secret," MECA CP, B2, F1/189.

To Fight Terrorism as Though There Is No Political Process

July 1946–
August 1947

5 "The King David Hotel Crime"

On Monday July 22, 1946, shortly after being pulled from the debris of the southeast wing of the King David Hotel,[1] Sir John Shaw, the chief secretary of the Mandate administration,[2] cabled the colonial secretary and the British ambassadors in the Middle East, Washington, and Moscow. A particularly large bomb had exploded in the Chief Secretariat at approximately 12:30 p.m., he wrote. He added that an entire wing of the King David Hotel had collapsed and that the damage and destruction were apparently widespread. Badly shaken, Shaw could only promise that he would send a full report as soon as he was able. Shaw was just the acting high commissioner, but he continued to work out of his office in the Chief Secretariat. (The cable itself was sent from Government House, because the telegraph facility in the hotel was destroyed.) Shaw survived because the Chief Secretariat was located in the hotel's southeast wing, which was only slightly damaged. The explosion occurred at 12:37 p.m.[3]

Cunningham was at the last place he would have chosen to be when the news reached him—Whitehall, where he was attending a meeting at the Ministry of Defense, the height of a triumphant visit to London to reap the fruits of his offensive in Operation Agatha. On his third day in the capital, he seemed to be having success in explaining to the government the connection, as he saw it, between the military's action, the cessation of the Jewish insurgency and the Jewish Agency's enlistment in the fight against terrorism, and the one possible political solution: partition. But the news from Jerusalem set him on a different course. Within a few months, he would be pushed, entirely against his will, into dealing with terrorism as a separate issue in itself, rather than as part of the political process. Cunningham's gradual exclusion from diplomatic activity after July 22 was brought about by the army, the Foreign Office, and even the Jewish Agency.[4]

This was not the high commissioner's first encounter with terrorism since arriving in Palestine. Heretofore, however, the violence had remained within the Yishuv's institutional framework and taken the form of street demonstrations and guerilla-like operations. These actions were carried out under the aegis of the Jewish Agency, a legally constituted body against which the administration could act, as in Operation Agatha. In contrast, the classic terrorism perpetrated by the breakaway groups, and not coordinated with the Jewish Resistance Movement, straddled the fault line between criminality (robbery, abduction) and senseless brutality (the murder of British soldiers in their sleep in Tel Aviv, in April 1946) of a type that infuriated the organized Yishuv. Cunningham and his aides had previously turned the terrorism to their advantage, invoking it to exert effective pressure on the Jewish Agency, which bore responsibility. From this perspective, the primary goals of Operation Agatha were to moderate the Zionist leadership ahead of a political settlement, and to prove its responsibility for Haganah and Palmah guerilla actions. A secondary goal was to induce the Jewish Agency to take action against Etzel and Lehi, though these entities were not targeted in the operation.

Even if Cunningham tried to deny it, the King David Hotel event represented a quantum leap compared to past actions. With the exception of Government House itself, there was no more sensitive, symbolic, and operational target than the King David Hotel, whose southern wing housed the Chief Secretariat (the Palestine government) and army headquarters. The terrorists struck at the very heart of the administration, with all the implications this entailed.

The King David Hotel, which was owned by the Jewish-Egyptian Mosseri family, opened its doors to the public in late 1931. From the beginning, the King David was an extraordinary international and intercultural meeting place in Palestine and indeed throughout the Middle East. Britons, Jews, and Arabs mingled at the bar and in the frequent parties held at the hotel. The guests came from all over the world: kings, princes, and leaders—whether genuine or self-styled—along with politicians, intelligence personnel, journalists, artists, businessmen, jurists, men of the military, administration officials, and anyone who wanted to see and be seen, obtain information, forge ties of various kinds, or close a deal. During the Second World War, Palestine as a whole and Jerusalem in particular were an island. The King David Hotel was emblematic of that reality. Terrorist attacks had occurred in Jerusalem before July 1946, but this tragedy marked the end of an era for the King David, for Jerusalem, and for the entire country.

The outrage on July 22 set new heights—or depths—of indiscriminate cruelty. Ninety-one people were murdered and 476 wounded. One member of the Etzel terrorist squad was killed. The dead included forty-one Arabs, twenty-eight Britons, seventeen Jews, two Armenians, a Russian, a Greek, and an Egyptian. Only a minority were enemies of the Yishuv, even as defined by the perpetrators. Among them were administration officials, army personnel, and civilian and military auxiliary staff. Some of the victims were hotel employees. People were hurled onto the walls of the YMCA building across the street. More than three months later, John Fletcher-Cooke, who was sent to replace the financial secretary, a victim of the blast, found, to his horror, human body parts on a flowerpot next to the hotel.[5]

In the spontaneous discussion held by the Ministerial Committee on Defense when news of the atrocity arrived, Cunningham probably "counted to ten" before requesting the floor. Two elements of his remarks remained constant in his reaction to the attack in the period that followed. First, the perpetrators must be punished meaningfully; second, the response would be declarative and specific. The British authorities must not go to extremes. Despite everything, the Jewish Agency was a necessary partner for a political settlement. This approach was favorably received by the ministers. Like their cabinet colleagues, they were pursuing an attempt—which still looked viable that week—to achieve an agreed settlement of the Palestine question together with the United States (see previous chapter). In line with Cunningham's wish, the committee decided that he should return immediately to Jerusalem, and he left London that same day.[6]

On August 3, as part of his regular monthly summary, Cunningham sent the Colonial Office a detailed account of the King David Hotel events. The comprehensive survey was forwarded to others in London and throughout the empire. His sense of shock comes through strongly, together with an uneasy feeling about those responsible. On that day, Cunningham estimated the number of dead at more than one hundred, in addition to forty-seven wounded. All seven departments of the secretariat and the army were affected. The worst hit were the financial, economic, and manpower units, which were housed in the hotel's southwest wing. Nearly all these units' British personnel were killed (of whom the most senior was Julius Jacobs, the financial secretary—English, Jewish, Zionist). "Even the centuries['] turbulent annals of the Holy Land record few crimes worse than the outrage perpetrated by The Irgun Zvai Leumi on the 22nd July," the shaken high commissioner wrote. Cunningham did not absolve the Yishuv of political and moral responsibility. The crime, he believed, was a direct result of years of twisted propaganda put out by all the Yishuv institutions and parties.[7]

Cunningham, who urged a moderate approach where possible and was at odds with the activists in his administration, with the military in Palestine, Cairo, and London, and with the British government, was compelled to admit that in the eyes of many Britons, the Jews' hands were steeped in the blood of their friends and colleagues stationed in Jerusalem. Despite this, his reports to London after the attack reflect his effort to preserve equanimity and a judicious approach in order to block irreversible militant actions. Above all, Cunningham feared the dynamics of the bloody cycle into which he too had been swept: the Night of the Bridges, Operation Agatha, the King David Hotel—and what next? His aim was to extricate all those involved—the administration, the security forces, Britain, the Jewish Agency, the Arab Higher Committee, and the entire population of the country—from the cycle of violence. In this cycle, the breakaways' terrorism was a marginal issue from his perspective. The actions perpetrated by Etzel and Lehi were, in the end, a function of the administration's inability to lock hands with the Jewish Agency in a struggle for partition and against terror. It was convenient for him that Etzel took responsibility for the King David Hotel attack. He did not know, and probably did not want to know, about the Jewish Agency's involvement (through the Haganah) in the atrocity. (According to the latest research, the Haganah definitely had a hand in approving the attack. What is in dispute is whether the Haganah tried to delay or annul the operation and whether the final decision to go ahead was made by Etzel alone.)[8]

Once the initial shock wore off, the high commissioner was determined to use the tragedy to bring about a return to the necessary political process. Its buds, he felt, had been clearly visible in the first half of July, after the Yishuv had been dealt a political and military blow in the form of Operation Agatha.

Cunningham now faced four missions in the Palestine domestic arena. First, he had to curtail the natural inclination of his staff and of the military to seek revenge. Second, it was necessary to get the administration working normally again. Cunningham ordered the urgent rebuilding—symbolic no less than concrete—of the southern wing of the King David Hotel in order to restore the administration's severely damaged status. With extra-budgetary help from the Treasury in London, the hotel was repaired and another story added.[9] The third task was to prevent the incensed and hurting Arabs from taking the law into their hands. The fact that most of those murdered in the attack were Arabs, many of them senior officials in the administration and members of distinguished families, was of great significance. The fourth and most complex mission was to try to persuade the Jewish Agency to resume its cooperation in the campaign against terrorism and in favor of partition. The danger that the agency would revert to terrorism, even against its will, was now palpable, the high commissioner thought.

A great many of the administration's civilian and military staff members had a friend or an acquaintance who was killed or wounded in the attack. Given the accumulated experience of his first months in the country, the high commissioner already had good reason to be concerned about morale. Indeed, the British community in Palestine was in a state of shock, and Cunningham sought to play this up in order to protect British subjects, his administration, and his policy. He knew that his superiors did not understand the implications of what had happened in Jerusalem on July 22, 1946, whether for good (in terms of the effect terrorism exercised on the political process) or for evil (in terms of London's willingness to aid him in combating terrorism). With great reluctance, Cunningham suggested to the colonial secretary on August 5 that serious consideration be given to the immediate evacuation of about two thousand nonessential British men, women, and children. At the same time, the administration's activities in Jerusalem could be headquartered in one small area to enable the physical protection of British civilians and local employees of the administration. Cunningham made clear his view that the time for this step—an idea he had first broached at the beginning of 1946—had not yet arrived. However, he would not be able to delay such preventive measures for long if Yishuv violence persisted.[10]

The effect such moves would have on his staff's morale was not lost on the high commissioner. But he was determined to take whatever steps were necessary to protect administration personnel. This would be done without disrupting the life of the local population or the routine activity of the civilian administration and the security forces. The plan to evacuate the "nonessentials" was based on a concept devised by his predecessor in office, Field Marshal Gort. The execution would be rapid, mainly through Haifa, with the possibility of an interim stop in Egypt, although Cunningham preferred to avoid this because of the security situation there. He was disturbed that some of his staff, particularly the veterans of the colonial service and the armed forces, did not have a home of their own in Britain.[11]

Hall submitted Cunningham's ideas to the cabinet, which agreed that a plan should be drawn up for the territorial concentration of the administration and the evacuation of nonessential personnel. The colonial secretary asked Cunningham what he thought should be done about the wives and family members who were scheduled to leave for Palestine to accompany a father who had just been posted there in a civilian, police, or military capacity. The War Office instructed the commander of the Middle East Theatre, General Dempsey, to cooperate with the Mandatory administration in the event of an evacuation. The Foreign Office suggested that the ambassador to Cairo should inquire about the Egyptian government's response to the possible short stay of the evacuees in Egypt, on their way to England. In the case of a decision to enact the plan, the ambassador would give the Egyptians advance notification. The Ministry of Transport, which would be in charge of actually moving the people, asked to be notified three to four weeks before the target date.[12]

Cunningham was taken aback by London's quick and positive response. His subsequent hesitancy might be considered surprising, as he himself had suggested the plan. In his August 9 reply to Hall's go-ahead, he noted that his wire of August 5 had apparently not made clear that he was still talking about a plan, definitely not implementation. Indeed, he hoped that the plan would not have to be implemented. Under the circumstances, he emphasized, the idea must remain an absolute secret. Publicizing the plan might encourage Jewish terrorism and also give rise to the old accusations that he was defensively minded. Cunningham informed Hall that he wished to delay the move for two reasons: because those slated for evacuation had no suitable abode in Britain and because morale, already low, would decline even further. Nor should the Colonial Office delay the arrival of the new families: it was important for movement in and out of the country to proceed as usual. The evacuation was duly postponed, but beginning in July 1946 it was on the agenda of the Colonial Office and the Mandatory administration. Its time would come.[13]

The King David Hotel attack left the administration's staff deeply anxious, particularly those based in Jerusalem. On July 27, Chief Secretary Sir John Shaw, the most senior official of the administration, was dispatched to London to explain the situation in Palestine firsthand. His mission was a continuation of the high commissioner's abruptly curtailed visit, and in addition Shaw could provide an updated situation appraisal. On August 3, Cunningham learned that Shaw intended to leave London for Jerusalem within the next forty-eight hours, without first informing him. The high commissioner asked Hall to delay Shaw's return. The hotel bombing had left the chief secretary mentally scarred, as was only natural, Cunningham wrote. Shaw had survived, but many of his staff members were among the casualties. He had pulled some of them out of the rubble with his own hands. In addition, his life was under threat from Lehi. Writing with unabashed empathy, Cunningham noted that when he sent Shaw to London he had the feeling that the latter was on the brink of collapse. He had suggested a two-week stay, at least, and possibly that Shaw not return at all. Shaw had protested vehemently, Cunningham reported, as he would be perceived to have deserted amid a war. At the same time, he had not turned down the idea outright, saying only that he was obliged to return to Jerusalem for at least a month in order to be with his staff at this difficult period and arrange for an orderly succession. Cunningham informed Hall that he had rejected such a plan and explained to Shaw that matters could be arranged to avoid the appearance that he had fled. Shaw, for his part, had retorted with an irrefutable argument: his two sons were with his wife in Jerusalem for their summer vacation. To this, Cunningham had no answer. He urged Hall to try to delay him, at least. It would be a relief if he did not come back to Palestine at all: protecting him was a burden.[14]

Nevertheless, Shaw returned on August 6. He persuaded Cunningham to let him stay on until the middle of September, both for appearances and because he had no home in England. Shaw resumed his duties under an intolerable cloud. If you cannot offer him a new posting at this time, Cunningham urged Hall, at least announce that he is leaving to take up a new position.

The humiliated and worn-out Shaw was not alone in having his morale shaken, the high commissioner saw. Every employee of the administration was badly rattled. Beyond personal considerations, displaying at least a semblance of stability was crucial for governing Palestine at this time. Through no fault of his own, Shaw, who had guided Cunningham into office efficiently and loyally, had become a burden to the high commissioner. His dejected mood could have repercussions for the entire administration. This was the very opposite of what was needed to calm Cunningham's staff, the army, and indeed himself so that rational decisions, uninfluenced by emotion, could be made. London authorized him to announce that Shaw was about to receive a new albeit unspecified assignment. The chief secretary had to strike a posture of business as usual, without letting on that he would be leaving within weeks. It was essential to keep this secret in order to maintain public image and morale. However, rumors of Shaw's imminent departure spread and generated new threats to his life. On September 12, Cunningham told Shaw specific information had been received that Lehi was targeting him for assassination before he left. Accordingly, he was sending him clandestinely to Cairo and thence to London. Only after Shaw departed would an announcement be issued stating that the chief secretary had been compelled to leave suddenly for personal reasons—indeed, no one would understand why he had left without having been offered a new post. Shaw left Palestine secretly on September 13, 1946. He had sympathized with the Zionist enterprise in his way, though that had not prevented Lehi from wanting to liquidate him.[15]

From the end of July on, the Colonial Office and the high commissioner conducted a search for a new chief secretary. Cunningham wanted someone of stable mind, sanguine, in his mid-forties (at least), and with rich experience. Every position in Palestine in this difficult period, above all the head of the civilian apparatus, demanded a fusion of mental fortitude, managerial ability, and an impressive résumé. The Colonial Office was hard-pressed to meet the requirements laid down by the high commissioner. Ambitious junior civil servants were more readily available than senior officials or those well up the ladder. Attention focused on Sir Henry Gurney, the colonial secretary of Ghana who was then serving as the colony's acting governor and almost certain to become the next governor. It was up to Hall to persuade Gurney to forgo a senior appointment for an assignment of lower rank and in a country beset with serious problems. Hall assured Gurney that he would not lose out, as change was afoot in Palestine and he would only have to hold the post of chief secretary for a short period before resuming his career track. Cunningham protested to Hall. He hoped that by a short period he meant not less than a year or two—that is, if the situation in Palestine was not transformed radically before then.[16]

Cunningham knew that success in the campaign against terrorism was conditional on the general public's refusal to cooperate with the perpetrators. Nor did he absolve the Mandatory police—that is, his administration—of responsibility. In his frustration, he turned to what was under his control. Discreetly, to avoid offending the police and its Criminal Investigations Department, which ran the intelligence aspect of the antiterrorism campaign, Cunningham asked Hall to arrange for the services of Sir Charles Wickham, a police antiterrorism expert who had acquired most of his experience in Ireland, for ten days. Wickham was in Greece at the time, on a similar mission. After visiting Palestine, he made recommendations that Cunningham implemented. Their gist was to reorganize the police as a civil body subordinate to the administration and to place the army in charge of operational antiterrorist activity.[17]

The Arabs' response to the King David Hotel attack was cause for concern to Cunningham. He believed that only poor organization kept the Arabs from taking violent action, but that such action was only a matter of time. The danger would increase as the political process toward partition gained momentum. Indeed, it was precisely on these grounds that the high commissioner expected the Jewish Agency to dissociate itself immediately from the path of terrorism and rejoin the front with him (and against the Arabs to a degree) in favor of the political process. He did not delve deeply into the Arab issue. From the outset, he argued that Operation Agatha had not calmed the Arabs. Their desire to take action was actually greater, even if they feared an "Arab Agatha." They had reached the conclusion that Najada, a partially armed Palestine Arab youth group, should take its cue from the Haganah, both in its character and in being directly subordinate to the Arab Higher Committee. According to Cunningham, the Arabs felt that they had the most to gain from the King David Hotel outrage. Their leaders described the Arabs killed in the attack as martyrs whose blood infused the national struggle with purpose and strength. Cunningham quoted Emil Ghoury, a member of the Arab Higher Committee, who declared at the funeral of two of those killed in the attack that they and the other martyrs had made the Arabs more determined and thereby benefited their cause. Revenge would be exacted and would be painful. Overall, Cunningham concluded, the attack on the King David had aggravated interethnic hatred in the country. Nor could he see the Arabs accepting a political solution that did not include guarantees against violence by Jewish extremists.[18]

The Arabs' hatred of the Yishuv, Cunningham noted, had only been intensified by the events of July 22. They saw the government's White Paper of July 24—which showed a direct connection between the Jewish Agency Executive and terrorism, based on the findings of Operation Agatha and wiretapping—as legal grounds for dismantling the Jewish Agency and deporting its leaders.[19] The Arabs viewed the events of 1946 through the prism of the Arab Revolt of 1937: Britain's measures now, in the wake of Jewish violence, should be as harsh as those taken nine years earlier. This expectation, coupled with the Arabs' organizational ineptitude, was all that stood in the way of a new eruption, Cunningham believed. And the attack on the hotel had heightened their expectations from the British.

At the same time, Cunningham maintained, the moderate wing of the Arab leadership was now willing to contemplate a federation under British auspices as the only alternative to violence and its unavoidably harsh consequences.[20] No one in the Arab camp wanted a meeting with the Jews in London, still less a partition solution. Cunningham was aware that an independent moderate such as Musa al-Alami wielded less influence vis-à-vis the Arabs than Chaim Weizmann did on the Jewish-Zionist side. (Alami was known as "the Arab Weizmann" in Britain.) Knowing comparatively little about the Arabs, Cunningham tried at least not to anger them. He could not meet their expectations of a renewed offensive against the Yishuv following the King David Hotel outrage. Nevertheless, he continued to expect them to accept partition, which was their only choice in light of the government's readiness to use force, however limited, against the Jews, and by implication against the Arabs as well.[21]

Cunningham could not afford to leave the King David Hotel attack without a response of some kind, not least in order to pacify the Arabs and lift the low spirits of the British personnel. With this in mind, he suggested two possible immediate declarations, which would have the appearance of a rapid and drastic reaction. The first was a total stoppage of Jewish immigration. Cunningham's approach on this subject was clear, even without the concrete context of the July 22 atrocity: he wanted to put a stop to Jewish immigration until a political solution was reached. The second measure entailed the confiscation or freezing of the Jewish funds. Cunningham requested authorization to promulgate regulations allowing him to place an immediate freeze on the monies of the Jewish National Fund, Keren Hayesod (the Foundation Fund), and other Zionist institutions. The advantage of these declarations was that they could be executed speedily, within a day or two.

In the meantime, forty-eight hours after the hotel attack, nothing visible (and visibility was crucial) had been done. Cunningham's strategy was to issue and implement immediately high-value policy declarations that would boost morale, and commit the military when he was good and ready. It was a calculated response that embodied his method of keeping a lid on the flames: display a semblance of aggressiveness and take punitive action that would not adversely affect the political process. "I have repeatedly stated that in my view immediate partition is the only solution which gives a chance of stability [in Palestine]," he wrote at the conclusion of a cable urging swift, drastic action.[22]

Drawing on Cunningham's ideas, which integrated political pressure with moderate economic and military pressure, the GOC Palestine, Lieutenant General Barker, ordered his officers and soldiers not to fraternize or do business with Jews. The Jews, he asserted heedlessly, need to be punished "by striking at their pockets." Appalled, Cunningham informed Hall that even though he did not object to a temporary economic boycott of the Jews, this was an unfortunate expression. Once more, the duality of the high commissioner's approach came into play: he wanted to burn forest undergrowth but also ensure that the whole forest did not go up in flames. As with "Wanted" posters put up by the army in Tel Aviv without his authorization in June 1946, he condemned the nature of the deed, not its content. Barker's sentiment, however undesirable, dovetailed with the acute declarative and economic actions taken against the Yishuv following the King David Hotel attack. This approach made for a useful division of roles: Barker as the bad cop and he, the high commissioner, as the good cop.[23]

Cunningham wanted blistering declarations, not irreversible actions. For starters, as noted, he wanted declarations on immigration and the economy. Whether this would be a smart move—given that the first to be affected in the Yishuv would be the merchants and industrialists, who were generally on the moderate side of the political map—was far from clear. However, the British government, increasingly hamstrung in its Palestine policy because of its differences with the United States, was determined to avoid not only unnecessary actions but also harmful phraseology. Cunningham found himself to the right of the government in his call for an immediate response to the attack.

Hall informed him, in the name of the Ministerial Committee on Defense, that no drastic and immediate measures had been approved, about either immigration or the economy. It was a mistake to make abrupt decisions, even short-term, the colonial secretary explained, before reaching agreement with Washington on long-term policy. The need for immediate action was understandable, Hall noted in another cable, but it would be counterproductive to act against the entire Yishuv just when new policy was being drafted that was based on positive proposals (in conjunction with Washington) about the future of Palestine. Only those directly involved in terrorism should be targeted. In other words, forget about a financial boycott or a complete halt to immigration. Proposals for immediate action, particularly in regard to immigration, would have implications for joint British-American policy.

The government wished to be able to inform the House of Commons that the new committee of experts (Morrison-Grady), which was trying to salvage the recommendations of the Anglo-American Committee, had agreed on policy. The major stumbling block of those recommendations was the call to allow 100,000 Jewish refugees to enter the country immediately—a challenge with which the British government believed it could not cope. London was ready in principle to operate against the terrorists (Etzel and Lehi), the high commissioner was informed, but would not condone large-scale arms searches. The last thing the government wanted was for passions to run high in the United States, but also at home, on the eve of the parliamentary debate on August 1. Indeed, until then no action was to be taken even against the terrorists.[24]

The government was pushing at an open door—though whether it was the right door is another question. Cunningham, meanwhile, was intent on pursuing his strategy of duality: firmly worded declarations to placate the Arabs, his distraught staff, and the army, combined with limited operations against the terrorists, thus ensuring that the diplomatic process would continue. He had no problem with the government's restrictions. Indeed, they matched those he himself had imposed on the army on July 24, before being directed by the government on how to proceed. Where he differed with the government was over acts of declaration: political headway would be untenable without the appearance of extensive action (economic, political, and military) against the Yishuv following the King David attack. The Arabs would not condone the high commissioner's silence—and rightly so. A hunt for terrorists was not enough on its own. He understood the government's need to inform the House that political progress was being made, but this was apt to be interpreted by both Arabs and Jews as a victory for terrorism, he thought. Furthermore, the provincial autonomy plan, which the government intended to endorse, effectively left Britain responsible for continuing to govern in Palestine. In that case, it was certainly wrong to show that terrorism pays. If the administration was fated to confront one of the sides, that side should be the Yishuv. Its ability to fight back was much reduced after Operation Agatha.

Cunningham also took issue with the decision not to announce the confiscation of Yishuv funds. He reminded his superiors that this was largely a declarative act and involved the confiscation of a small amount of money. However, the impact on the debate between moderates and extremists in the Yishuv and on the atmosphere in the Arab community would be considerable. Accordingly, Cunningham suggested that the government reconsider his proposal.[25]

To mollify the high commissioner, Hall informed him that his suggestions would be reconsidered by the government on July 29. Cunningham had no ready reply to this. The government's discussions and decisions reflected a desire to calm the situation with a view toward a possible political breakthrough that he sought no less ardently than London. Once more, though, Cunningham felt that only he was capable of seeing the full complexity of the situation. He saw eye to eye with the government on the need for a political solution; where they differed was over the content of the solution and the way to achieve it. In the long run, he agreed, it was right to ignore terrorism on the road to a political solution, because only such a solution could put an end to terrorism. At the same time, he was upset by London's disregard of what he perceived as an urgent need to take controlled action against the terrorists after the King David attack. The result would be to diminish his ability to rule until the achievement of a political solution, which no one, he pointed out again, advocated more consistently than he.

Hall finally acceded in part, authorizing Cunningham to conduct a limited antiterrorist operation on July 30. That, he agreed, could buttress the government's statement on July 31, on the eve of the parliamentary debate. Let it be clear that the government intends to remain active in Palestine in the short term, too, even before the planned Arab-Jewish conference in September.[26]

In addition to approving the King David attack, according to the latest research, the upper ranks of the Haganah displayed unconcealed envy for the target's high quality and the method of operation, which they considered "simple and beautiful." Cunningham, like many others, thought Etzel alone had been involved. He accepted at face value what he termed the organization's "arrogant confession"; he did not probe whether there had been an advance warning telephone call, minutes before the explosion. "I am under no illusions," he wrote to the colonial secretary on July 29, that a warning, even if given, was not motivated by contrition or a sense of humanity, as the organization involved had inscribed on its banner the sword and blood in the spirit of the Maccabees.

Furthermore, the high commissioner did not look deeply into the chain of command and the contacts that had led Etzel to target the hotel. The organization's guilt was convenient for him politically as much as militarily. He instructed the army to exercise patience and not be tempted to take the seemingly easier route of raiding rural settlements, which were Haganah territory exclusively. No arms searches were to be conducted in the kibbutzim. He was after the terrorists from the breakaway organizations, and their centers were in the big cities, primarily Tel Aviv, not in the countryside. The operative difficulty was as clear as the political significance was crucial. Cunningham understood that despite the largely urban character of the Jewish community in Palestine, its identity and ethos derived from the collective farming settlements, which were also the hubs of Haganah activity, both operationally and symbolically.[27]

The army wanted a large-scale operation. Cunningham refused. The military, headed by Montgomery, had to capitulate, as the government in this case backed the high commissioner. Moreover, Operation Agatha had cemented his absolute authority as the head of both the civilian and military branches in Palestine.[28] Cunningham ordered the army to plan a "surgical" operation against the breakaways in the cities; his assumption was that the organized Yishuv would pitch in. The atrocity of July 22 could thus be utilized to bring the Jewish Agency, which had been battered in Operation Agatha, back on board, in a way recalling the "hunting season" against Etzel and Lehi, which Cunningham believed had been beneficial to both the British and the Yishuv. He would use the breakaway organizations as a punching bag, to set an example, in order to boost British morale and, more important, to pointedly avoid attacking those with whom a political solution could be worked out. He drew a distinction between searching for the Haganah's illegal weapons (only partially illegal, it must be said), which was an essentially political act, and the struggle against the terrorists, an approach that freed him from taking measures against the organized Yishuv and specifically the Jewish Agency.

Cunningham gave Barker sufficient time to prepare for a search of the cities. He did not declare a state of emergency or martial rule, measures to which he objected in principle. In addition to reliable intelligence, the Tel Aviv operation would require at least two divisions. Taking into consideration London's request not to rush into action, Cunningham agreed to Hall's request to set July 30 as the earliest date for the operation. The army wanted to avoid confronting the Jews and the Arabs simultaneously. Its aim was to exploit the attack on the nerve center of British rule in Palestine to disable the Yishuv's military capability before a possible Arab outburst. Barker therefore requested authorization to extend the search to ten rural settlements, even though they had no connection with Etzel. Cunningham informed him that this would be authorized only if the political situation were to change; that is, if the rift between the British and the Jewish Agency were to be aggravated. In contrast to Operation Agatha, which was aimed almost exclusively at the organized Yishuv's bastions in the rural areas, the security forces now geared for an assault on the urban centers, in line with the high commissioner's guidelines. It was the cities that provided the staging ground and centers of support for the breakaways.[29]

The primary target of Operation Shark, as it was code-named, was Tel Aviv. Before dawn on July 30, some 20,000 troops and police descended on the city, which was placed under curfew. On August 1, Cunningham reported to Hall that 644 people had been arrested in the morning, among them apparently some long wanted by the authorities in connection with acts of murder and sabotage. The most significant detainee was Yitzhak Yzernitzky (afterward Shamir, prime minister of Israel, 1983–1984, 1986–1992), a member—with Israel Eldad and Nathan Yellin-Mor—of the triumvirate that led Lehi. Yzernitzky was exiled to Eritrea. Caches of light arms intended for terrorist actions were uncovered. Cunningham took particular note of the weapons cache found in the basement of a school on Lilienblum Street in Tel Aviv. A large number of forged government bonds were found in the city's Great Synagogue. (These discoveries so incensed the high commissioner that he noted them in his monthly report.) Cunningham's reports on the operation were accurate down to the number of rounds of ammunition and the documents found in a taxi. The curfew was suspended every day for two hours so that people could buy food and other provisions. A group of Jews attacked a roadblock manned by soldiers from the Sixth Airborne Division. A warning volley was fired, aimed low, wounding a few of the assailants in the legs. The curfew was lifted on the evening of August 1.[30]

The high commissioner's announcement to the Jewish and Arab public on the morning of July 30, as the search operation began, sums up his position after Operation Agatha and the King David Hotel attack, and on the eve of a possible political turning point. The declaration is important, because it shows a correlation between what he said in private forums and in public. Its gist was that the operation was intended to arrest terrorists and was the direct result of the outrage committed in Jerusalem. At the same time, he promised minimal disruption to everyday life. He reminded the public that an intensive political effort was being made to find a solution to the Palestine question. Talks would be held with Arabs and Jews alike (ahead of the planned London conference in September, which never took place). The violence, he noted, hampered and delayed this mission, and ultimately might render it impossible. In other words, continued terrorism meant no political process. In the central section of the statement, the high commissioner addressed the Jewish public directly:

I wish to make it clear that the military operations now proceeding in the Tel Aviv area have as their objective the search for detention of terrorists and are a direct result of the vile and horrible crime committed in Jerusalem on Monday, 22nd of July, through which over one hundred innocent civilians lost their lives [actually ninety-one] including women and boys, of British, Arab and Jewish birth.

In making this announcement I do not depart one jot from my statement of the June [*sic*]. It has been and is my earnest wish that if as a result of violence directed against the Government military action is forced on us, it should have as its objective the forces responsible for that violence and that military operations and restrictions should interfere as little as possible with the normal life of the country.

The remedy therefore is plain to see. Should violence be eschewed normal occupations will take no harm and endeavor of all for the betterment of the future of Palestine can continue in peace.

Moreover I would remind all the peoples of Palestine of the great and urgent activity now proceeding to find an early solution of the Palestine problem. Discussions are to be held with both Arabs and Jews. Violence can only make the task more difficult and lengthy if not impossible.

In this instance a shameful and barbarous crime has been committed. A crime which lays a blot on the history of the Yishuv. It must be evident to every right minded man that mere protests are not sufficient to remove stains of this kind. No movement of terrorist character would have a chance of survival against the wishes of the people from whom it springs. . . . It lies with the Yishuv to decide whether they will help or hinder the design of rooting out canker which if it remains can only recoil on the head of the Yishuv under whatever conditions the future may hold for them.[31]

The Yishuv leadership and the Jewish press, while condemning the atrocity—too feebly, in Cunningham's view—cast the blame on the administration and the British government, refusing to accept even a shadow of responsibility themselves. Disappointed, the high commissioner noted that he had not found readiness to cooperate with the administration's antiterrorist activity. Indeed, he saw a connection between the inability to advance his diplomatic and political agenda in the wake of Operation Agatha and the Yishuv's preoccupation with deploring "Weizmann's defeatism" rather than the mass murder in the King David Hotel.[32]

Cunningham also took offense at remarks made by Ben-Gurion at a press conference in Paris. The chairman of the Jewish Agency Executive held the Mandatory administration—in other words, Cunningham—responsible for the events at the King David. In Ben-Gurion's view, the government bore absolute responsibility for every terrorist attack or violation of the law. He made his remarks with reference to a white paper issued on July 24. The document spelled out the findings of Operation Agatha, with an emphasis on Jewish Agency ties to terrorism. The high commissioner was apparently too immersed in the ugly atmosphere following the attack, and too preoccupied with harnessing the Yishuv in the campaign against terrorism, to catch the hints contained in Ben-Gurion's comments. Ben-Gurion did indeed absolve the Yishuv of responsibility, but he also remarked on "the appalling tragedy, the mass slaughter at the King David Hotel in Jerusalem." Perhaps because it was politically inconvenient for him, Cunningham did not respond to Ben-Gurion's remarks at the press conference that the high commissioner was "an honest man. . . . I do not want my words to be construed to mean that he is pro-Jewish, but . . . in every meeting with him my impression has been that I am negotiating with a person who is businesslike and frank."[33]

Cunningham was ultimately less concerned about who was responsible for the terrorism than with its political impact. At the beginning of August, before the decision of the Jewish Agency Executive in Paris to stop engaging in violent resistance, the approach that had led him to implement Operation Agatha seemed to have failed. From his perspective, the lack of interest displayed by both the Jews and the Arabs in a rumor about a possible new government-sponsored partition plan was the most serious result of the King David Hotel attack.[34]

The Jewish terrorism in general, and the atrocity of July 22 in particular, left Cunningham less empathetic with the Yishuv than he had been. At the same time, the terrorism heightened his impatience with the Arabs. From this point of view, his assessments were more pessimistic than those emanating from London.

Both the War Office and the Colonial Office, which closely followed Zionist politics in Palestine and elsewhere, tended to allow their approach to the subject to color their assessments, even if these were not always consistent with the information they themselves possessed. An example of this type of misguided evaluation was their conclusion that the moderate elements in the Yishuv—such as the Ihud party (whose leaders came from the Brit Shalom movement and other peace groups), Hashomer Hatzaʿir, the Craftsmen's Association (which, as an economically oriented body, was inherently inclined to moderation), and the Young Worker group in Mapai—were becoming stronger. This conclusion flatly contradicted reports possessed by intelligence personnel in London to the effect that both before and after the King David Hotel atrocity the moderates had been defeated time and again in forums of the Yishuv's national institutions. Furthermore, both the Foreign Office and the Colonial Office knew that Weizmann had been prevented from entering into negotiations with the British government and that his ideas had been rejected by the Morrison-Grady Committee, while support had increased for the orientation espoused by Ben-Gurion, whom the British considered an extremist.

Indeed, British policy-makers were apprised of internal violence and threats by the breakaway groups against collaborators with the government. In fact, cooperation between the official bodies and the breakaways was said to be growing at the grassroots level. The breakaways were reportedly flaunting their new alliance with the national institutions and with the Jewish Agency in particular, notably in connection with the agency's backing for the Jewish Resistance Movement. The only plausible explanation for the disparity between the field reports and the conclusions drawn lies in London's desire to align itself more closely with Washington's approach and obtain its cooperation for the perceived desirable solution in Palestine.[35]

In contrast to London, Cunningham was focused on the real developments in the Yishuv and in the Zionist movement. Although he wished to strengthen the moderates and supported their desire for a less aggressive leadership than the one headed by Ben-Gurion, he could not accept the assessments from London. Cunningham was aware of the infighting—at the highest level of the Yishuv, in the Jewish Agency, and in the Zionist movement—over whether to maintain violent resistance. He wanted to impress upon the Jewish Agency that now of all times, with the British government moving—hesitantly but irrevocably—toward partition, pursuing violence instead of cooperation would be a historic mistake. As it happened, the Jewish Agency seemed to respond positively to the challenge posed by Cunningham and his government by adopting moderate resolutions in Paris. However, the high commissioner found himself without tenable interlocutors. He himself had jailed the leaders, moderate and otherwise, in Latrun and would not release them unconditionally. His main demand, overriding even a commitment to desist from terrorism, was political: support for partition. As for those not in detention, they were in Paris for the Jewish Agency conference.

Cunningham summed up the violent summer of 1946 in a note to Hall. There had been "the storms of July," which had peaked with the bombing of the chief secretariat and army headquarters followed by the massive manhunt in Tel Aviv, followed in August by a tidal wave of anti-British feeling in the Yishuv. On the other hand, August had seen a relative lull in the violence. This he attributed, on the Jewish side, to the impact of Operation Agatha, namely, the absence of the Yishuv leaders; on the Arab side, meanwhile, was the monthlong Ramadan fast and the inclination to opt for a nonviolent political struggle under the auspices of the Arab Higher Committee and an Arab League summit meeting in Alexandria.[36]

Overall, though, Cunningham remained pessimistic. The Yishuv press went on fanning the flames, and there was no sign that anyone in the Jewish community was assuming responsibility for the bloody events of the recent past. The impact of the citywide search in Tel Aviv was heightened by fanciful horror stories, the deportation of illegal immigrants to Cyprus, death sentences given to nineteen Lehi militants, and the government's policy declaration on Palestine. But the inhabitants of the Yishuv, instead of criticizing the Jewish Agency Executive, vented their fury at the "military governors" from Britain. The Arabs, for their part, resented the administration's failure to mount a full-scale reprisal operation against the Jews, and their simmering anger was fueled by rumors about the resumption of stepped-up illegal Jewish immigration.[37]

A sense of impasse prevailed in Government House at the beginning of September 1946. After almost a year in Jerusalem, Cunningham for the first time interiorized the two parties' radically opposed approaches to the conflict. This perception colored his response to specific events. As an example, he noted the opposite reactions by the Jews and the Arabs to President Truman's pro-Zionist declarations. The Jews, he thought, considered them irrefutable proof of Washington's conclusion that the Jewish question could be resolved only in the Land of Israel; the Arabs, by contrast, considered the statements a mere election ploy. Among the Jews, Cunningham identified fright, a sense of infinite victimization, and a historic inability to engage in self-criticism; among the Arabs, an unquenchable thirst for revenge.[38]

The high commissioner's patience seemed to be wearing thin; or worse, things might be slipping out of his control. By the end of August, the restraint he had imposed on the military in Operation Agatha, and still more stringently in Operation Shark, had vanished. He authorized the army to conduct searches on August 28 in two kibbutzim in the northern Negev,

Dorot and Ruhama. In contrast to Agatha, in which documents, leaders, and commanders were targeted, and to Shark, which sought terrorists, the aim this time was to uncover weapons. Given the arms cache discovered in Kibbutz Yagur during Operation Agatha, Cunningham had little choice but to allow the search operation.

The two kibbutzim lay on a route along which surplus weapons of the British Army could be smuggled from the Western Desert and Egypt, serving as transit stations on the way to the central arms stockpile at Yagur. The bitter residue left by Lehi's brutal murder of seven British soldiers in their sleep at the end of April was deepened by the events of June–August and by the Haganah's removal after Operation Agatha of most of its arms from the kibbutzim.

The troops, seething because of the events and frustrated when no arms were found in the two kibbutzim, went on a rampage of destruction and humiliation targeting the kibbutz members. Nothing like it had been seen in previous operations. Friends of the Yishuv in the British Parliament, led by Richard Crossman, claimed that the army, not the Mandatory administration, was running the show.

The episode hurtled Cunningham into the situation he most feared: he truly seemed to be losing control.[39]

NOTES

1. This chapter's title comes from Cunningham to Hall, August 5, 1946, NA CO537/2418.

2. Born in 1894, Shaw was chief secretary of the Mandate administration in Palestine from December 1943 to September 1946. He had joined the colonial service in 1925, and was posted in Ghana (Gold Coast) until 1935. He later served as assistant to the chief secretary in Palestine (1935–1940) and with the War Office (1940–1943). After his tenure in Palestine, he was colonial secretary in Cyprus (1946–1947) and governor of Trinidad and Tobago (1947–1950). In 1955, he chaired the commission of inquiry into the industrial dispute and riots in Sierra Leone.

3. Chief secretary to the colonial secretary, July 22, 1946, MECA CP, BI, F1/158; Thurston Clarke, *By Blood and Fire*, New York 1981. This study, subtitled "The Attack on the King David Hotel," is vitiated by its lack of understanding of the period and the context. At the same time, as far as I know, no one before or since has researched the events so thoroughly.

4. Ministerial Committee on Defense, July 22, 1946, NA CAB131/1; Cunningham to Hall, July 15, 1946, MECA CP, B1, F1/169; and also July 13, 1946, NA CO537/171.

5. Clarke, *By Blood and Fire*, p. 227. John Fletcher-Cooke, passages from a letter to the historian Elizabeth Monroe, February 23, 1966, MECA GB 165–0107, p. 3.

6. Ministerial Committee on Defense, July 22, 1946, NA CAB131/1. Two days later, Cunningham was already cabling from Government House; e.g., Cunningham to Hall, July 24, 1946, MECA CP, B1, F1/169.

7. The July report was written by Newton, signed by Cunningham, NA, Co537/1708; Cunningham to Hall, August 3, 1946, NA, Co537/1708.

8. Cunningham to Hall, August 3, 1946, NA, Co537/1708; Shealtiel, *Always a Rebel*, pp. 285–287; Teveth, "Puzzling Exercise," pp. 77–78; Avizohar, introduction to Ben-Gurion, *Toward the End of the Mandate*, pp. 6–10; Cunningham to Hall, July 24, 1946, July 25, 1946, MECA CP, B1, F1/169, 174.

9. Cunningham to Hall, July 24, 1946, July 25, 1946; "Visit of the High Commissioner for Palestine—January 1947. Subjects Dealt with in Discussion with the Colonial Office and Other Departments," January 20, 1947, MECA CP, B6, F3/25–31.

10. Louis, *The British Empire*, p. 430; Cunningham to Hall, August 5, 1946, NA Co537/2418.

11. Cunningham to Hall, August 5, 1946.

12. Hall to Cunningham, August 8, 17, 1946, NA Co537/2418.

13. Cunningham to Hall, August 9, 1946, NA Co537/2418.

14. Cunningham to Hall, August 3, 1946, MECA CP, B6, F5/10a.

15. Cunningham to Gater (Colonial Office), August 13, 1946, MECA CP, B6, F5/12a; [First name unavailable] Gutch for high commissioner to colonial secretary, August 16, 1946, MECA CP, B1, F2/33; Cunningham to Hall, August 31, 1946, MECA CP, B1, F2/65. Shaw repeatedly emphasized his loyalty to the high commissioner: e.g., Shaw to Cunningham, June 13, 1946, MECA CP, B6, F5/34; Cunningham to Gater, August 13, 1946, MECA CP, B1, F2/12a, and Cunningham to Gater, September 12, 1946, MECA CP, B1, F2/95; Hall to Cunningham, August 22, 1946, MECA CP, B1, F2/49; Cunningham to Hall, August 24, 1946, MECA CP, B1, F2/53; Gater to Cunningham, August 27, 1946, MECA CP, B1, F2/57; Arthur Dawe (Colonial Office) to Cunningham, August 30, 1946, MECA CP, B1, F2/65; Cunningham to Shaw, September 14, 1946, MECA CP, B6, F5/35; Cunningham to Gater, September 25, 1946, MECA CP, B1, F2/123. Shaw's wife later related that her husband never recovered from the events of July 22, 1946, particularly the accusation that he had ignored a telephone warning that a bomb had been planted in the hotel. Clarke, *By Blood and Fire*, p. 233. In an interview years later, Shaw espoused a sharply anticolonial and clearly pro-Zionist approach, MECA GB165–0282, 3.

16. Hall to Cunningham, August 22, 1946, MECA, CP B1, F2/49; Cunningham to Hall, August 24, 1946, MECA, CP, B1, F2/53; Motti Golani, *The End of the British Mandate for Palestine, 1948: The Diary of Sir Henry Gurney*, London 2009.

17. Cunningham to Hall, August 1, 1946, CP, B1, F2/5; Rivka Itzhaki-Harel, "Toward a State: British Rule, the Yishuv Leadership, the Police Force, and the Supernumerary Police, 1918–1948," PhD dissertation, University of Haifa, 2004, pp. 214–216 (Hebrew).

18. Cunningham to Hall, August 3, 1946, NA C0537/1708.

19. Slutzky, *History of the Haganah*, III, 2, p. 901, admitted that the evidence contained in the White Paper was "quite well-grounded."

20. This is an interesting observation. At the end of 1946, Britain backtracked from partition ideas—which it had reprised briefly that summer—in favor of a solution involving federative national autonomies within a one-state framework.

21. Cunningham to Hall, August 3, 1946, NA C0537/1708.

22. Cunningham to Hall, July 24, 1946, MECA CP, B1, F1/169–170.

23. Cunningham to Hall, July 30, 1946, MECA CP, B1, F2/14.

24. Hall to Cunningham, July 25, 1946, MECA CP, B1, F1/174–176.

25. Hall to Cunningham, July 28, 1946, MECA CP, B1, F1/179; Cunningham to Hall, July 27, 1946, July 29, 1946, MECA CP, B1, F1/177–178, 181.

26. Hall to Cunningham, July 28, 1946, MECA CP, B1, F1/179; Cunningham to Hall, July 29, 1946, MECA CP, B1, F1/177–178, 181.

27. Cunningham to Hall, July 29, 1946, MECA CP, B1, F1/181, and also August 3, 1946, NA C0537/1708; Shealtiel, *Always a Rebel*, pp. 262–264; Teveth, *Kinat David*, pp. 748–751.

28. Two days after the King David Hotel bombing, Montgomery wrote to Dempsey, the GOC Middle East, "We shall show the world and the Jews that we are not going to submit tamely to violence." Louis, *The British Empire*, p. 430.

29. Cunningham to Hall, July 24, 1946, July 27, 1946, MECA CP, B1, F1/169, 178; Louis, *The British Empire*, p. 430.

30. Cunningham to Hall, August 1, 1946, NA C0537/1713; and Cunningham to Hall, August 3, 1946, NA C0537/1708; Slutzky, *History of the Haganah*, III, 2, p. 902, maintains that the searches continued until the evening of August 2; on Shamir, see p. 903 of the same text.

31. Cunningham sent the text to Hall for ratification on July 29, MECA CP, B1, F1/181; the text also appears in his cable to Hall, August 3, 1946, NA C0537/1708.

32. Ibid.

33. Ibid.; Teveth, Kinat David, p. 747; Ben-Gurion, *Toward the End of the Mandate*, pp. 90–97.

34. Cunningham to Hall, August 3, 1946, NA C0537/1708.

35. Major [First name unavailable] Telfer-Smollett (War Office) to Trafford Smith (Colonial Office), "Summary of Reports for the Period 20th July to 3rd August," August 19, 1946, NA C0537/1713.

36. Cunningham to Hall, September 3, 1946, NA C0537/1708.

37. Ibid.

38. Ibid.

39. Cunningham to Hall, September 27, 1946, NA C0537/1712. Slutzky's report, *History of the Haganah*, III, 2, pp. 904–905, suggests that the weapons had been removed from Dorot and Ruhama even before Operation Agatha. The groundlessness of this claim, equal to that of the more general claim that the Yishuv had advance knowledge of the operation, is shown by the fact that the central arms cache at Kibbutz Yagur was not removed before Operation Agatha.

6

The High Commissioner's "Conciliation Policy"

On November 20, 1946, Field Marshal Montgomery, the chief of the Imperial General Staff, launched a concentrated attack on Cunningham's policy. Meeting that day with the Cabinet Defense Committee and the Chiefs of Staff Committee, Montgomery explained that the "conciliation policy" in Palestine had failed and that the limited initiative achieved by the army—not the high commissioner, who had initiated and managed Operation Agatha—had vanished as though it had never been. The security situation was deteriorating and army and police casualties were rising. Unauthorized attacks on innocent Jews by members of the security forces in retaliation for acts of terrorism were a direct result of this feeling of helplessness, the field marshal explained, without condemning the manifestations of retaliatory rage.

Montgomery's solution: to reinforce the police and the army in Palestine. As for the high commissioner, he is not the right man for the job at this grim time, Montgomery told the committees; he is reprising the weaknesses that he displayed in the Western Desert, particularly his defensive mind-set. If he cannot be removed (as far as is known, Montgomery did not dare demand this explicitly, if only because it was not within his purview, a matter of great weight in the British system), then the cabinet must order him to stop interfering and allow the police and the army to gather intelligence freely, and to conduct searches and set up roadblocks based on their professional opinion. In short: let the army win.[1]

The debate over how to deal with Jewish terrorism dated from autumn 1945, when the Jewish Resistance Movement was formed. However, until the tail end of 1946 the issue was overshadowed by the political effort. By November 1946, it was clear that the commissions of inquiry had been unproductive. On the eve of the Jewish-Arab "last-chance conference," scheduled for January 1947, and against the looming British evacuation from India and Greece, a political and military reassessment seemed necessary in Palestine as well. In the policy debate, the Colonial Office acted as a buffer between Cunningham and his adversaries in London, mainly in the Foreign Office. On the terrorism issue, the confrontation was a direct one, as the high commissioner was the supreme commander of the army in Palestine, the operative superior of the military commander in the country and parallel in authority to the Cairo-based chief of the Middle East Command. The latter was directly accountable to the CIGS and the War Office, whereas the high commissioner received his instructions from the Colonial Office. Day to day, Cunningham worked with General Miles Dempsey, the commander of the Middle East Land Forces, and with the army commander in Palestine, Lieutenant General Evelyn Barker. Both were Montgomery's men and, not coincidentally, were appointed to their posts on the eve of his becoming CIGS, toward the end of June 1946. Indeed, Montgomery sought to groom Dempsey as his successor. The two supported their superior's approach unreservedly. In this situation, Cunningham and Montgomery clashed head-on.[2]

The governmental bodies represented by Cunningham and Montgomery had long been engaged in a battle over the Palestine question, as over other colonial issues. From the War Office's point of view, the Second World War naturally strengthened the army, at least temporarily. Britain's postwar situation—the collapse of the empire and the onset of the Cold War—left the Colonial Office in something of a shambles, but in the final analysis also reduced the stature of the War Office and the military. It was the Foreign Office that gained at these two agencies' expense. However, at the end of 1946, not all those involved, particularly the army, understood which way the wind was blowing. The situation was compounded by the two men's strikingly different personalities and by the bitter memories that colored their relations; substantive disagreements became personal and made consensus between them impossible. Montgomery's view of Cunningham's policy as soft, not to say defensive—a view derived from the Western Desert events of 1941—seemed amply confirmed during Montgomery's visit to Palestine in June 1946 and in the months that followed.

The source of the complaints about Cunningham that reached the chiefs of staff and the Defense Committee in London was apparently Dempsey. Immediately upon taking over as commander of the Middle East Land Forces in June 1946, Dempsey clashed with Cunningham over the implementation of the forces in Operation Agatha, having been influenced by his joint visit with Montgomery just before the operation and by Barker's reports. The disagreement between the army commander-in-chief and the high commissioner was evident from the outset of Barker's tenure in May 1946: the dissemination of the names of the wanted individuals on Tel Aviv's streets in June, the differences of opinion regarding the implementation of the army in Operation Agatha (Barker was personally briefed by Montgomery and Dempsey), Barker's antisemitic remark following the King David Hotel tragedy, and in particular the high commissioner's growing feeling that he could not count on the loyalty of the army chief—a not unwarranted suspicion considering Barker's close relations with Montgomery.

The rift between Barker and Cunningham was further exacerbated by the former's loathing of the Yishuv in contrast to the latter's basic sympathy. Mistrustful of Barker, Cunningham summoned him to express his criticism to his face and to either support or oppose his response to the disparaging remarks made about him by Montgomery in the Cabinet Defense Committee. After Barker voiced his backing for the high commissioner's line of action, Cunningham wrote to Arthur Creech-Jones, the new colonial secretary, that there was no reason to believe that the source of the rumors about his defensiveness and about the restrictions he was imposing on the army lay in "the general here," nor had the theater commander said anything to him to suggest that he was the source. Cunningham could not say, either, how long it would be before the commander of the army in Palestine would cease to obey him, under the influence of the distinguished CIGS. In the meantime, Cunningham and Barker were of one mind, he assured the colonial secretary.[3]

Montgomery was a professional soldier in the narrow sense. In his opinion, only force, pure and simple, would persuade the Jews to desist from terrorism. Tactlessly, he spoke shortly after the Second World War about "a war against the Jews." Toward the end of 1946, he stated: "The policy of appeasement which had been adopted during the last few months had failed. . . . The police and military forces were placed in a most difficult position. . . ." He accused the authorities in Palestine of slackness, manifested in the release of the Operation Agatha detainees and the revocation of death sentences meted out to Jewish terrorists. The government, he insisted, must order the high commissioner to utilize all the forces at his disposal to preserve law and order in Palestine. Because the high commissioner was not answerable to him, he railed at first against Cunningham's civilian masters in the Colonial Office and did not hesitate to speak out against the soft hand of the prime minister himself. In short order, he moved to a direct attack on Cunningham. The attitude of the CIGS toward those who were handling the Palestine question on behalf of Britain was later summed up by the minister of defense, Victor Alexander: "Montgomery [is] anti High Commissioner, anti Secretary for the Colonies and perhaps even anti Government, for what he believes to be a lax way we are handling Palestine affairs."[4]

One can write off Montgomery's simplistic approach, which assumed that what was not achieved by force would be achieved by more force. Such an approach also ignored the situation of the British Empire at the time, ignored the Cold War—by then already a hard reality—and most of all ignored the simple fact that the Second World War was over and that actions acceptable in wartime could no longer be condoned. Montgomery also had a simplistic approach to dealing with a civilian population and a concrete misunderstanding of the distinctive character possessed by the Jewish community in Palestine. Altogether, he struggled to understand the political situation in the Middle East, and specifically in Palestine. The problem was that this oversimplified view was held by the chief of the Imperial General Staff in the critical period from the end of June 1946 until May 1948. And it was this same august personage who relentlessly reminded Cunningham—if only by dint of his being "Montgomery of Alamein"—of an episode Cunningham himself had consigned to oblivion. Personal matters aside, Cunningham, as the head of the civilian apparatus in Palestine, rejected Montgomery's approach out of hand. These were the opening positions from which the two locked horns in a policy debate that raged from November 1946 until well into 1947.[5]

As it turned out, the high commissioner had a pleasant surprise from London. On November 21, a day after Montgomery attacked him in the cabinet committee, the colonial secretary cabled the two antagonists, asking them to elaborate their positions. Creech-Jones was inclined to support "his man" but wanted to be sure of where the two stood. He asked them three questions: What had been the goal of Operation Agatha? Had there been a change recently in the high commissioner's instructions to the army concerning antiterrorism activity? And how could the mode of work between the civil administration and the army be improved?

Cunningham spent two days working on a detailed reply, which he divided into two cables expounding his doctrine on the terrorism question. He was clearly bent on reassuring his superiors of his sure-handedness and minimizing the damage done by Montgomery, who exercised considerable influence on the cabinet. To begin with, the high commissioner recalled that Agatha had not been intended as an operation against the terrorists (Jewish breakaway groups). It followed that the army's allegation that the troops were muzzled in the operation lacked a basis. Second, his instructions had not been amended recently, other than in one matter: he could not in good conscience accept Montgomery's call for reprisal measures, which in essence would mean collective punishment aimed at the entire population. How could divisions of troops eliminate resistance actions that were carried out by no more than a few hundred terrorists who operated in small squads, bore no identifying marks, lacked proper bases, and possessed no discernible logistical or even political infrastructure? This was police work, Cunningham explained. He also reiterated his view that Britain wanted the cooperation of this very population in its campaign against terrorism, and cited the examples of Ireland and the Arab Revolt to back up his argument. Even if we have not reached a situation as dire as those just cited, the high commissioner wrote, operations of the kind advocated by Montgomery could turn the majority in the Yishuv against the administration. True, the Yishuv is not yet ripe for a practical campaign against terrorism as in the past, but it condemns the practice and concrete action to block it would not be long in coming.

Referring to Montgomery's allegation that he was harming troop morale, Cunningham noted that he considered this an important issue. However, it would be a mistake—and this was his basic argument—to scuttle the prospect of cooperation by the Yishuv, and even more the possibility of a political solution, which was the only viable solution in Palestine, solely in order to avoid harming the soldiers' morale. Third, Cunningham stated that he saw no need to modify his way of working with the army. He denied that problems existed in the relations between the political/civilian echelon and the military echelon in Palestine. The solution, he concluded, was to leave matters as they were and upgrade the responsibilities of the police. Indeed, Cunningham added, Montgomery was playing into the hands of the terrorists by advocating a position according to which the worse things get, the better they will be. In fact, for the past four months, since Operation Agatha, the organized Yishuv had not engaged in violent resistance, placing Montgomery in an awkward situation.[6]

Then Cunningham had a change of heart and that same evening sent Creech-Jones a follow-up cable. This was "private and personal" ("for your eyes only," Cunningham wrote to his secretary), rather than "secret and personal," as his previous cables to the minister concerning relations with the army were designated. Under the British working code, messages with the former tag were intended personally for the minister but had other addressees as well, and the minister was at liberty to show them to anyone he wished, at his discretion. But not in this case of a "private and personal" missive intended exclusively for the recipient. Cunningham noted that he wanted to take advantage of the present opportunity to offer a frank description of his relations with the military. Montgomery, he said, felt no need to enlist facts in belittling the high commissioner. Already during his visit in June, Cunningham related, before Operation Agatha and before acquainting himself with the situation, the chief of the General Staff had accused him of curbing the army. So wrongheaded and mistaken was such a stance that the previous Middle East commander-in-chief, General Paget, who was accompanying Montgomery, saw fit to write to the previous CIGS, Field Marshal Alanbrooke, that these accusations were unwarranted. Montgomery's last experience in Palestine was during the Arab Revolt, Cunningham added, and he continued to think in those anachronistic terms. The high commissioner avoided digging any deeper into the past and dredging up the unresolved issues from the Africa campaign between him and Montgomery of Alamein.[7]

Dempsey, the commander of the Middle East Land Forces, is not speaking to me, Cunningham informed Creech-Jones. This he attributed to a cable from Montgomery to Dempsey, which was in Cunningham's possession, stating that as a military man, he should not interest himself in the problem's political dimension. Perhaps there was nothing personal here, Cunningham wrote, but communication with Dempsey was critical to get the job done. He was even more scathing about General Barker, the army commander in Palestine. He had had his fill of Barker, and wanted him replaced immediately. Barker is aware of this, Cunningham continued, so he is careful to agree with everything I say. Barker also expressed to the high commissioner his fervent desire to remain in his post at least until the beginning of February 1947. Cunningham had agreed to this request for reasons he did not want to bother the minister with, he wrote. Barker's request was almost certainly prompted by his highly intimate relationship with Katy Antonius, the widow of the Palestinian historian George Antonius. Cunningham would pay dearly for not putting his foot down in this case.[8]

Creech-Jones accepted Cunningham's approach. On the twenty-sixth of the month, he asked the prime minister for his opinion. Attlee, who had been a recipient of the high commissioner's first cable, of November 23, was not obliged to reply. His private secretary related that the prime minister found Cunningham's observations to be reasonable. This response did not satisfy Creech-Jones: he suspected that Attlee had not actually seen the cable. He sent him another copy, and this time Attlee responded personally: ". . . I fully endorse the views expressed by the High Commissioner." He left further discussion of the matter to the Cabinet Defense Committee. This was support of inestimable value, which would stand the high commissioner in good stead in the confrontation with the chief of the General Staff.[9]

Montgomery did not need his generals in the Middle East in order to hurl accusations at Cunningham. As we saw, his opinion of the high commissioner was set in stone well before the events of summer 1946 and before his preparatory visit in June. However, he now faced a formidable array: not only the high commissioner but also the prime minister, the colonial secretary, and his colleagues in the Chiefs of Staff Committee, who were disinclined to accept his approach. Working against him as well was the partial warming that fall of relations between the British government and the Jewish Agency.

Before replying to the colonial secretary's questions and before the Defense Committee could decide between him and Cunningham, as well as to consolidate his opinion firsthand, Montgomery visited Palestine for his first time as chief of the General Staff. He and Dempsey spent forty-eight hours in Jerusalem (November 29–December 1, 1946), which were extremely uncomfortable for the high commissioner. Montgomery took Dempsey to a meeting at Government House on November 29. The aim of the meeting was to agree on a formulation ahead of the Defense Committee's reassessment of the policy concerning the use of the army in Palestine. Among the subjects discussed were the divergent views on the implementation of the army and the clarification questions forwarded by the colonial secretary on November 21, including Cunningham's reply of November 23. Once again, Montgomery did not pass up the opportunity to put Cunningham in his place. On the evening of November 30, break-aways attacked the police station in the Mahaneh Yehuda market in Jerusalem and scattered mines on area roads. There were no British dead. The CIGS noted sarcastically that the one firm decision made in Jerusalem that evening was to cancel the festive dinner at Government House, for fear the guests would be unable to arrive because of the road mines.[10]

Cunningham was not about to repeat his mistake. It was exactly five years earlier, also in November, that a superior officer had visited him at his headquarters, with disastrous consequences. Accordingly, he announced, a precondition for the present meeting was an apology by Montgomery. He would not allow his reputation to be tarnished mortally again. Before the meeting, the chief of the Imperial General Staff must retract his statement to the effect that he, General Sir Alan Cunningham, the

high commissioner and supreme commander in Palestine, had supposedly kept the army on a leash and not allowed it to act against the terrorists, even when intelligence existed enabling a preemptive operation to be
carried out. With the prime minister behind him, Cunningham felt safe
in making the demand. Montgomery did in fact "take back what he had
said" and apologized. Cunningham thus joined an exclusive group before
whom the hero of El Alamein would swallow his pride. Among those not in
the group were, for example, field marshals such as Gort, Wavell, Auchinleck, and Alexander, senior political figures such as Attlee, Bevin, and Defense Minister Alexander, as well as many others. Others on the exclusive
list included Churchill, Eisenhower, and Field Marshal Alanbrooke. The
distinction was that Montgomery admired the latter three, to the point of
self-effacement before them, whereas for Cunningham he had only contempt. The eccentric CIGS had apologized to a man he detested. Cunningham would pay the price.[11]

The high commissioner came well prepared to the meeting on Friday
November 29, 1946. He had drawn up a comprehensive, very clear survey
demonstrating that his use of military force was unmistakably in line with
the government's decisions in the past year. General Cunningham was
convinced that the two men sitting across from him—senior officers like
him but still in active service—had no conception of the reality in Palestine. In any event, he believed that if they had their way, British interests in
Palestine would suffer incalculable harm. Their proposed policy of collective punishment and massive reprisal raids might well induce the majority, who were not tainted by terrorism, to actively confront the Mandate administration. The soldiers would bring disaster on the population—and
on him. In November 1946, Cunningham was even more convinced than
he had been in June that a dialogue with the Jewish Agency was essential
to suppress terrorism. It followed that the discussion must focus on Britain's policy and not on the use of the army and the police. He would not
have mounted an operation like Agatha in the conditions that prevailed in
November. But that was exactly the desire of the two senior officers, whose
visit was hardly a courtesy call.[12]

No sooner had he apologized to Cunningham than Montgomery fished
for a quid pro quo. First, he placed on the table a document bearing his
signature. It contained a description of the army's gloomy state under the
present guidelines. Replete with military jargon, the paper analyzed the
army's missions and noted the restrictions imposed on its activity by
the high commissioner. The conclusion was clear: the restrictions were

so sweeping that the army was effectively unable to carry out its tasks. A "political solution" was required, the CIGS noted, appropriating the high commissioner's term. However, if no such solution was forthcoming—and Montgomery assumed it was not—the army must be allowed to act as it deemed necessary. To Montgomery's surprise, Cunningham endorsed the document.[13]

Why? Had the apology been enough for him? Was he again unable to cling to his views in the face of military authority? Probably, he felt intimidated by Montgomery, like many others before and after. In any event, Cunningham stood alone against Montgomery and his reputation, now bolstered by Dempsey. Beyond the criticism of the high commissioner's policy, Montgomery's remarks were rife with contempt, as was his wont. Cunningham did not know that the acclaimed officer of El Alamein had labeled his policy "cowardly" and derided him as spineless in a cable to the War Office in London. In his diary, Montgomery called the high commissioner no more than "a broken reed." What Cunningham did know was that the chief of the General Staff was accusing him of tying the army's hands even when there was good intelligence and salient targets for attack.[14]

But there was something more. Montgomery's formulation, after all—that Cunningham controlled the army and not vice versa—was on the mark. The high commissioner could hardly fail to agree with such a successful, and unexpected, way of looking at things by the CIGS. Agreement was thus reached on a plan that Dempsey proposed with Montgomery's backing; namely, that until the cabinet revised its instructions to the high commissioner in the spirit of the chief of staff's wishes, the campaign against terrorism would be based on force confined to passive defense. The main force would consist of army-initiated mobile missions, and a total curfew would be imposed on staging areas for terrorism, with an effort to rid them entirely of weapons. That said, Montgomery and Dempsey remained unalterably convinced that the constraints imposed on the army by the responsible civilian echelon, namely, Cunningham, were so stringent as to prevent its optimal performance.

The high commissioner drew on the policy decided by the cabinet at the end of 1945, following the outbreak of the Jewish uprising. Only a new cabinet decision could amend that policy. The decisions then in effect had ruled out aggressive military action a year earlier and provided the rationale for the "soft arrests" and the takeover of the Yishuv's power centers, as in Operation Agatha at the end of June 1946. What had been a thorn in the side of the inexperienced Cunningham in 1945 was now a vital prop. As a former military man, Cunningham had believed it was possible to disarm the country, even if it took a year or two; as high commissioner, he believed that this was not the way. He had no intention of honoring the oral agreement with the two generals who had come and—more important—had gone.[15]

Montgomery summed up the situation to himself arrogantly: "I have told Cunningham that it is my opinion that his methods have failed to produce law and order in Palestine and that it is my opinion that he will have no success unless he organises his police in a proper way and uses the police and army properly and adopts a more robust mentality in his methods to keep the King's peace." In November 1946, the high commissioner had to listen to a similar sentiment, exactly five years after Lieutenant General Alan Cunningham was removed in disgrace from command of the Eighth Army in the Western Desert for thinking defensively instead of offensively.[16]

Knowing he had no chance in a direct confrontation with the popular chief of staff, Cunningham beat a tactical retreat. The experience of the past few months had shown him that he could evade a clash with Montgomery: the work would be done for him in London. Cunningham informed Creech-Jones that Montgomery was about to acquaint the Defense Committee with the paper the two had agreed upon. Accordingly, he was sending the colonial secretary a copy so that he could prepare. Cunningham conceded that the document described accurately the limitations he was imposing on the army. But he disagreed with the chief of staff over the conclusions to be drawn from this. Montgomery had failed to account for the political implications of his proposal and the impact on the Jewish community; he viewed the Yishuv through the barrel of a gun. Cunningham, for his part, remained convinced that the only way to eradicate terrorism was through cooperation with the Jewish Agency. After Montgomery left Jerusalem, gloating over his achievements, the high commissioner, in the spirit of his agreement with the army, issued a sweeping order to cancel extensive army search operations planned for Tel Aviv, Petah Tikva, and Ramat Gan in the wake of the early-December wave of terrorism. Barker, after all, was not Montgomery. Creech-Jones responded to the challenge. Henceforth, Cunningham would wage his struggle against Montgomery successfully through the colonial secretary in London. Together, they would take advantage of Monty's foibles: his haughtiness, his problematic behavior in interpersonal relations, and his lack of understanding of political issues in general and the Palestine situation in particular.[17]

At the same time, the breakaway groups in Palestine played into Montgomery's hands. Terrorism, as noted, intensified in December 1946. On at least two occasions, the terrorists targeted Barker himself. Thus, for example, on December 2 the Irgun and the Stern gang set a joint ambush for the army commander's convoy near Motza, outside Jerusalem. Barker took a different route, but a military jeep was hit, killing four soldiers. A successful assassination attempt on Barker could well have brought Cunningham's mission crashing down. Even as the terrorism raged, Cunningham pinned his hopes on Whitehall and, in large measure, on the participants at the Twenty-second Zionist Congress, which was then under way in Basel.[18]

Cunningham believed he could be sunk by either the army or the Yishuv. Even as he deployed for a confrontation with the army, he set out to persuade the Yishuv leaders that their interests would best be served if they gave him their support. However, he had no one to talk to, as virtually the entire Zionist hierarchy was in Basel. There remained Yitzhak Ben-Zvi, the president of the National Council. The two met three times at the beginning of December. Cunningham was under no illusions about the status and political power of his interlocutor, in contrast to his former hopes for Weizmann. Ben-Zvi was a moderate, though, and might at least be a faithful emissary to the leaders of Mapai. Accordingly, Cunningham concentrated his message to the Yishuv leadership in one sentence, which Ben-Zvi probably could not perceive, because he knew nothing about the relations between the high commissioner and the army. He noticed only that "unusually, the high commissioner was tense." Nothing more. Cunningham informed Creech-Jones that he had told Ben-Zvi that the Jewish Agency "did not seem to realize that the Government stood between them and the Army." As it happened, it was not the administration that was a buffer between the army and the Yishuv. Rather, Cunningham himself stood between Montgomery's desire to launch "a war on the Jews" and a possible further effort by the Jewish Agency to take action against the breakaway groups.

The high commissioner told Ben-Zvi as much as he could. His inclination—in the best colonial tradition, it must be said—not to share developments with the locals worked to his disadvantage. The leaders of the Jewish Agency were immersed in the political and diplomatic issues that arose at the talks in London and the congress in Basel, not to mention the "affront of the Black Sabbath" (Agatha). The residues from the latter event apparently kept them from harnessing the high commissioner's approach to the needs of the Zionist cause, an oversight that would exact much blood from Britons, Jews, and Arabs alike. For the first time since his arrival in Palestine, Cunningham admitted that if the Jewish Agency gave the breakaway groups a free hand he might be forced to let the army have its way with the Yishuv. That possibility frightens them, Cunningham reported hopefully. It frightened him too. If the murders of administration personnel and soldiers continued, he would have no choice but to step aside and allow the army to deal with the Jewish community, he told Ben-Zvi. The Haganah, for its part, took no action against either the British or the breakaways, which resumed their operations without coordination with the Jewish Agency.[19]

On December 19, the positions of the parties to the intra-British controversy were summed up in a memorandum prepared for the Cabinet Defense Committee. Although the attribution was to the War Office and the Colonial Office, in practice the positions represented were those of Montgomery and Cunningham, respectively. Each of the two rivals wanted to eliminate Jewish terrorism. For Montgomery, the ultimate solution was a large-scale preemptive military operation in which the country would be flooded with mobile forces that would seize the initiative from the terrorists. Cunningham's way was to strengthen the moderates, which would guarantee both a falloff in terrorism as well as the goodwill of the Jewish Agency in a political settlement, a result then desired by the government. Cunningham's whole past and present seemed to be encapsulated in this discussion and its outcome.[20]

The meeting as such constituted an expression of no-confidence in Cunningham's handling of terrorism in Palestine. Finally, the dispute, which had been simmering for six months, was about to be addressed formally and produce a compromise or the capitulation of one of the adversaries. Neither capitulation nor resignation was an option for Cunningham. Seemingly, his approach had been defeated even before the discussion began. But even beyond the problems inherent in Montgomery's proposals, Cunningham had three good cards to play: the question of whether the army was operationally capable of executing the chief of the General Staff's plan; the desire of the government, and of the foreign secretary in particular, for the success of the political conference due to convene January 18 in London; and, above all, the fact that nothing in the discussions to date had undermined the formal bureaucratic structure of the Mandate administration, in which the high commissioner bore supreme authority. Stripping him of that authority would have required the installation of a military regime, an extreme option that no one had broached, not even Montgomery.

On January 1, 1947, the Defense Committee met and instructed the colonial secretary and the defense minister to formulate new guidelines—in coordination with the high commissioner and the CIGS—for dealing with the terrorism in Palestine, and to submit them for the committee's approval. In the meeting, Creech-Jones was left on his own to face a coalition of Foreign Secretary Bevin and Defense Minister Alexander. Montgomery, who also attended the meeting, refuted one by one the arguments put forward by the colonial secretary to the effect that the policy of restraint in Palestine had produced good results. The ministers did not have the tools to judge between the two, but Monty's reputation was a cogent factor, along with the humiliating flogging administered to British soldiers on December 29 by the Irgun. On the day in question, Binyamin Kimhi, an underage Irgun activist, was given eighteen lashes in the Central Prison in Jerusalem after he was caught pasting leaflets on walls. In retaliation, members of the Irgun administered the identical number of lashes to a British officer and three sergeants. Flogging was standard British punishment for underage offenders; the Irgun made it a matter of national honor. Both sides were outraged. In this state of affairs, the colonial secretary could not vote against the new guidelines; certainly not against Bevin, his patron. He opted for a different route. After the meeting, Creech-Jones took two steps: he asked Montgomery to prepare new guidelines for the high commissioner regarding the campaign against terrorism, and he summoned Cunningham to London.[21]

Montgomery was puzzled by the request but acceded willingly. He saw it as an admission of defeat by Creech-Jones and proof that the colonial secretary's assessment of the high commissioner was similar to his. The gloves are off, he wrote with satisfaction, and everything is now ready for a battle between the War Office and the Colonial Office. He did not know that Creech-Jones was in possession of a draft of Montgomery's directives to the high commissioner for the campaign against terrorism—the same paper that had been placed on Cunningham's desk in Jerusalem in November and was the basis for the proposal about to be submitted by the

CIGS. Creech-Jones had had ample time to study the proposal, grasp its simplistic character, make his plan, and coordinate his response with the high commissioner. He also knew that Montgomery's tight schedule—he was to leave on January 3 for a visit to the Soviet Union—would prevent him from taking part in the discussion on the eve of the submission of the final document to the ministerial committee. The idea was to fuel Montgomery's arrogance and diminish his vigilance.

Certain he would succeed, Montgomery hurried to submit his former plan, padded with a few improvements. He also agreed to attend a brief meeting at the Colonial Office on the day of his departure for Moscow, at which the high commissioner would be present. Creech-Jones would chair the meeting and ensure agreement on the basis of Montgomery's draft proposal. This was only natural, after the colonial secretary, rather than the war secretary or the minister of defense, assumed the role of mediator immediately after Montgomery had berated Cunningham in the Defense Committee meeting of November 20 and again on January 1.[22]

Cunningham left Jerusalem on January 2, making a stop in Malta. He arrived in London on January 3 and departed January 16, the day after the Defense Committee met to decide between him and Montgomery about the campaign against terrorism. Despite the short notice, the colonial secretary and his staff scheduled meetings for Cunningham for a two-week visit. The Colonial Office was aware of the significance of the cabinet committee's decision. Cunningham received a cable containing Montgomery's proposal while Cunningham was in transit in Malta: the colonial secretary wanted to be sure that Sir Alan would arrive prepared for the meeting, which was to take place immediately upon his arrival. Because of Montgomery's departure that day, Creech-Jones and Cunningham had only a few hours to devise a response to Montgomery. Without having a chance to rest or even change his clothes, Cunningham proceeded directly from the airport to the Colonial Office at Whitehall, where Creech-Jones was waiting for him. The two had a bit of time in private to coordinate their moves. They were then joined by Montgomery and by two senior officials from the Colonial Office. This time, it was Montgomery who found himself in "foreign territory" and, in contrast to the situation with the Defense Committee, very much in the minority.

The Cunningham encountered by Montgomery in London was not the same person who had sat across from him in Jerusalem, grateful for his apology and ready to accept anything the chief of the General Staff said (and then to cry on his minister's shoulder). The human component made the difference. The following paraphrase of the discussion on January 3, 1947, will enable the reader to understand what transpired:

> Creech-Jones: The Defense Committee wants more vigorous measures to be taken in dealing with the terrorism in Palestine, and Monty has prepared a draft proposal for action, which in his view can be considered as new guidelines for the high commissioner.
>
> Cunningham: The army has never been prevented from acting to the best of its ability against terrorism. However, this is essentially police activity, as is agreed by the expert we brought in, Sir Charles Wickham. The best weapon the police have is the assistance of the civilian population, and I hope that is about to increase.
>
> Montgomery: The restrictions placed on the army effectively prevent it from taking action. It is barred from acting unless there is proof of an imminent terrorist act [a "ticking bomb"]. The army has to wait for the terrorists to perpetrate an attack, so it is always on the defensive. What we should be doing is "turning the place upside down" without waiting for proof. It is impossible to avoid harming the life of the public, but nothing will happen if the Jews tire of this interference and decide to cooperate in the battle against terrorism. General disarmament may not be possible, but the number of people bearing arms must be reduced considerably and they must be kept under supervision. That approach succeeded in the Arab Revolt.

Asked how much time he would need to suppress the terrorism, Montgomery replied that he could not predict but that the army must be instructed to act in the spirit he had indicated, even if this entailed bringing in reinforcements from Germany or Egypt. In any event, if the Haganah wanted a fight, he would be glad of the opportunity to take them on.

> Cunningham: The army is under no restrictions. Moreover, most of the Jewish settlements in the periphery are against the terrorism. The terrorists are concentrated in the cities, and searches in the settlements will generally hurt an innocent population. The Jews will react in a manner we are familiar with, namely by sparking a conflagration that will probably compel us to evacuate women and children. An all-out war means the end of a chance for a political settlement.

The colonial secretary noted that the situation had been relatively calm of late and that the strength of the moderates had risen discernibly.

Creech-Jones: In my conversation yesterday with Ben-Gurion, he deplored the terrorism, and the Zionist congress in Basel did likewise. A military operation of the kind being suggested by Monty will make a political solution difficult to achieve. A war against the Haganah will be a war against the entire Jewish people.[23]

Montgomery: I am ready to run roughshod over the lawbreakers and the terrorists in Palestine.

Creech-Jones: Those are two different matters. The violations of the law are related mainly to immigration. They stem from the Zionists' view that the government's policy has no moral foundation. It is impossible to persuade them otherwise on this subject. The terrorism is a completely different matter.

Montgomery: It might be better to talk about "keeping the king's peace."

George Gater (permanent undersecretary of state for the colonies): There is still a civil administration in Palestine.

Montgomery: So the only possibility is to impose a partition by force on the two sides.

Creech-Jones: We are ready to append the transcript of this meeting to Monty's memorandum.

Montgomery: It is not our affair to say how the guidelines should be implemented. That is a matter for the high commissioner to conclude with the army in Palestine.

Creech-Jones: As for implementation, it would serve no purpose to conduct a thorough search in places where there are no indications of a terrorist presence. On the other hand, areas where there is good reason to suspect the existence of terrorist activity should be given appropriate treatment by the army.

Montgomery: Will the high commissioner be ready to give the army commander a free hand in applying the guidelines?

Cunningham: That is out of the question; as high commissioner, I must also take into account the political-diplomatic aspect.

Creech-Jones: Thanks, Monty, for making his position so clear and helping to moderate the army's operatively. Further thought will be given to the question of how best to implement the guidelines for dealing with terrorism.[24]

To understand this brief discussion, we must remember the personal residues that each side brought to the meeting. Although the gist of the matter was clear, there were two surprises. One was that the debate was not over the final goal. Everyone, including Montgomery, agreed that the solution must be political and, no less important, that it must be partition. The disagreement was whether the goal could be reached by force or by persuasion, with the latter route leading to the Jewish Agency's cooperation in eradicating terrorism and a joint thrust for a political solution along the lines then being discussed in London under the aegis of Bevin and Attlee. In any event, the foreign secretary and prime minister, like the other members of the Defense Committee, would see the minutes of this discussion, which would be appended to Montgomery's original plan. The approach advocated by the colonial secretary and the high commissioner would be no less clear than that recommended by the CIGS. The forum convened on January 3 at the Colonial Office wielded influence largely in regard to the antiterrorism effort, which might affect Britain's readiness to cooperate in promoting the partition idea.

The second surprise of the meeting was the resolute stand taken by Cunningham—but that was apparently only a seeming surprise. The key figure at this stage was the colonial secretary. It is useful to consider his moves from November 21 until the decision by the ministerial committee in mid-January and, in particular, in the meeting on January 3. Montgomery came to the meeting with no inhibitions and equipped with a 1930s-type solution involving a declaration of "war on the Jews," as though he were referring to enemy divisions in World War II. This need not have been a surprise. His remarks represented an anachronistic hybrid synthesized by a division commander in the 1930s and an army commander in the 1940s. From his lofty post, he announced his willingness to send reinforcements to Palestine from Egypt and also Germany. The response by Cunningham and Creech-Jones that such a move would eliminate any prospect for a political settlement and that it would balloon into a war against "the entire Jewish people" left a certain impression on him, which was duly recorded and brought to the attention of the cabinet ministers afterward.[25]

Did Cunningham precoordinate his responses in the meeting with the colonial secretary? Probably. In this connection, it is noteworthy that the two did not argue with Montgomery but only set forth their views. When George Gater, who had not been at the previous meeting, tried to argue with Montgomery's approach, his remarks had no backing or follow-up.

Creech-Jones remarked only that the transcript of the discussion would be appended to Montgomery's proposals and praised the CIGS for helping moderate the army. Cunningham had arrived straight from the airport, and Montgomery went directly there after the meeting. His memoirs indicate that he did not recognize the trap that had been laid for him. He thought the meeting had produced another victory for him over the defensive high commissioner from the Western Desert. He set out for the Soviet Union and confidently left to Creech-Jones the work of drawing up the final formulation of the new guidelines by which the high commissioner was to fight terrorism.[26]

From this point on, Creech-Jones and Cunningham engaged in a quiet and elegant maneuver that would satisfy the lion while saving the prey. In the days that followed, they held lengthy working meetings to prepare the new guidelines for the government's approval. Creech-Jones told the high commissioner in no uncertain terms what he thought about Montgomery's concept, as he understood it. The matter was simple: Montgomery wanted to turn over every stone in every place without need for proof of a connection between the terrorists and the place in question. It was clear to the CIGS, Creech-Jones wrote to the concerned high commissioner, that this method would harm the population; but according to Montgomery, nothing terrible would happen to them, and when they got tired of the harassment they would cooperate in eradicating the terrorism.[27]

Cunningham responded to Montgomery with restraint but left no room for misunderstanding: he was the head of a political entity in which military action was only one element, and not the main one, in the overall calculation of his available means and strategic considerations. To begin with, he made clear, as he regularly did when discussing military matters, and certainly in a confrontation with Montgomery, that he himself, as a military man, fully recognized the army's needs. Moreover, he noted, even under the existing guidelines the army was not excessively hampered, other than in regard to restrictions stemming from political or diplomatic factors, which in his eyes were supreme. Cunningham challenged Montgomery's approach directly in order to provide his minister with additional ammunition ahead of the final "battle" (Montgomery's word) in the Defense Committee. If we react inordinately, he argued, and follow Montgomery's lead, we will find ourselves in a full-scale confrontation with the Yishuv and we will scuttle every prospect of a political settlement. Montgomery's approach will inflame the population, the great majority of which is against terrorism, with the result that even the Haganah (through the Palmah, the Haganah's impressive force, the high commissioner explained) will join in and perpetrate "high quality" terrorism. As for himself, Cunningham said, he had never feared the terrorism of the breakaway groups; they were a great nuisance, but no more. Terrorism's true danger lay in its potential to drag the Mandate administration into a broader confrontation with the Yishuv. The possibility of another uprising by the entire Jewish community, along the lines of that enacted by the Resistance Movement from October 1945 to July 1946, was troubling. And that, in one form or another, Cunningham explained to the colonial secretary, is what Montgomery will inflict on us if he has his way.[28]

At this time, one should recall, major policy decisions made by Britain, particularly in regard to Palestine, were intimately bound up with the postwar situation of the British Empire and with Anglo-American relations. The latter were becoming increasingly paramount because of Britain's bleak economic situation. Amid the debate just described, Attlee decided in principle that Britain would leave India, Greece, Burma, Egypt, and Palestine. At the same time, concrete implementation of the policy in Palestine resulted from negotiations of the kind held January 3 between London and Jerusalem.[29] In November 1946, just before the debate over how to deal with Jewish terrorism reached its peak, Cunningham told Moshe Shertok:

> The widespread impression among the Jewish public . . . is that the administration is a monster beneath some sort of disguise, that the government consists of a gang of murderers or a band of crooks and cheats. This, however, is a completely false impression. The administration is composed of human beings who consider themselves decent and honest and who are making an effort, in a very difficult situation, to do their difficult work faithfully. They [meaning Cunningham] are duty-bound to carry out the orders they receive, but try as best they can to ease the situation rather than make it more difficult in every trying time.[30]

The cabinet convened on January 15, 1947, the Defense Committee alone being insufficient given the importance of the question at hand. Creech-Jones submitted a recommendation in the spirit of Cunningham's approach and emphasized that the high commissioner was ready, in coordination with the chief of the Middle East Command, to examine ways to heighten the efficiency of the security forces' operations against Jewish terrorism as reflected in the army's approach. The colonial secretary informed the cabinet that, in any event, new and more aggressive guidelines had already been issued following the events of the end of December and the beginning of January—the latter referring to the flogging episode—as was apparent in the response of the Mandate administration. The guidelines were formulated to enable the high commissioner to utilize his forces more aggressively, but at the same time the matter remained solely at his discretion.[31]

The cabinet endorsed the remarks of Creech-Jones. The ministers acceded to Montgomery's requests without diminishing Cunningham's powers. The high commissioner lost no time in demonstrating the significance of the cabinet decision by revoking in principle the order to flog terrorists. In response, Montgomery wrote to Dempsey, the chief of Middle East Command, that the latter did not have the authority to revoke Cunningham's directive; even though the failure of the soft-hand approach was manifest, he must coordinate operative actions with the high commissioner.

The army was frustrated by the new reality, particularly Montgomery and Dempsey, Monty's man in the Middle East. Junior officials can sometimes give expression to feelings that their superiors must be wary of uttering in public. A case in point is Lieutenant General Harold Pyman, at the time Dempsey's chief of staff in Cairo. There is no chance of an aggressive policy in Palestine unless Cunningham is replaced, he wrote to a colleague, adding, "You will remember that he gave in at Sidi Rezig in December 1941 forty-eight hours too soon." It makes no difference for our purposes that Pyman got both the date and the place wrong. (The event occurred in November 1941 at Eighth Army headquarters, when Cunningham considered adopting a defensive posture after the lines were breached on the Libya-Egypt border and Rommel, heading a not especially large column, raced eastward into Egypt.) The point is that Cunningham's defensive image still clung to him in 1947 and was readily invoked to discredit him.[32]

On December 16, the day after the cabinet meeting and two weeks after he left Palestine, Cunningham departed for Jerusalem. No one saw him off at Heathrow, for reasons probably related to his personal security: the Jewish terrorist groups were after him. But his solitary departure was also a metaphor for the high commissioner's situation, the condition of his administration, and, not least, Britain's status in Palestine. Cunningham had bested Montgomery in a battle, but had he won the war?[33]

NOTES

1. Nigel Hamilton, *Monty: The Field Marshal, 1944–1976*, London 1986, p. 636; Charters, *The British Army*, p. 101.

2. Hamilton, *Monty*, pp. 636, 678; Smart, *Biographical Dictionary of British Generals*, pp. 20–21, 82.

3. Cunningham to Hall, September 27, 1946, NA C0537/1712; Cunningham to Creech-Jones, "secret and personal," November 23, 1946, NA C0537/1712.

4. Louis, *The British Empire*, p. 447; Alexander to Attlee, March 17, 1947, NA C0537/1712.

5. Charters, *The British Army*, pp. 100–101; Hamilton, *Monty*, pp. 694–695; Cunningham to Creech-Jones, "secret and personal," November 23, 1946, NA C0531/1731.

6. Cunningham to Creech-Jones, NA C0531/1960-1.

7. Cunningham to Creech-Jones, "private and personal," NA C0531/1966.

8. Ibid.; Tom Segev, "Katy and the General," *Ha'aretz*, June 15, 1979, pp. 16–17, 19.

9. Prime Minister's Office to Colonial Office, November 26, 1946, NA C0537/1731; Attlee to Creech-Jones, NA C0537/1731.

10. CIGS to his deputy, November 29, 1946, NA C0537/1731; Montgomery, *The Memoirs*, pp. 468–469.

11. CIGS to his deputy, November 29, 1946, NA C0537/1731; Hamilton, *Monty*, p. 694; Kenneth Harris, *Attlee*, London 1995, p. 310; Montgomery, *The Memoirs*, throughout.

12. Cunningham's memorandum for his meeting with the CIGS, November 29, 1946, "Directives to High Commissioner on Use of Armed Forces in Palestine," NA C0537/1712.

13. CIGS to his deputy, November 29, 1946, NA C0537/1731; Cunningham to Creech-Jones, December 3, 1946, NA C0537/1712.

14. CIGS to his deputy, November 29, 1946, NA C0537/1731; Cunningham to Creech-Jones, December 3, 1946, NA C0537/1712; Montgomery, *The Memoirs*, pp. 467–469; Hamilton, *Monty*, pp. 665–667.

15. Cunningham to Creech-Jones, "secret and personal," December 3, 6, and 12, 1946, NA C0531/1731; Charters, *The British Army*, pp. 100–103.

16. Hamilton, *Monty*, p. 667; Auchinleck to Cunningham, November 25, 1941, NAM 8303–104/28.

17. Cunningham to Creech-Jones, December 6 and 12, 1946, NA C0531/1731; Creech-Jones to Cunningham, December 19, 1946, NA C0531/1731.

18. Cunningham to Creech-Jones, December 6 and 12, 1946, NA C0531/1731; Creech-Jones to Cunningham, December 19, 1946, NA C0531/1731; Slutzky, *History of the Haganah*, III, 2, p. 912; Charters, *The British Army*, p. 118.

19. Cunningham to Creech-Jones, December 6 and 12, 1946, NA C0537/1712; Ben-Zvi report on his conversation with the high commissioner, December 3, 1946, CZA S25/22.

20. "Use of Armed Forces," Part I: War Office views; Part II: Colonial Office views, Defense Committee, December 19, 1946, NA C0537/1731.

21. Defense Committee, January 1, 1947, NA C0537/1731; Montgomery, *The Memoirs*, p. 469; Niv, *Campaigns of the Irgun Zvai Leumi*, Vol. 5: "The Revolt (1944–1946)," pp. 70–77 (Hebrew); Slutzky, *History of the Haganah*, III, 2, p. 915.

22. Montgomery, *The Memoirs*, pp. 469–470.

23. Creech-Jones conversation with Ben-Gurion, December 2, 1946, Ben-Gurion, *Toward the End of the Mandate*, pp. 304–309.

24. "Notes on the Conference at the Colonial Office on 3rd January, 1947. Present: Mr. Creech-Jones, Field-Marshal Lord Montgomery, General Sir Alan Cunningham, Sir George Gater, Mr. J. M. Martin," NA C0537/1731.

25. Ibid.

26. Ibid.; Montgomery, *The Memoirs*, pp. 469–470.

27. "Diary of Sir Alan Cunningham's Visit to London January 2nd–January 16th 47," MECA, CP, B6, F3/24–31; "Brief of the S.O.S [Colonies] for the Cabinet 15.1.47," NA C0537/1712.

28. "Brief of the S.O.S [Colonies] for the Cabinet 15.1.47," NA C0537/1712.

29. Louis, *The British Empire*, pp. 98–99.

30. Sharett, *Imprisoned with Paper and Pencil*, p. 427.

31. Cabinet meeting, January 15, 1947, NA CAB128/9.

32. Montgomery to Dempsey, January 16, 1947, LHCMA, Pyman 6/1/2; Harold Pyman to [First name unavailable] Hobert, January 17, 1947, LHCMA, Pyman 6/1/2.

33. "Diary of Sir Alan Cunningham's Visit," MECA, CP, B6, F3/24.

7 Martial Law

On January 17, 1947, the day after his return from London and another ephemeral victory, Cunningham summoned Ben-Gurion and told him he was disappointed that the Jewish Agency's promises to fight terrorism were not being translated into action. The Yishuv leader, of course, could not have known what had prompted the high commissioner to raise this long-standing complaint again now.[1]

In any event, even before Cunningham could bask in the sun of his political success in London—encapsulated in the approval of his plan for cooperation with the Jewish Agency in combating terrorism—reality stepped in. Etzel and Lehi, enraged by the caning, at the end of December, of a Jewish youth who took part in a bank robbery, by the possibility of a political settlement arising from the British-Jewish-Arab conference in London on January 18, and by the confirmation of the death sentence imposed on Etzel activist Dov Gruner on January 24, launched a new wave of terrorism. Soldiers, policemen, and civilians were targeted indiscriminately. Worse, the breakaway groups viewed the families of administration and army personnel as "legitimate" targets. On January 26, Etzel kidnapped a British intelligence officer, Major H. A. Collins, in Jerusalem, followed the next day by the kidnapping of a judge, Ralph Windham, from Tel Aviv District Court. The perpetrators threatened to kill both men if Gruner—who had been arrested on April 23, 1946, following an Etzel raid on the Ramat Gan police station to steal weapons—were executed.[2]

On the afternoon of January 29, Cunningham sent an urgent cable to the colonial secretary. He asked for a reply by the next morning: "[The] terrorist organizations have now proved that they will not stop short of reprisals on British Civil Community in Palestine. The Police and Army have informed me that they are unable to protect civilian [sic] under conditions of normal civil life which obtain at the present."[3]

Cunningham hoped that the condemned would appeal to the Crown for clemency, a move that would abate passions, but this was not the style of the breakaways. Unlike other Yishuv prisoners, those from Etzel did not request clemency and thereby bring about the revocation of the death sentence. Gruner had actually asked for a pardon but was compelled to retract his request in the face of Etzel's argument that this constituted legitimization of British rule in the Land of Israel.[4]

The high commissioner did not intervene in the judicial process, although as the caning episode showed, doing so was his prerogative. It was clear to him that the operation of the civilian government would be severely hampered under conditions of rampant terrorism. He presented two alternative courses of action and indicated his preference. One would place the army in charge and dismantle the civilian component of the Mandatory administration; the other would organize the work of the civilian authorities so that they could continue to function under the new conditions. The first option was both undesirable and untimely, argued Cunningham, whereas civil government could operate under different conditions. Whatever the decision, Cunningham wrote, women, children, and nonessential personnel should be sent home to Britain so that the security forces could act freely to restore law and order.

The high commissioner, then, was ready to pay a steep price to ensure the administration's continued functioning. A passive posture made more sense than a more activist approach, he maintained. The latter would make life in Palestine intolerable for both the administration and the Yishuv, cause irreversible damage, and make British rule dependent on military coercion. Even though the removal of families and nonessentials would be a victory for the terrorists and a setback to Britain, the administration, and not least to Cunningham personally, the high commissioner wasted no time in promoting such a course. He ordered the immediate preparation of a plan to remove the families and nonessentials, and reported to the minister that it could be implemented within forty-eight hours. Leaving no doubt about his mood and intentions, he added that after the families and others had left he would be able to carry out Gruner's sentence.[5]

As will be recalled, the idea to send home the families and nonessentials was not new. It first arose during the period of uncertainty in the Second World War, 1940–1942, and again at the start of the Yishuv-wide resistance struggle toward the end of 1945, during the tenure of High Commissioner Gort. In January 1946, Cunningham contemplated fencing off the King David Hotel and concentrating all the administration's activity there. However, he soon dropped the idea: official personnel could be protected in this way, but not the whole British civilian community living in Palestine as an adjunct to the Mandatory regime. In August 1946, after the King David Hotel atrocity, a detailed plan to remove nonessentials was drawn up but again rejected. But now, at the beginning of 1947, the time had come. In the balance was the subjective ability of the administration's employees and the public in Britain to tolerate terrorism against civilians. In August 1946, a political solution still seemed possible and there was hope. But half a year later, the feeling in the administration had changed with the looming failure of the conference in London. As in the past, the evacuation plan was linked with a plan to concentrate the administration's everyday activity in a protected area. This would make more sense if those in the British community who could not be so easily protected were to leave the country.[6]

Cunningham, determined not to backtrack and of course not to falter or embarrass his superiors, exercised the full force of his imagination. Removing families and nonessentials bore serious implications, but not as serious as ceding control to the army. That would certainly unleash a tidal wave of terrorism, not to mention a wider confrontation between Britain and the Yishuv, and possibly even between the Jews and the Arabs throughout Palestine. He refused to accept the defeat of what he perceived as the commonsense approach—Yishuv-British cooperation in combating terrorism—either by the rule of violence under the Jewish terrorists or by the militancy of Montgomery and his supporters. Both believed in force alone.

Operation Polly—the removal of the families—was authorized by the colonial secretary that very evening, January 29. Cunningham was also given the go-ahead to concentrate the offices of the administration and its agencies in security zones, based on the August 1946 proposal. The British used two terms in this connection: *evacuation*, referring to the removal of families and nonessentials from Palestine; and *withdrawal*, which, in addition to its operative military connotation, served the internal British discourse about leaving Palestine and every other imperial outpost.[7]

On January 30, it seemed for a moment that Dov Gruner would request clemency. Cunningham immediately informed the colonial secretary that should this transpire, there should be no rush to remove the families, certainly not while Gruner's appeal was pending. He added his hope that three weeks to a month of quiet would come as a result of the appeal.[8]

The high commissioner and colonial secretary agreed that evacuation would be problematic generally and should be presented as part of the natural development of the situation in Palestine. In the meantime, that same evening it became clear that Gruner, under pressure from Etzel, would not appeal. Etzel preferred Gruner to be hanged rather than give the appearance of kowtowing to the British.[9] Cunningham accordingly informed Creech-Jones that he was withdrawing his suggestion to postpone the removal of the civilians and the creation of a security zone. At first, he considered accepting King Abdullah's offer to move the families through Transjordan. However, this was ruled out by the absence of a suitable infrastructure in the kingdom. Instead, the evacuees should first be taken to British Army bases on the Suez Canal, even without consulting with Cairo, owing to the pressure of time. The Egyptian authorities would undoubtedly be prepared to absorb them by February 4. This was the right course, the high commissioner believed, to avert harm to civilians who were not administration personnel. He informed London that he would make an announcement the next day, adding that despite the precautions being taken, civilians and soldiers alike were still in danger of being kidnapped.[10] He also gave the Jewish Agency an ultimatum whose gist was that if the Jewish Agency did not strike at the terrorists, the army would do so in its way.[11] Overall, the message to the agency was an embarrassing mix of threat and plea. He accused the agency's leaders of being dishonest, making false promises, and sowing incitement.

When Chief Rabbi Isaac Herzog came to ask for the commutation of Gruner's death sentence, Cunningham noted that although the Yishuv's cup of troubles might have flowed over, as the rabbi said, now the administration's cup, too, had spilled over. Herzog, formerly the chief rabbi of Ireland, noted in response that the Yishuv merited the same treatment as the Irish, who were not subjected to collective punishment, prompting the Irish-born Cunningham to blurt out, "But they were ours. . . ." Alarmed by his own remark, he promised that he did not intend to impose martial law. At most, he said, special measures would be introduced.[12] Cunningham did not want to burn his bridges with the Jewish Agency (which was fearful of a military regime). From Herzog, he learned that the Yishuv perceived the removal of the families and nonessentials as a threat: a license for the army to run wild.[13]

Both Creech-Jones and Cunningham were concerned about how the removal of the families and the nonessentials would be construed. This apprehension was well founded. The colonial secretary and his high commissioner were in the minority in terms of Palestine policy, both politically and militarily. The removal of the families was a setback to them after they had trumped the army over the past two months. In any event, the implications of the move had to be played down, so as not to encourage the terrorists or further damage Britain's status in Palestine and in the international community, particularly as Palestine was likely to be on the United Nations agenda very soon. Creech-Jones suggested that the evacuation be conducted secretly; Cunningham replied that this was impossible. To avoid undesirable alternatives being put forward, such as martial law or even a rapid withdrawal from Palestine, the high commissioner suggested issuing a statement that the evacuation would enable the civilian and military authorities to maintain law and order without interference.[14]

On January 31, an immediate departure order was issued for some two thousand nonessential British and Irish nationals. The group did not include administration officials—Britons, Jews, and Arabs alike—who were ordered to work at locales close to the central administration offices, where there was surveillance of those entering. Some of those assigned to the security zones were accommodated in the homes of Jewish families, who were moved to alternative housing. (The Arab families remained in place.) This was collective punishment of the type Cunningham had wished to avoid. Those over whom the administration had no control—journalists, businessmen, and others—were warned that the authorities could no longer be responsible for their security. British subjects who were not administration personnel—such as staff members of medical institutions, emissaries or employees of religious institutions, Jews (and the families of everyone in these categories)—were not on the list of evacuees.

Some in the administration accepted the decrees in a good spirit, but others reacted with fright. A degree of agitation was shown by those who felt they had been wronged either by being told to pack up and leave or by being forced to stay without their families. The evacuees were flown to Egypt and thence to Britain.[15]

In the winter of 1947, Cunningham's defensive posture (removing the nonessentials and entrenching the administration) was severely tested by Montgomery's offensive approach and his call for martial law to be imposed. The advocates of a military regime had their case strengthened by the Jewish Agency's unwillingness to cooperate in fighting terrorism. It was precisely to avoid rule by the army, or at least delay it as long as possible, that Cunningham had ordered the removal of the nonessentials. But the move undermined the morale and motivation of his staff, although how much would be difficult to gauge. More important, it was a boost to Etzel and Lehi and perhaps also to the Jewish Agency, which, together with the overwhelming majority in the Yishuv, declined to cooperate in the struggle against terrorism. Thus, by his ideas and his decisions at the beginning of 1947, Cunningham brought on himself what he wanted least of all: Montgomery's way.

On February 3, amid Operation Polly, Creech-Jones wrote to Cunningham, "[I]n the event of recurrence of serious outrages you will authorise some form of military control in particular areas and this will involve withdrawal of many facilities provided by civil administration."[16]

The directive was a complete debacle, Cunningham saw at once, notwithstanding the cautious phrasing. The successes of the campaign that he and the colonial secretary had waged in January against the CIGS were snuffed out. The high commissioner fired off a speedy reply. Purposeful and lucid, he seemed to return to his old form, in a style that had been lost with the decision to execute Operation Polly: "In regard to [military control], as short term policy I propose to *take* [emphasis in original] action . . . in first instance only for a limited period, after which civil administration would be restored if possible. . . . Complete military control does not seem a feasible answer, as long as [a] large part of the country can continue to function normally, which under any circumstance which can be foreseen immediately, seems possible." Cunningham added that he intended to convene the army's senior officers for a joint situation appraisal, as though wishing to make clear who was in charge of sending the army into action, should the need arise.[17] The colonial secretary accepted Cunningham's viewpoint in principle, but was less optimistic. What, he wanted to know, would Cunningham do if the Jewish Agency again rejected his latest ultimatum to cooperate in the battle against terrorism? Both officials favored cooperation but were apprehensive about the implications should the agency refuse.[18]

About two weeks after this exchange, the possibility of martial law became a concrete option. Foreign Secretary Bevin and his aides were unable to get the parties in the second London conference, held in January–February 1947, to agree to the amended provincial autonomy plan or, for that matter, to any other plan. On February 18, Bevin, on behalf of the government, publicly raised the possibility that absent an agreed political settlement Britain would refer the Mandate to the United Nations. The atmosphere of withdrawal from key bastions of the empire—India, Greece, Burma, Egypt, and others—facilitated the transfer of power to the army for an interim period until the final departure. More specifically, Operation Polly, though aimed at enhancing the work of the civilian authorities, helped pave the way for a possible military regime by thinning out the British civilian presence and placing the bulk of the administration behind walls and fences.

Saturday March 1, 1947, was a particularly violent day. The breakaway organizations attacked British civilian and military installations in Haifa, Beit Lid, Kfar Yona, Netanya, Petah Tikva, Rehovot, and Akir (Tel Nof). The most vicious assault was perpetrated by Etzel against a British officers' club on King George V Street in the center of Jerusalem. The club was destroyed. Twenty British personnel were killed in eighteen terrorist attacks during the day—two officers, eight soldiers, ten policemen—along with others, probably staff of the hotel in which the club was located; thirty-one people were wounded. Etzel, mindful of the King David Hotel carnage, chose the Jewish Sabbath for the attack, at a time when civilians were unlikely to be in the area. The organization claimed that the assault was a reaction to Bevin's announcement two weeks earlier that Britain would refer the Mandate to the United Nations—a base deception, according to Etzel. In fact, the breakaways appear to have been indifferent to British actions; they were determined to pursue their campaign of terror. Cunningham seems to have grasped this reality. On March 2, the government in London authorized the high commissioner to impose martial law. At the latter's suggestion, the military regime was limited in time and place: about two weeks in the urban areas where the breakaways' main bases were located. Cunningham was bent on restricting the operation, while the army claimed, without evidence, that the Haganah had also been involved in the attacks. According to Middle East Command, the Haganah carried out an attack on a garage in the Haifa port on March 3. (This allegation is uncorroborated.) Once again, Cunningham found himself perched between the breakaway groups and the army.[19]

From the high commissioner's and the government's perspective (though not the army's), martial law was intended to put pressure on the Jewish Agency for not cooperating in the campaign against terrorism. Martial law was imposed across most of Tel Aviv, along with Givatayim, Bnei Brak, Ramat Gan, and Petah Tikva (Operation Hippo), as well as small areas of Jerusalem (Operation Elephant). The first clause of an order issued by the military governor of Tel Aviv, Major General Richard Gale, the commander of the First Infantry Division, reflected Cunningham's perception of martial law and his guidelines to the army: "Martial law shall be declared. It is not to be viewed as a punishment, although there will be no avoiding suffering caused to residents through the fault of irresponsible individuals."[20]

Like High Commissioner Arthur Wauchope before him in the period of the Arab Revolt, Cunningham equated martial law with the liquidation of the Mandatory civil authority. Yet, like Wauchope, he could not ignore its necessity in the face of highly disruptive terrorism, whether by Arabs or Jews.[21] Creech-Jones, whether because he grasped the duality of Cunningham's approach or because he wanted to protect himself and the high commissioner, made clear that the latter had acted in consultation with the military authorities in the Middle East and in Palestine: "[T]he High Commissioner took this decision in full collaboration with the military authorities. . . . On hearing the High Commissioner's decision, and with the concurrences of the Prime Minister and Minister of Defense, I at once cabled my full approval of the course he had adopted."[22]

The imposition of martial law had serious implications for both the Yishuv and the administration. Cunningham tried to avert a situation in which the district governor would transfer his powers to the local military commander. However, this is precisely what occurred during the short period of sixteen wretched days in which he transferred his powers—in the areas in which martial law was declared—to Montgomery, at least in principle. Where martial law was declared, all the powers of the civil authorities were annulled, vesting the military governor with the same authority as the high commissioner. He could impound land, buildings, and means of transportation; impose curfews, make arrests, and conduct a speedy trial in a military court. Soldiers bore police powers. The areas under martial law were cordoned off; access was only possible by means of personal permits. The Jewish neighborhoods in Jaffa, which were not under martial law, were cut off from their Tel Aviv base. Children could not get to school, where some received their only hot meal of the day. And many Jaffa Jews were unable to reach their place of work in Tel Aviv. The result was that the Jewish population in Jaffa remained at the mercy of the Arab-run Jaffa municipality. Food was available, but if the present situation continued those unable to get to work might not have money to buy basic commodities. Within a few days, Jaffa residents started to sneak into Tel Aviv to work and buy food, which the military authorities made sure was in plentiful supply there. Two other points are noteworthy: the leniency shown to the Hebrew-language newspapers based inside the area of martial law and the imposition of all the regulations of martial law on the Arab villages in the area.[23]

Under the aegis of the high commissioner, who sometimes flouted his own directives, the new GOC Palestine (as of February 1947), Lieutenant

General Gordon MacMillan, tried to alleviate the plight of the population. For example, Cunningham refused to sign an order compelling the mayor of Tel Aviv to close the municipal court. Cunningham and MacMillan worked hand in hand to make the military regime tolerable—with greater success than anyone could have anticipated. Tel Aviv was a major center of employment, and the productive cooperation between the army and the municipality led to requests from residents of areas adjacent to the city—now cut off from Tel Aviv—to incorporate them within the boundaries of the military regime. Martial law was indeed extended to parts of Jaffa for this reason. The mayor of Tel Aviv, Israel Rokach, was given access to Mandatory radio so that he could deliver a calming message to the city's inhabitants. In his remarks, he took note of the facilitations granted the city. The Tel Aviv municipality and nearby local authorities were grateful for the military's approach. Rokach was in constant contact with Major General Gale, who did his best to solve problems and ease the situation for the civilian population.[24]

As for Barker's removal as GOC Palestine after serving only ten months in the position, this proved a felicitous development during the period of martial law. Cunningham had wanted to dispense with Barker's service months earlier, after the crises of summer 1946, not least because the GOC was constantly targeted by the breakaways, but had agreed to hold back for a time, at Barker's request. MacMillan was more inclined than his predecessor to work with the high commissioner. Like Cunningham, he understood that a cooperative population was likely to be quiescent. Nor was MacMillan—in contrast to Barker—prone to say one thing to the high commissioner and another to his officers. Years later, MacMillan noted that he saw himself as more of a Mandatory official than a military commander, and that his mission had been to work for the benefit of the population. In the case of the Jews, this meant working for a national home. The limitations of oral testimony notwithstanding, these remarks are of value against the background of the approach taken by MacMillan's superiors in Cairo and London. MacMillan's attitude came as a great relief to Cunningham, who felt he was losing control to the army. The army's efforts, under the high commissioner's guidelines, offset somewhat the impact of the collective punishment and prevented the eruption that Cunningham had feared. The anomaly of martial law reinforced what Cunningham already knew: the majority of the Jewish population wanted only a quiet, secure existence, a good livelihood, and the services they needed.[25]

But despite the authorities' approach, soldiers accidentally shot an adolescent boy on a Tel Aviv street on the first day of martial law. Immediately, the voices the high commissioner feared and had warned against were heard. Pinhas Lavon, a Mapai moderate (later Israel's defense minister), declared, "Just as we cannot accept the operations of the breakaways, we cannot accept the operations of the government, [which amount to] inflicting collective punishment on hundreds of thousands of innocent people, in order to cause the economic strangulation of our enterprise in this country."[26] Despite his good relations with MacMillan, Cunningham was extremely worried about the possible consequences of martial law. His belief that the military way was wrong was only reinforced during the two weeks and more of martial law.

Montgomery in London and Dempsey in Cairo both felt that they had no one in Jerusalem as a counterbalance to Cunningham. Dempsey, the GOC Middle East, reminded MacMillan that he must insist on having a free hand from the high commissioner. He added that martial law would remain in force until it produced satisfactory results from the army's viewpoint. Two weeks was a minimum, Dempsey wrote, all the while feeling that his man in Palestine was too close to the high commissioner.[27] The theater commander saw what the high commissioner saw, but read it differently. There were murderers in Britain just as in Palestine, he noted, but in Britain they were apprehended whereas in Palestine they were not, because the public there was hostile to the law enforcement authorities. This was patently a provocation vis-à-vis the high commissioner, an avowed advocate of cooperation with the local population.[28] Montgomery, who ostensibly got what he wanted—martial law, albeit limited—told Dempsey that now was not the time for saying "We told you so." Success depended on the army, if it fielded sufficient manpower fired with the right level of determination. If political limitations were continuing to cause us to lose the initiative, the CIGS summed up, he needed to know about them. In other words, if Cunningham interfered again, Montgomery should be notified at once and would do everything possible in Whitehall to ensure that the high commissioner would not be able to hamstring the military.[29]

However, Cunningham did not back down. With martial law at its height, he pursued every possible channel to persuade his superiors in London not to extend this drastic measure. The Yishuv was showing signs of tension, he wrote—at this stage, more in words than deeds, but the danger of an eruption existed.[30] Cunningham pointed out to Creech-Jones that the economic damage inflicted on the Yishuv also had an effect both direct (nonpayment of taxes) and indirect (not immediately measurable) on the budget of the Mandatory administration. An excessively lengthy operation would harden the Yishuv's attitude toward the administration and possibly spark civil revolt and violent demonstrations. In other words, the broad, nonviolent Jewish public (99 percent, in the British estimate) must not be thrust into the cycle of violence. Just because the public was not providing information about the breakaways did not mean that it was taking an active part in terrorism. Cunningham could draw on material published by the Tel Aviv municipality showing a disparity between the declarations of political figures and the close and surprisingly fruitful cooperation among the army, the administration, and the municipal authorities during the period of martial law.[31]

At midday on March 17, the sixteenth day on which martial law was in effect, the measure was lifted. The British military and civilian authorities agreed that the results had been lukewarm. Sixty "extremists" were arrested (the army cited a figure of seventy-eight), including twenty-four wanted men from Etzel and Lehi. Some of the arrests were made thanks to tacit cooperation by the Jewish public, which, as it happened, enabled arrests to continue even after martial law was lifted. Twenty-four people were killed: thirteen from the security forces, one British civilian, and ten Jewish civilians. It is unclear how many of the Jewish dead were classified as terrorists. At least one youngster was shot by mistake, as already noted. The continuing arrival of ships carrying illegal immigrants during the period of martial law stretched the security forces to the limit. In the army's view, the public did not offer a quid pro quo in the form of information about the terrorists. Dempsey and Montgomery proved more adept than MacMillan at offering explanations for the incomplete success at an early stage of the operation and immediately afterward. Their remonstrations were aimed at both the Jewish population and the administration, but not at the security forces in Palestine and their commander.

The administration did not dispute the army's principal conclusion: that the hoped-for level of cooperation with the civilian population in combating terrorism had not been achieved. Although some progress had been made in terms of assistance rendered by the Jewish Agency, the National Council, and the public itself, Government House and the Colonial Office were united in their assessment that the cooperation of the Yishuv establishment in rooting out terrorism had been ineffective. Still, the incipient cooperation by the street led the administration and the army to ask the public, over the heads of its leaders, to pass on essential intelligence for the campaign against terrorism.[32]

Was martial law lifted only because a two-week period had been mentioned from the outset? Probably not. The colonial secretary's memorandum of March 19 to the prime minister, which also contained the high commissioner's opinion, expressed unequivocal opposition to martial law. A week later, the Chiefs of Staff Committee conveyed its summation to Attlee. Surprisingly, the paper explicitly rejected Montgomery's policy, even though he was of course a member of the committee. Its wording was a clear victory for Cunningham, both in its analysis of the situation in Palestine and its conclusions about what had been done and what remained to be done. The chiefs of staff agreed that the Yishuv by and large deplored Jewish terrorism, but not to the point of providing specific information against its perpetrators. At the same time, the Haganah and the Palmah were maintaining quiet, although initial indications suggested they were taking independent action against the terrorists, which might become more effective in time. The memorandum noted that even if the Yishuv showed little taste for terrorism, the public was committed to Jewish immigration. In this connection, the chiefs of staff recalled the promise of the Yishuv leadership—which they did not accept—that increasing the immigration quotas would increase the Yishuv heads' willingness to cooperate in the campaign against terrorism. On the other hand, they warned that extending martial law was apt to push elements in the Haganah and the Palmah into the arms of Etzel and Lehi. The terrorists, a small minority, were trying to set a trap: they wanted to drag the administration and the army into inflicting collective punishment, believing that this would reverse the low esteem in which they were held among the moderate Jewish majority. Moreover, the economic havoc wreaked by martial law would push the jobless into the terrorist organizations. In the view of the document's authors, the Yishuv's satisfactory economic and political condition would ensure the public's continued opposition to terrorism. It followed that the extension of martial law could well serve primarily the terrorists: Etzel and Lehi.

There must be no yielding to the blackmail of the Jewish minority, the chiefs of staff stated; their aim was to provoke Britain into taking rash action in Palestine. The result would be an expansion of the cycle of terrorism and the sabotage of Britain's ability to promote a political solution. The military also recommended not revoking the death sentence given to Dov Gruner (even if the hope shared by the British and the Yishuv—that Gruner would ask for clemency—did not materialize) and four other Jewish militants. Backing away from the death penalty would project weakness in the perception of both the Yishuv and the Mandatory administration and army. The chiefs of staff agreed that the use of martial law and of force in general against the Jews in Palestine should be limited. The nerve centers of terrorism were in the big cities, particularly Tel Aviv, and a military effort against them might well reduce their capacity to act. That, indeed, was the purpose of declaring martial law in Tel Aviv. Nevertheless, the most effective tool against terrorism was the cooperation of the civilian population and of the institutions on behalf of which the terrorists were supposedly operating.

The chiefs' six-page report devoted only three lines to the Arabs. The Arabs were not presently causing problems, the authors noted, but were quick to complain of being harmed as a result of British action against the Jews. The document proceeded to analyze the options for dealing with terrorism. Martial law was counterproductive, the chiefs of staff concluded: first, because it would ultimately only increase the need for military operations; and second, because the army lacked the resources to handle all the civilian tasks that martial law called for. They conceded that, in contrast to their past claims, the present forces were insufficient to deal with Jewish terrorism. The existing situation—namely, the continuation of the civil administration—should be allowed to remain intact for the coming six months, with martial law to be imposed only in extreme cases. It stands to reason that this conclusion was reached with the aid of MacMillan, the senior British officer in Palestine.[33] Cunningham could not have summed up the episode of martial law better himself.

The content of the memorandum was seemingly unexpected. Montgomery remained adamant in his approach, but his colleagues took a different view. In this instance, the human relations problems incurred by the CIGS worked in Cunningham's favor. Since assuming his post about a year earlier, Montgomery had not been getting along with the two other members of the CSC, Admiral John Cunningham (no relation to the high commissioner) and Air Marshal Arthur Tedder. He therefore often dispatched his deputy, Lieutenant General Frank Simpson, to routine meetings in his place, but Simpson was junior in rank to the two others and their view prevailed. Montgomery may have succeeded Field Marshal Alanbrooke as CIGS, Land Forces, but Tedder became chairman of the CSC. The committee strove for unanimity of opinion; the chairman was rarely called upon to cast the deciding vote. Montgomery had no taste for this form of group dynamics. It is difficult to assess to what extent the memorandum on Palestine reflected the interpersonal relations on the committee. In any event, its contrarianism was blatant: the committee fully accepted the approach that Montgomery rejected and for which Cunningham fought.[34]

The CSC was almost certainly also influenced by the crossing of lines by General Dempsey himself immediately after the lifting of martial law. The GOC Middle East, Montgomery's man, had backed his superior but then recanted. One reason for this might have been that Dempsey, who had been marked as Montgomery's successor, was now about to retire from the armed forces, not necessarily of his own volition. However, the main reason for his change of mind was his recognition that the army was incapable of performing civilian missions. From the time he arrived in Cairo, in June 1946, Dempsey had witnessed a continuing confrontation between the high commissioner and the GOC Palestine, Barker. He was impressed by the fruitful cooperation between Cunningham and MacMillan beginning in February 1947 and, in particular, during the period of martial law in March. At the end of May, Dempsey grasped what MacMillan had seen immediately: that Cunningham knew the Jewish community better than both of them and that it was sensible to work with him, not against him. The fact that the high commissioner insisted on consultation and did not authorize every operation did not mean he was intervening in the army's operation. The joint cooperation between Cunningham and MacMillan produced more effective results than martial law. Dempsey visited Jerusalem to see the "miracle" for himself. Because the War Office had requested that either he or MacMillan should come to London for the deliberations about martial law, and the Colonial Office had requested Cunningham's presence for the same purpose, Dempsey suggested that the high commissioner and MacMillan make the trip. He did not want to undermine the good working relations between the two. In the end, MacMillan went alone to present the view of both the administration and the army. Dempsey thereby put another nail in the coffin of Montgomery's approach, while Cunningham gained support from an unexpected quarter.[35]

Cunningham's success was manifest. The lifting of martial law, which had been imposed against his will, was ultimately a key victory of both substance and image and a positive step in terms of rehabilitating his status both generally and regarding his standoff with Montgomery. The memoranda produced by the colonial secretary and the chiefs of staff left no room for doubt. It wasn't every day that harmony prevailed between the Colonial Office and the War Office. On March 27, the day before the chiefs of staff submitted their memorandum, the cabinet decided against imposing statutory martial law in Palestine. In the wake of this decision, the provisions of the defense (emergency) regulations were improved and a new term introduced—*controlled area*—which in practice meant a closed military zone. Cunningham's hand can be seen in this development.[36]

However, Jewish terrorism did not abate with the lifting of martial law. Cunningham was rattled by reports of a significant decline in British candidates for the Civil Service in Palestine. The reason, he believed, resided in a play of opposites: natural human fear, together with the inability, since Operation Polly, to bring one's wife and family. The only course at present, he insisted, was to persist in trying to obtain the Yishuv's cooperation in the campaign against terrorism. At the same time, he was encouraged by signs of direct independent activity, with the Haganah taking action against the perpetrators of terrorism at the behest of the Jewish Agency.

However, because these actions were not enough, and against Britain's referral of the Mandate to the United Nations "without recommendations" at the beginning of April 1947 (although this decision was made by the government in February, after the failure of the London conference, and approved by the House of Commons, the formal request to the secretary-general was only made now), Cunningham proposed that Britain ask the UN to declare an interim period without terrorism as a condition for a political discussion on the future of Palestine. He was impelled by the quest for a political solution, a positive approach to the referral of the Mandate to the UN, and the assumption that the Yishuv also preferred this arena of discussion.[37]

The episode of martial law continued to haunt Cunningham, in the first place because the continuing terrorism ensured that it remained on the agenda as an option. In addition, he was eager to persuade London of the logic of his approach. Immediately after the curfew was lifted in Tel Aviv, the high commissioner directed his staff to compile data for a secret memorandum that would consolidate his case in the debate over the usefulness of martial law and collective punishment. He was heartened by the stirrings of Jewish Agency cooperation, such as the Haganah's preemptive operation in Beit Hadar (Citrus House) in Tel Aviv on June 18, 1947. The operation—which prevented the demolition of the army's headquarters in the building by Etzel—cost the life of a Haganah man. Ze'ev Verber was killed in an explosion while probing a tunnel dug by Etzel beneath the building. Clearly, the disastrous King David Hotel incident had not persuaded Etzel to change its ways, as the attack on the British officers' club in Jerusalem and the attempt in Tel Aviv showed. The Tel Aviv operation was an important boost for Cunningham's approach to the question of how to deal with terrorism. With the necessary caution given the fraught public atmosphere, the high commissioner sent a Jewish official from the district office of the administration to represent him at the mass funeral for Verber.[38]

In a short memorandum to Creech-Jones on June 19, 1947, Cunningham drew a comparison between the Arab "disturbances" in the 1930s and the actions of the Jews at present. The memorandum, which was also circulated to the Foreign Office and to the British embassies in the Middle East, was more than a little critical of the approach of the War Office, the army, and the Foreign Office. It opened with a clear allusion to the position advocated by Montgomery: "It is sometimes suggested that if measures similar to those taken during the Arab disturbances of 1936–39 were adopted against Jewish terrorism more success would be achieved than has resulted from the measures actually employed. The purpose of the memorandum is briefly to explain the essential differences between two situations."[39]

The gist of his historical-political analysis was that the Arab Revolt had encompassed the entire Arab population—even those who did not take part lent their support. The administration had been effectively paralyzed for entire days. British military activity in the 1930s sometimes lasted for days at a time and aimed to seize territory, in order to prevent the insurgents from installing—even temporarily—an autonomous government in the areas under their control. The present situation regarding the Jews is completely different, the high commissioner noted. The troublemakers now were an extremist minority whose relations with the majority of the public were generally even worse than its relations with the administration. The Jewish Agency's approach to the terrorists fluctuates, he said, but the thrust is clear. In its propaganda and in its policy, at least since July 1946, the agency has rejected terrorism and considers it a threat to the Zionist cause. The leaders of the Jewish Agency are unwilling to cooperate openly with the British, but in some cases they take independent action and work tacitly with the Mandatory security authorities.

Cunningham also addressed the method of collective punishment employed against the Palestine Arabs in the 1930s: martial law, curfew, deportation, house demolitions, and the like. Such actions have no effect on the Yishuv, he argued. The Arabs, he explained, were habituated to collective responsibility from time immemorial, whereas the Jews followed an individualist Western approach. Consequently, he summed up, there was no basis for a comparison between the British confrontation with Arab terrorism a decade earlier and the treatment of Jewish terrorism. Although somewhat apologetic in tone and flawed in its historical accuracy, the memorandum authentically reflected the contemporary reality in Cunningham's perception.[40]

The high commissioner also explained why he had not resorted to house demolitions as a form of punishment. The experience of the Arab Revolt—when some two thousand homes were demolished by the British—showed that excessive use of this practice had the effect of transferring responsibility for imposing order to the district governors and their staff, and ultimately to the army, down to the level of the local commander, who acted according to on-site considerations. House demolitions also drew more people into the terrorist fold, spurred by a desire to avenge injury done to the innocent. Cunningham was determined to prevent this consequence. Another aspect of his very different response to Jewish terrorism, as compared against the efforts in the 1930s to suppress the Arab insurgency, involves the number of those deported for their involvement in terrorist attacks: only five Arabs throughout the Arab Revolt, but 444 Jews since October 1945, nearly all of them from Etzel and Lehi. (These figures do not include the many Arabs who fled the country for fear of reprisal by the authorities from 1937 onward, or the Jewish refugees deported to Cyprus beginning in the summer of 1946.) From 1945 on, the administration's approach was driven by a desire to avoid imposing collective punishment.[41]

Cunningham backed up his conclusions with the data compiled by his staff. The key element here is not the validity of the data but the high commissioner's efforts to validate his approach. Thus, according to the memorandum, 9,461 terrorist events were reported during the period of the Arab Revolt, whereas from late 1945 until April 1947 there were 758 cases of Jewish terrorism. Even if this was only half the time of the Arab Revolt, the disparity is impressive. The overall number of fatal casualties also reflects responses of a different character by the Mandatory administration and the army. During the period of the Arab Revolt, 1,791 Jews and Arabs were killed in actions by the Arabs, whereas during the period of the Jewish Resistance Movement, until April 1947, 158 Jews and Arabs were killed in attacks by the Jewish terrorists. The Arab Revolt took the lives of 265 members of the Mandatory police (British, Jews, and Arabs); in the Jewish insurgency, 103 policemen and soldiers (including both Jews and Arabs) were killed in the period under discussion. The small difference in the number of British nationals killed was due to the relative efficiency of Jewish terrorism. The numbers are even more instructive in regard to those classified as terrorists and killed by the security forces: 2,150 Arabs from 1936 until 1939, as compared with ten Jews from October 1945 until April 1947. From 1937 to 1939, 12,622 Arabs were placed in administrative detention (arrest without trial) under the emergency laws on suspicion of being terrorists. The number of Jews arrested under the same rubric in a period of twenty months stood at 2,431 (excluding those detained in Operation Agatha for a few hours or days). It is also significant that 108 Arabs were executed in the first period, as compared against four Jews in the second period—the four Etzel members who were hanged on April 16, 1947. No dramatic rise occurred in the number of Jews executed afterward: the total was twelve, of whom eleven were from Etzel or Lehi. Two of them, the assassins of Lord Moyne, the British resident minister in Cairo, were put to death in the Egyptian capital, outside the jurisdiction of the Mandatory administration.[42]

These data were consistent with Cunningham's view of the proper way to handle Jewish terrorism. Collective punishment was pointless, the army must not be allowed to lead the struggle and its contact with the Jewish population should be minimized, executions served no purpose, and a political horizon should be proposed and economic growth encouraged. These methods would be more effective against terrorism than Montgomery's "turn every stone" approach. Martial law must be limited in time and in territory.

On June 21, two days after the memorandum was sent, Montgomery arrived in Palestine for a lightning visit on his way to India (the same route he took upon assuming his new post). After landing at Akir airfield (today's Tel Nof) at 4:30 p.m., he was driven to Sarafand base, near Ramle, for tea, an update from General MacMillan, and rest. He left Palestine, again from Akir, at 4:30 a.m. on June 22. The high commissioner was informed of the visit only hours before it took place. "How" is sometimes more important than "what." Shortly before midnight on June 20, MacMillan received a personal cable from Montgomery asking him to inform the high commissioner that given the brevity of his visit he did not wish to bother him and therefore would not come to Jerusalem. Cunningham, he was certain, would understand, he added. MacMillan duly passed on the message. There is no known response by Cunningham to the affront.[43]

Notwithstanding the frequent crises in spring and summer 1947, Cunningham continued to advocate the supremacy of the civilian authorities over the military. His civil-oriented approach on the question of martial law was probably justified, even if nothing seemingly changed. The Yishuv's pattern of behavior—the Jewish Agency's failure to cooperate directly with the British against the breakaways' terrorism (even if it acted independently against them), and its tendency to concentrate its resistance activities in the form of illegal immigration and the political discourse—continued unchanged even after martial law was lifted. However, this time Cunningham did not wait for the Jewish Agency. He struck at the terrorists in the most effective way possible. Without a systematic discussion, but nevertheless consistently and clearly, the growing terrorism by Etzel and Lehi in April–July 1947 left the high commissioner and the administration unmoved, literally. In short, the administration effectively ignored the acts, and it is axiomatic that terrorism that does not elicit a reaction loses its influence.[44]

The unfolding larger events also played into Cunningham's approach. Britain's referral of the Mandate to the UN, the special General Assembly session held in May 1947, and the arrival in Palestine of the United Nations Special Committee on Palestine (UNSCOP), together with the dramatic episode of the immigrant ship *Exodus*, overshadowed the terrorism of summer 1947. The Yishuv, too, focused its attention on these events, while the breakaways carried out violent reprisals following the death sentences given to their comrades, who were forbidden to request clemency. To the administration, as well as to the majority in the Yishuv, the struggle by Etzel and Lehi seemed beside the point. Cunningham actively advocated a policy of ignoring terrorism. Beginning in May 1947, he believed—though his superiors in London were less certain—that a political option existed in cooperation with the UN. In a meeting at Government House with members of UNSCOP, Cunningham assailed those who urged force as the only answer to terrorism. Turning his back on the terrorists also served his aim of showing that he was in control of the situation and that the British government had been right to accept his approach over Montgomery's about martial law.[45]

Suffice it to compare Cunningham's approach to the terrorism perpetrated in January–March 1947—he removed families and nonessential personnel and imposed martial law, clear victories for the terrorists—to his near indifference from late March until the beginning of August. The Acre Prison break staged by Etzel in May, together with dozens of terror events every week in July—in reaction to the possibility that the executions would go ahead—were reported in a businesslike, not to say technical, manner to the Colonial Office. The reports carried no recommendations, made no requests, offered no suggestions for a publicity line, and shunned the idea of declaring martial law. It was as though terrorism were no more than a reality of daily life. London had already announced that martial law would not be imposed in any event. The new situation created by the removal of the families and the establishment of the administration's security zones also contributed to this new approach. Cunningham no longer dealt with acts of terrorism personally, leaving the role to his aides. He himself signed the monthly intelligence reports. An undersecretary, Vivian Fox-Strangways, signed off on the weekly reports, and an official from the chief secretariat, G. G. Grinwood, signed most of the daily reports, when there were any.[46]

Only an extreme event could have placed terrorism back at the top of the high commissioner's agenda. He, like his staff in the administration, the government in London, and indeed British public opinion, was very sensitive to humiliations. An attack on a policeman or a soldier stirred rage and often a harsh reaction. In most cases, though, the response to terrorism was measured, or entailed an operation with additional goals beyond punishment, deterrence, or revenge. Although there were exceptions (such as the arrest of Rabbi Fishman-Maimon on the Sabbath at the start of Operation Agatha, or the rough search of the two Negev kibbutzim in August 1946), the British authorities, both civilian and military, generally made an effort to carry out searches in a dignified manner. Terrorism was a price that could be tolerated and did not even enter into the discussions of the decision-makers in London and Jerusalem about Britain's goals in Palestine. However, the ultimate humiliation was inflicted on the British at the end of July 1947.

On July 12, Etzel kidnapped two unarmed British field-security sergeants from a café in Netanya. They were sitting with a local "Jewish official," possibly an informer, who was also snatched but soon released. The two sergeants, Clifford Martin and Mervyn Paice, disappeared. They were held as hostages, their lives dependent on the fate of the Etzel men sentenced to death.[47]

Cunningham did not resort to force immediately. True to form in this period, his response was moderate. He warned that if the two officials were not released by July 14, the Netanya region, a terrorist center since January 1947, would be declared a "military controlled area," in the spirit of the cabinet's guidelines following the period of martial law in March. However, the ultimatum was ignored, forcing Cunningham to make good on his threat. He emphasized that the restrictions—code-named Operation Tiger—were intended solely to facilitate the search for the missing soldiers and avert additional terrorism. This was also the gist of his report to the cabinet in London. The quantum leap in terrorism was reflected in the now-daily reports on terrorism, though their style remained unchanged: date, curt description, number of casualties. Cunningham instructed his staff to go on essentially ignoring acts of terror.[48]

Days and weeks passed, but the missing sergeants were not found. In the meantime, the *Exodus* crisis erupted and the testimonies to UNSCOP reached their height; tension ran high as the committee moved to Geneva to draw up its final report. Interest in the abduction seemed to wane among members of the Mandate administration, even though the soldiers were not freed. Etzel threatened retaliation in kind if the death sentences on its men were carried out. Cunningham's only solace lay in his assessment that the Yishuv itself was deeply worried about how the administration would react if Etzel fulfilled its threat. This, together with the furor over the political process and illegal Jewish immigration, gave him cause not to be apprehensive about carrying out the death sentence on the Etzel prisoners.[49]

The executions took place on July 29. Three Etzel men who had been condemned to death on June 19 for their part in the Acre Prison break on May 4—Yaakov Weiss, Avshalom Haviv, and Meir Nakar—were hanged. Two days later, the bodies of the two sergeants were found. At midday on July 31, the chief undersecretary informed the Colonial Office that the bodies had been discovered at 9 a.m., hanged from trees in a British-planted eucalyptus grove at Umm Uleiqa near Beit Lid, east of Netanya. Notes affixed to the soldiers' clothing said that they had been executed by Etzel for being British spies. The bodies were found by members of the Jewish police force, who had summoned the British authorities to the site. The area had been mined, and an explosive device was planted below the bodies. A mine went off as the first body was being lowered and blew it to bits. An officer of the Royal Engineers backed off in time and suffered only minor face wounds. The bodies, one shattered and the other whole, were taken to the forensic institute at Abu Kabir, in Tel Aviv, for identification.[50]

The entire character of the event—the kidnapping of unarmed soldiers from a café, their execution by hanging, the booby-trapping of the bodies, the obliteration of one of them, and the wounds sustained by an officer who was releasing the bodies from their humiliating condition—triggered a furious reaction. On the evening of July 31, policemen and soldiers "ran amok," as Cunningham put it in a cable to the minister, damaging twenty-five stores in Tel Aviv and murdering five Jewish civilians and wounding sixteen. Cunningham was aware of his staff's feelings. On July 17, in a meeting with the members of the UN Special Committee at Government House, he related the story of a British soldier who had lain wounded in the street and been ignored by passersby. At the same time, both he and the colonial secretary were appalled at the violence perpetrated by the security forces. It was clear to them that the rampage was above all a blow to British interests. In the meantime, protest demonstrations were held in Britain and angry questions fired at the colonial secretary in the House of Commons and the House of Lords. An unshakable belief in the chosen path and nerves of steel were needed to resist the temptation to move from "military controlled area" to full martial law.[51]

Cunningham's great triumph in March on the issue of martial law evaporated in an instant. Anything other than a Montgomery-style response was likely to be taken as proof—as in November 1941—of cowardice or unwarranted defensiveness. Cunningham tripped precisely over the issue that had brought him his greatest achievements in Palestine: how to deal with terrorism. The experience he had gleaned had taught him to avoid the defensive and go on the offensive. In a "secret and personal" cable to Creech-Jones sent just hours after the two bodies were found, he noted that he had not been surprised: he had been contemplating the possibility that Etzel would carry out its threat for some time. With Creech-Jones sure to face questions in Parliament, the high commissioner would provide relevant information that would be best heard from the colonial secretary. Cunningham reported that he had imposed a closure in the Sharon area and that searches were under way and arrests being made. A list had been drawn up of fifty-eight key individuals who supported Etzel and Lehi and provided the terrorists with shelter and political and physical support. By August 5, thirty-four of them were in custody. However, this was a short-term battle, and as such, Cunningham reprised ideas from a year earlier, following the King David Hotel attack: restrictions on immigration—the Yishuv's chief objective—combined with economic sanctions and the detention of leaders. The high commissioner and his aides believed that the Yishuv was expecting an Agatha-type operation and had probably begun to destroy documents.[52]

Nevertheless, after a year drenched in terrorism Cunningham was far from certain that these measures would produce the coveted cooperation with the Jewish Agency. Worse, the result might be an end to the low-level cooperation that existed and to the Yishuv's independent action against the terrorists since the period of martial law in March. And looming in the background was the UNSCOP report now being drawn up, which would profoundly influence the future of the Mandatory administration and, concomitantly, his own future. In June 1946, Cunningham had acted with presence of mind and a long-term view. Now, in August 1947, under pressure of time running out and patience that had expired, he decided to exploit the tragedy to coerce the Jewish Agency into doing what it had refused to do since his arrival in the country: cooperate with him in the battle against terrorism. The Yishuv leaders were frightened at the possibility that martial law would be declared again, he believed. In this spirit, he accepted the suggestion of Golda Meyerson, the acting head of the Jewish Agency's Political Department, for the administration to do nothing until the Jewish Agency Executive made a decision on whether to cooperate or not—and that would happen quickly, she assured him. She hinted that the organized Yishuv was determined to take action to suppress terrorism. The high commissioner, keen to believe her but just as keenly suspicious, requested an immediate reply. Time, he knew, was limited.[53]

Amid the negotiations with the Jewish Agency and the consultations with the military, the reactions in Britain were reported. Harsh as they were, they were by no means the cause for Britain's decision to withdraw from Palestine—a decision that was effectively made, albeit not yet formally, with the Mandate's referral to the United Nations. Indeed, it was precisely because of a process already under way signaling Britain's withdrawal, compounded by the humiliation inflicted by the murder of the two sergeants, that the reactions were so grim. The responses in Britain were further intensified by the frenetic pace of the developments bringing about the end of the empire. The historic decision to leave Palestine influenced the methods chosen to combat terrorism and humiliation more than they influenced the decision to leave.

Creech-Jones succinctly described the situation in Britain: "Reaction here has been strong, indignation and horror has swept all over United Kingdom." On July 31, he was compelled to confirm to the House of Commons the news about the hangings, quoting from the report he had received that morning in Cunningham's name. The colonial secretary, although certainly not wishing to fan the flames, did so unintentionally, forcing Cunningham to mount an exceptional reaction in order to extricate everyone involved safely from the debacle. Distraught, but anticipating the opposition's assault, Creech-Jones stated, "In the long history of the violence in Palestine there has scarcely been a more dastardly act than the cold blooded and calculated murder of these innocent young men. . . ."[54]

On August 1, questions were put to the colonial secretary by members of the House of Lords, mostly dealing with the personal security of British nationals serving in Palestine. Creech-Jones asked the high commissioner for his input. Cunningham, in a characteristic response, noted that this would be an opportune time to mention the many successes of the administration in preventing terrorism, heretofore unnoticed. Moreover, he added with wounded pride, no terrorist attack or kidnapping had occurred since the declaration of "military controlled areas." At the same time, he could not provide full personal security in a situation in which the security forces were the major target of the kidnapping attempts, and not civilians, be they British, Arab, or Jewish. Even if he provided data about the security forces' success in preventing terrorism, his description revealed a situation that hardly merited pride. The reality was that the governmental community in Palestine was generally shut behind fences and barbed wire and could only move about with a military or police escort. The tacit implication was that there was little awareness of this in Britain and that the public and the government did not really care what happened in Palestine, as long as there were no British casualties.[55]

Reading the transcript of the parliamentary debate, which he received shortly after its conclusion, Cunningham could note two trends, neither of them new. They boiled down to the school of the high commissioner versus the school of the chief of the Imperial General Staff. Some members of Parliament had reservations about dealing a blow to the Zionist cause and wanted to know whether the Jewish Agency had condemned the hangings and was ready to cooperate; others demanded the immediate declaration of martial law. The colonial secretary was at a loss to reply to the first group, as Cunningham was just then talking to the Jewish Agency. As for the second group, the colonial secretary, knowing that martial law was no longer an option, related that after the sergeants were kidnapped the area had been sealed off and thorough searches conducted. Creech-Jones seems to have thought that the double murder did not justify a revision of the cabinet decision to eliminate the option of martial law. He heaped praise on the civilian and military authorities in Palestine, and sent personal words of encouragement to Cunningham. The surprise came, unexpectedly, from Jerusalem.[56]

On Friday evening August 1, Cunningham felt increasingly hemmed in.

Atop the reactions in Britain and the rampage by the police in Tel Aviv, he was deeply disappointed by Golda Meyerson's reply. We are ready to go a long way against terrorism, she said, even to the point of civil war. However, we cannot order our people to cooperate with you fully.[57] Indeed, the Jewish Agency had launched a third Saison against the Jewish terrorists. But even if the agency's campaign, begun during the period of martial law in March, was now much intensified, it remained uncoordinated with the administration.[58]

Anything less than full cooperation was not an option for Cunningham. The reason was not operational: the organized Yishuv would be no more successful in fighting terrorism than the army. Cooperation was needed to salvage the image of Britain, the administration, the Colonial Office, and his own leadership. In the light of the Jewish Agency's refusal, it was clear to him that his suggestions for punitive measures involving immigration and the economy no longer met London's call for drastic measures. Given his repeated rejection of martial law, his response to the situation came as a surprise. Regrettably, he informed Creech-Jones, he had been compelled to accept the advice of the consultative council (a Mandatory body whose advice the high commissioner took if he wished); namely, that if the Jewish Agency persisted in its refusal the only viable alternative would be to declare martial law throughout Palestine.[59]

After the government itself had ruled out martial law at Cunningham's behest, he himself was now calling for just that remedy, a situation in which he would forgo civilian rule in favor of the military. This would amount to collective punishment, an outcome promoted by the same high commissioner who only two weeks earlier had told UNSCOP that those who believed force was the optimal way to handle terrorism were dead wrong.[60]

The army's response was also seemingly surprising. Middle East headquarters in Cairo was uneasy about Cunningham's threat, veiled or not, to declare martial law in Palestine. The military was not prepared for anything on that scale. Nor, in truth, was Cunningham. He seems to have wanted the idea to remain only that—an idea. His remarks were aimed both laterally, at the War Office and the army, and upward, at the Colonial Office and the government in London. From the government, he expected an announcement that martial law was being given serious consideration. He needed an announcement in that spirit as much as, and perhaps more than, he needed additional forces to implement it.[61]

Cunningham was well aware of the problematic nature of his new stance. Determined not to fall into the pit he had dug for himself, he turned to the source from whom the worst might come, in order to make him a partner to potential success—or to failure, if that were the result. On the thirty-first of July he discovered, to his surprise (and possibly also his chagrin), that with the troops at his disposal Lieutenant General Mac-Millan could impose martial law on Tel Aviv only, and barely even that in order to maintain routine security in the rest of the country. MacMillan also informed him of talk in the army of an imminent downscaling of forces in the Middle East in the wake of the government decision of July 30. This would rule out a March-style military regime. On August 1, the day after the hanging of the British sergeants, Cunningham sent a personal message via MacMillan—and after consultation with him—to General John Crocker, the new GOC Middle East. He explained that in the present conditions the possibility of imposing protracted martial law in Tel Aviv was an essential bargaining card for the administration. It followed that an excessively rapid thinning out of forces would have the opposite effect. He concluded with a remark that could be construed as a threat; certainly it reflected his mood at the time: "I am sending a copy of this telegram to the Secretary of State for the Colonies for unless sufficient forces are maintained here it might be necessary to reorient Palestine policy generally."[62] Cunningham believed that in order to maintain civilian rule, suppress Jewish terrorism, and be ready for a violent eruption by the Arabs—if they felt that the administration had been weakened or that the British were responding to Jewish terrorism less harshly than to the Arab Revolt—he needed to have available larger forces than those he had in August 1947.[63]

This was not just empty bluster. The situation in summer 1947 was inimical to Cunningham as he turned to the military option—although not necessarily because of Jewish terrorism, which he viewed as marginal in the British perspective of the time. In the broader picture, Britain was about to take the historic step of relinquishing its rule in India on August 15 (a development that had a dramatic impact on the strategic importance of Palestine) and was preparing to withdraw from Greece and reduce its military presence in Egypt. Cairo, pressing for the withdrawal of British forces from the Suez Canal in line with a treaty of 1936, had taken its case to the United Nations. Britain had known since August 1946 that it would have to remove most of its forces from Egypt. Until then, Palestine in general and Haifa in particular were perceived as a good alternative to Egypt. But a year later, in the light of international developments and the work of UNSCOP, such a relocation of troops was an anachronistic assumption, even if the army stuck to it.

The UN allowed Britain two more years to maintain forces on the Suez Canal. The government wished to relocate some bases to Kenya as quickly as possible. The situation was aggravated by the severe postwar economic recession in Britain. Hence, the government made its decision on July 30, the day before the murder of the sergeants, to accelerate the downscaling of its armed forces worldwide, particularly in the Middle East. Even had it wished to do so, London was manifestly incapable of committing forces to implement martial law in Palestine. The government was made uneasy by UNSCOP's progress. The decision-makers in London thus had no choice but to deal in short-term planning for redeployment—no more than two years where Palestine and the Middle East were concerned.

The War Office was accordingly instructed to plan a reduction of forces. MacMillan was notified of this development by the end of July, including the possibility that Palestine itself would be affected. From Faid (near the southern end of the Suez Canal, to which Middle East headquarters had been moved from Cairo in view of the planned cutbacks and the concentration of forces on the Suez Canal), he was informed that Field Marshal Montgomery would be visiting the region in the wake of the government's decision. The question of the redeployment in Palestine would be decided in the visit. Montgomery would not leave Egypt, MacMillan was informed, until a decision was made concerning the reduction of forces and redeployment in Palestine. On August 3, MacMillan arrived in Egypt in order to present the viewpoint of the Mandatory authorities, civilian and military, concerning future deployment and immediate needs, on the eve of a possible declaration of martial law throughout Palestine. Faid, he found, was in the grip of an atmosphere of reorganization, and terrorism in Palestine was not at the top of the agenda. MacMillan was not promised reinforcements but was assured that no troop reduction would take place in Palestine at least until the discussions with Montgomery.[64]

It is not clear whether Crocker himself was aware of Cunningham's revised approach on the question of martial law. However, veteran officers in Egypt noticed the change in the high commissioner's demeanor and were skeptical about the tough policy he suddenly wished to implement. Crocker, for his part, could only promise Cunningham and MacMillan all the help they would need. Still, he was not certain he could live up to his promise. After MacMillan left, Crocker hurried to apprise General Simpson, Montgomery's deputy, of the mood in Jerusalem, not omitting to quote the aggressive sections from Cunningham's letter. Crocker informed Simpson that in the present circumstances and considering the plans for the near future, he doubted he would be able to meet his commitment to the high commissioner to impose martial law, even of a limited character. Moreover, he emphasized, it was doubtful whether Britain would be able to maintain its responsibility for Palestine, or only at the expense of its other missions in the Middle East. Crocker then seized on MacMillan's report, after speaking with him that morning, concerning the Yishuv's attitude toward terrorism and the launching of a new Saison by the Jewish Agency. This was the type of argument, anyway, to which Cunningham often resorted. In any event, Montgomery was due to visit Egypt (August 6–8) to decide about redeployment in the Middle East. Because the CIGS had stopped dealing with Palestine since the failure of martial law in March, Crocker asked MacMillan to return to Faid on August 7 in order to brief the field marshal. Throughout this period, Montgomery avoided direct contact with Cunningham.[65]

Montgomery's formal summation following his meeting with Crocker and MacMillan contained a fascinating mix of the necessity to act within the constraints forced on him by the government and his approach to Jewish terrorism together with his undiminished antipathy toward the Yishuv and still more toward the high commissioner. Moreover, he was out to avoid giving the impression that he was curbing the army in its handling of terrorism, even though he was effectively doing just that. Montgomery used Crocker's report and recommendations from August 3 (which echoed the views and needs of the high commissioner) as the basis for his decision, while casting them in his own colors. As suggested by Crocker (in effect, Cunningham), Britain must strike hard against the criminal actions being perpetrated in Palestine. As for the indications (according to Cunningham and MacMillan, via Crocker) that the Jewish Agency was showing encouraging signs of cooperation, we should not make too much of them. It must not be forgotten, Montgomery continued, that the population is hostile to us, and cooperation with them, even if essential, must not divert us from the path of using force of arms against terrorism. On the contrary, he concluded, only a hard hand against the entire population will induce the moderates in the Jewish community to remain active in this regard.[66]

The bottom line, however, was not a recommendation of martial law but a slowdown in the reduction of British forces in Palestine, at least until March 1948, and partial troop reinforcement in the Middle East, enabling MacMillan to beef up his troop levels if needed. Thus, Montgomery ignored the high commissioner, reveled in his ostensible victory, and also did not give Cunningham what he wanted—namely, martial law (which demanded forces he could not provide under the government's new policy). In short, the CIGS, like the high commissioner, was compelled by the dwindling order of battle to prefer declaration to deed.[67]

Although Montgomery could not stem the reduction of forces, he was able to ensure troop reinforcements outside the region in case of need, so that a reasonable force would remain in Palestine. In an internal War Office memorandum, bearing neither date nor addressees, which was drawn up by Montgomery after his visit to Egypt and apparently unknown to the Colonial Office and the high commissioner, the CIGS emphasized the importance of cooperating with the Yishuv in this period and explained why he could not support martial law. The document was closer to Cunningham's basic approach than Montgomery's official summation after the Faid meeting. In this complex state of affairs, Crocker became the key figure charged with transforming Montgomery's thoughts into hard and clear policy. Like MacMillan, Crocker could not ignore Cunningham and had no wish to. On August 12, he met with the high commissioner at Government House to discuss ways of dealing with Jewish terrorism. By this time, the situation was somewhat calmer. The Haganah was doing increasingly effective work against Etzel and Lehi at the behest of the Jewish Agency. Crocker, with Montgomery's tacit backing, provided Cunningham with the military ladder he needed to climb down from the tree of martial law. On the day after his visit to Jerusalem, Crocker summed up the positions taken by the high commissioner between June 1946 and July 1947 in order to clarify Cunningham's decision against imposing martial law. The document was pure Cunningham, noting his objections to collective punishment, which would only heighten hostility; the need for the cooperation of the local population to suppress terrorism originating from within it; and the supremacy of the civilian echelon over the military. The army's role, he summed up, was to support the Mandatory administration, not overrule it. Birds of a feather . . .[68]

Cunningham was left uneasy by the developments in Faid, although not necessarily by Montgomery's disregard of him, which was equally convenient for him. This time, he had been the one to urge the use of military force. The declarative thrust of his call for martial law and his concern about the army's reaction to his unexpected suggestion are discernible in what he wrote to the colonial secretary even before the Faid meeting. Once more, his image formed the background. Irrespective of the army's stance, Cunningham reiterated that no request from it had gone unmet.

On the contrary, he wrote, he was now pressing the army to act, even if the roles were now reversed, at least seemingly. Cunningham expressed himself in this way throughout the crisis, an ongoing riposte to Montgomery.[69]

However, the high commissioner's verbal toughness left the army unimpressed. On September 1, after the majority recommendations of UNSCOP were made known—including a recommendation to end the Mandate—the chief of staff of Middle East Land Forces, Lieutenant General Harold Pyman, sent General Dempsey (GOC Middle East during martial law, in March 1947) an evaluation of Cunningham's performance during this period. Pyman knew Cunningham's history. He had been a junior officer in the Eighth Army at the time of Cunningham's removal in November 1941, had remained there until the Montgomery period, and had been Dempsey's chief of staff in Second Army headquarters in Europe. He accompanied Dempsey to the Middle East and was his chief of staff until 1949. Pyman's evaluation is of interest because it reflects the view of the high commissioner held by Montgomery, Dempsey, and perhaps also Crocker. Palestine is in trouble, Pyman wrote to Dempsey, and the new GOC Middle East holds the same negative opinion about Cunningham as do you. The high commissioner continues to wish for martial rule—we are vehemently opposed. Possibly, Cunningham will go the way of Wavell in India and admit that he can no longer continue serving in the position, leaving the army to remain in Palestine for two more years to end the affair. In fact, it was far from clear that Cunningham "wished for martial rule" that would be his salvation; but it's important that some in the army thought he did.[70]

Once more, Cunningham found support in the Colonial Office, with Creech-Jones, who regarded the high commissioner highly, pulling the chestnuts out of the fire for him. Even before the decision was made at Faid, the colonial secretary wrote Cunningham about the planned declaration regarding the possible introduction of countrywide martial law. It was clear to him that Cunningham did not intend to impose martial law; all he wanted was an announcement by Britain that the idea was under consideration. He asked Cunningham whether, after reexamining the situation, he still thought it was practicable and desirable to impose martial law throughout the country.[71]

In the same letter, Creech-Jones played a neat trick on Cunningham. He went back to the high commissioner's letter of August 1 to the GOC Middle East (of which the minister was also a recipient) explaining the plight of the army in Palestine, this in order to show that declaring countrywide martial law was unfeasible. He then cited Cunningham's well-grounded recommendations of the previous March, in which the high commissioner persuasively explained to the government why he—contrary to Montgomery—believed that declaring martial law in the Yishuv would not benefit British interests. All the changes since then, Creech-Jones noted, made martial law even less practical. The same was true in regard to enforcing martial law during Britain's continuing withdrawal from historic imperial bastions and the UNSCOP report. This could also be said of Cunningham's other suggestions about possible measures against the Jewish Agency. Britain did not wish to implement them—and was incapable of doing so. If, then, the minister—who was on Cunningham's side—continued, in what was almost a reprimand, you cannot impose martial law throughout the whole of Palestine, why make the threat? Creech-Jones added that he was certain Cunningham agreed with him that concrete steps were necessary but that they must be within the realm of Britain's capability: empty threats will only create a perception of hesitancy and weakness.[72]

Cunningham could almost have commissioned this message himself. Moreover, a clear message of support arrived from the government, expressing appreciation and understanding for the difficulties faced by those in the actual arena. The high commissioner's response to Creech-Jones's semi-reprimand was a masterpiece of fence straddling, taking into account both the need to respond and the even greater need to avoid responding. It was clear to him, as it was to the minister, he noted, that both at home and in Palestine action was expected of him, primarily by ill-wishers in both places. But it was equally clear that he must refrain from taking action, because Britain was fettered politically (the Palestine question having been referred to the UN), economically, and in its deployment capability (after the decision on force reductions, no one would impose martial law in any case); that a confrontation with the Jewish community in Palestine would be detrimental to British interests; and also that his personal image obliged a declaration without implementation.[73]

Taking into consideration Creech-Jones's problems on the domestic front, Cunningham led him by circular reasoning to the conclusion that declarations made today would be more meaningful than implementation tomorrow. This followed from his assumption and evaluation that the most disturbing element at present was the firm demand in the House of Commons and among the British public for action to be taken. Accordingly, a declaration was essential. Everything that could be done within the law and that ability and operational creativity made possible had been done, he wrote to Creech-Jones. He and the security forces were racking their brains for new ideas, but unproductively at this stage. Moreover, he noted, he had authorized a form of punishment to which he had objected vehemently in the past: the controlled demolition of houses. Journalists had been invited to cover the demolitions. In addition, for the first time not only the terrorist organizations—Etzel and Lehi—had been targeted but also their political hinterland. Cunningham admitted that he had hesitated initially but then had ordered the arrest of mayors with links to the Revisionist movement or who were known to sympathize with Etzel and had contacts with the organization. The organization's youth movement, Betar, a hothouse of young terrorists, would be outlawed. Newspapers identified with the Revisionist right would be shut down. These actions would mollify the army and the Palestine police. Betar was duly outlawed on August 5–6, and a few leading Revisionists, such as Aryeh Altman, Ze'ev Von Wiesel, and Isaac Remba, the editor of the newspaper *Hamashkif*, were arrested. Also taken into custody were Tel Aviv mayor Israel Rokach and heads of local councils such as Oved Ben-Ami (Netanya) and Avraham Krinitzi (Ramat Gan). Even though they belonged to the bourgeois right, they were considered suspect because they sometimes acted as liaisons with the breakaways, if only to prevent them from carrying out operations.[74]

Nevertheless, Cunningham was by no means certain that the British Parliament or public would appreciate the significance of these arrests of political figures, in any case of the second rank, in a kind of "mini-Agatha." The house demolitions were carried out mainly for domestic (British) consumption. If explosives and cameras were used in reasonable quantities, Cunningham thought perhaps it would be clear that something concrete was being done.[75]

The high commissioner noted, in conclusion, that he understood that exceptional actions were expected of him. He acknowledged that the actions he had taken, although aimed at specific targets and more effective than collective punishment, did not create a proper spectacle.[76] In passing, he rejected as unfeasible the idea, put forward in the House of Commons, of using the Royal Air Force in the battle against terrorism. That is out of the question, he wrote to the minister, particularly when nearly 99 percent of the population has nothing to do with terrorism—unless Tel Aviv, with its population of 180,000, were classified as a terrorist base. The only sensible way to deal with the situation was through a declaration of intent to place the entire country under martial law. Everything else had already been considered and tried, without success. To impose martial law, even partial, only on Jewish population concentrations, would make the British a laughingstock, as the terrorists would continue to act in the other regions. As for implementation: in any event, a declaration of a military regime would be little more than a formality, because the army was already stretched to the limit and the civilian administration could continue to function informally even under ostensible military rule. The important considerations were that the Yishuv very much feared such a move and that it would be greeted with satisfaction at home.[77]

And remind Parliament, Cunningham added in a separate cable to Creech-Jones a week later, about the wonderful work the administration and the army are doing, at the risk of life and limb. Explain to them that the situation in Palestine is such that we have to be ready to impose martial law at any moment. However, this option is being deferred in order to give the Jewish Agency the opportunity to fulfill its decisions and fight Jewish terrorism with determination and without mercy.[78]

Cunningham understood and accepted the minister's approach. From his point of view, the question centered on the cost to him in personal terms, particularly if he were forced to give up his powers to MacMillan under martial law. In any event, martial law, even full, would not solve the problem of terrorism. According to Cunningham, MacMillan was sorry he, Cunningham, had raised the idea of martial law, as he lacked sufficient forces, a situation that was unlikely to change given the reaction by Middle East headquarters in Egypt. To ensure he would not have to follow through on his martial law threat, the high commissioner back-tracked elegantly from his ultimatum to the Jewish Agency—that it must declare its full cooperation with him in the campaign against terrorism— to a more convenient position. He understood the agency's preference for independent action against terrorism, he wrote on August 4. That might not be the most effective method, but the agency's argument—that an announcement of cooperation with the British would undermine its authority and thereby leave it unable to act independently against the breakaway groups—should be accepted. Accordingly, he would not press now for a declaration of full cooperation with the administration in the struggle against terrorism.[79]

Thus, yesterday's unconditional demand and Cunningham's open disappointment at the Jewish Agency's response became today's haven, complete with an option for martial law—if and when—and also a good excuse to avoid that measure. From the start of the debate over martial law, in spring 1947, Cunningham had relied on the Jewish Agency's control of the Yishuv and its will to fight the terrorism of the breakaway organizations. In March, that reliance had been a good reason to terminate martial law and even rule it out as a future option. Now, in August, it would be enough if the Jewish Agency's Saison would give the administration the leeway to threaten martial law without having to make good on the threat.

Creech-Jones agreed wholeheartedly. Under martial law, he wrote, Britain could find itself in a full-scale confrontation with the Jews and also upset the Arabs, who themselves would be affected. It was important for the Yishuv to know that failure to cooperate in the effort to eradicate terrorism would harm its cause in London and might prompt Britain to take harsh measures. Antiterrorist action was also helpful to the Jewish position in Geneva, where UNSCOP was meeting. The Colonial Office grasped the duality, not to say contradictions, in Cunningham's approach to the question of martial law. However, the duality was not a problem in a situation in which none of the decision-makers truly wanted martial law—on the contrary.[80]

The decision was made, the thrust was clear: to avoid imposing martial law and buy time until the definitive decision was made in Geneva and New York. Indeed, the referral of the Mandate to the United Nations left Britain unable to take drastic measures. It was no longer a simple matter to introduce martial law or issue another white paper. The truly important question now was what UNSCOP would recommend to the General Assembly. Its report would change the agenda in Palestine. Chomping at the bit, Cunningham on August 6 fired off an urgent personal cable to the Colonial Office liaison officer in Geneva. Was it true, he wanted to know, that UNSCOP would announce its recommendations on the thirty-first of the month, as had been reported to him? From the perspective of those in Palestine, the date is of surpassing importance, he noted. But the reply was disappointing. After a two-week wait, he was informed by the liaison officer, Donald MacGillivray, that there was no chance of a statement by the committee before September 10.[81]

Disaster could strike Palestine at any moment. If Cunningham had not already known that he and his administration were living on borrowed time, confirmation came on the day that Creech-Jones authorized the high commissioner to impose "declarative martial law." The background was Etzel's detonation of a powerful bomb in the Mandatory administration's Labor Bureau in Jerusalem on August 5. Three people were killed, including a policeman, and the building was seriously damaged. The Labor Bureau was located in the former German consulate on the Street of the Prophets, in a Jewish area, outside the British security zones. Cunningham kept his promise that the security zones would be hermetically sealed, but nuances of location were not visible from London. Tough questions were hurled in the House of Commons. Cunningham explained that British subjects rarely found themselves in the area where the attack had taken place.[82]

Within a few days of the crisis brought on by the murder of the sergeants, Cunningham had regained his former patience. On August 10, after the impact of the murder and of the arrests made in its wake had abated, and as the outrage over the Labor Bureau attack had also faded, the high commissioner reaffirmed his credo: cooperation with the Jewish Agency and anticipation of a political solution. By the second week of August, the need for martial law had receded. A palpable expectancy regarding the UNSCOP recommendations began to be felt about three weeks before they were published.

As in similar cases, the emotions on the street anticipated those of the leaders. A feeling of fraught change hung in the air. The administration's weekly reports for August 1947 and its log of events in that period show a steady decline in the number of terrorist attacks by Etzel and Lehi against the British. The breakaway groups, whose activity had long harmed the Zionist cause, now became even less relevant in contemporary eyes. This atmosphere facilitated the Jewish Agency's campaign against them. But now an old-new front burst powerfully into the center of the arena: bloody clashes between Jews and Arabs spurred by the coming UNSCOP decision. The violence was especially intense along the Tel Aviv–Jaffa seam line. Most of the incidents were spontaneous, and they were not large scale, but the potential for trouble was ever present and generated pervasive anxiety. The administration counted about a thousand hours of confrontations (simultaneously) between Jews and Arabs in the two-week period beginning on the first of August, in most cases with casualties.

Not since the late 1930s had anything comparable occurred. The Arabs blamed a "mysterious hand" and the Jews; the Jews blamed the Arabs and the British. Increasingly, the administration and the security forces became preoccupied with curfew, closure, searches, arrests, and the like. Talk of a civil war had not yet surfaced in August, nor had the question of how the British authorities should react to such a development. However, the escalating situation allowed Cunningham to invoke the approach he had brought to Palestine in the first place: that of the mediating ruler who tries to advance a solution. On August 17, a little more than two weeks before UNSCOP would publish its recommendations, the high commissioner issued a public appeal to both sides in an effort to restore calm.[83]

Evidence of an incipient return to normality, at least from the administration's perspective, can be seen in the serious consideration given beginning on August 29 to the possibility of returning to Palestine the wives of the officials and police officers who had been sent home the previous winter. Despite the UNSCOP recommendations, to be published at the end of the month, or perhaps because of them, the feeling in the local British community was that the pressure of terrorism had receded. At the end of August, the day before the recommendations were made public, and with no connection to them, the cabinet decided on an additional troop reduction in the Middle East, and that in any event martial law would not be imposed in Palestine.[84]

Cunningham now faced a new and complicated task, which would occupy him until his departure from Palestine eight and a half months later. His mission was nothing less than to dismantle the Mandatory entity in an honorable manner—for Britain's sake and his own—a project made infinitely more problematic by being carried out amid an intensifying civil war in the country. From the summer of 1946 on, Cunningham, like his colleagues in Britain, had watched as the Zionist movement increasingly looked to the United States to advance its cause; and, from the following spring on, to the United Nations as well. Neither he nor they viewed the American orientation positively, although Cunningham did welcome the UN's involvement in Palestine. It was the end of a period, certainly from Cunningham's viewpoint.[85]

At the end of August 1947, before UNSCOP published its momentous recommendations, the high commissioner visited London. He returned to Jerusalem a month later, to a completely different reality.

NOTES

1. Cunningham to Creech-Jones, January 29, 1947, NA C0537/2418.

2. For the course of events, see Charters, *The British Army*, pp. 190–191, and Slutzky, *History of the Haganah*, III, 2, p. 920. On the caning episode, see chapter 6 and Amir Goldstein, *Heroism and Exclusion: The "Gallows Martyrs" and Israeli Collective Memory*, Jerusalem 2011, p. 106 (Hebrew).

3. Cunningham to Creech-Jones, January 29, 1947, NA C0537/2418.

4. Ben-Gurion, *Toward the End of the Mandate*, pp. 324–326; Goldstein, *Heroism and Exclusion*, pp. 106–110.

5. Cunningham to Creech-Jones, January 29, 1947.

6. Cunningham to Hall, August 3, 1946, August 9, 1946, NA C0537/1708; Hall to Cunningham, August 8, 1946; Cunningham to Hall, January 26, 1946, MECA CP, B1, F1/29.

7. Creech-Jones to Cunningham, January 29, 1947, NA C0537/2418.

8. Cunningham to Creech-Jones, January 30, 1947, NA C0537/2418, no. 208.

9. Goldstein, *Heroism and Exclusion*, pp. 106–110.

10. Cunningham to Creech-Jones, January 30, 1947, NA C0537/2418, no. 214.

11. Ibid.

12. Cunningham to Creech-Jones, January 31, 1947, NA C0537/2418, no. 214; "Conversation of His Eminence the Chief Rabbi I. L. Herzog with the High Commissioner, February 1, 1947," CZA S25/22.

13. "Conversation of His Eminence," CZA S25/22; Fletcher-Cooke (chief undersecretary for administration and finance, who was sent to Transjordan to assess conditions to absorb families there) to the historian Elizabeth Monroe, February 23, 1966, MECA GB 165–010.

14. Cunningham to Creech-Jones, January 30, 1947, NA C0537/2418, no. 217.

15. Cunningham to Creech-Jones, February 1, 1947, NA C0537/2418, nos. 221, 224, 228; A. J. Sherman, *Mandate Days: British Lives in Palestine, 1918–1948*, New York 1997, pp. 192, 201.

16. Creech-Jones to Cunningham, February 3, 1947, NA C0537/2418.

17. Cunningham to Creech-Jones, February 4, 1947, NA C0537/2418.

18. Creech-Jones to Cunningham, February 5, 1947, NA C0537/2418.

19. Commander-in-chief, Middle East, to the theater's director of operations (DMO), March 3, 1947, LHCMA, Pyman 9/13; "The Palestine Gazette Extraordinary 1558 of 2nd March 47 under Authority of Article 6, Palestine (Defense) Order-in-Council, 1937"; Niv, *Campaigns of the Irgun Zvai Leumi [Etzel]*, Part IV, pp. 102–104.

20. "Situation in Palestine, Memorandum by the Secretary of State for the Colonies to the Prime Minister," March 19, 1947, NA PREM8/864; "Orders of the Military Governor regarding Arrangements of the Military Government," as distributed to the population of Greater Tel Aviv in Hebrew, March 2, 1947, TAMA, Aleph-4-10.

21. On Wauchope's approach to the question of martial law, see Eyal, *The First Intifada*, pp. 175–220. Of course, the debate over this issue did not begin in Palestine; Ireland in the 1920s was a high-profile, precedent-setting case; Memorandum of colonial secretary, March 19, 1947, NA PREM8/864.

22. "Situation in Palestine, Memorandum by the Secretary of State," March 19, 1947.

23. "Orders of the Military Governor," March 2, 1947; David Idelson, Social Work Department in Tel Aviv, to Mayor Israel Rokach, March 5, 1947, TAMA, Bet-4-10; Dr. Schlesinger, Social Work Department, to Rokach, March 6, 1947, TAMA, Bet-4-10; Committee of the Maccabi Shanties Neighborhood in Jaffa to Rokach, March 7, 1947, TAMA, Daled-10-4.

24. Municipality circular to the residents, March 6, 1947, TAMA, Aleph-10-4; "Note on Points Raised by Mayors and by Representatives of Local Councils at Meeting with the Military Liaison Officers, TA, on the 6th March 47," TAMA, Aleph-10-4; Meetings of the Tel Aviv Situation Committee, March 8, 11, 12, 1947, Aleph-10-4; Broadcast by the mayor of Tel Aviv to the city's residents, March 8, 1947; Hila Friedman, "Activity of the British in Tel Aviv, March 1947–May 1948," seminar paper, University of Haifa, June 2003, pp. 3–8.

25. Interview with General Sir Gordon MacMillan, September 6, 1983, "End of the Empire Transcripts," Vol. 2, RHLO, Nss. Bit. Emp., S. 527.

26. Meeting of Tel Aviv–Jaffa Municipality Situation Committee and afterward of the Municipal Council, March 3, 1947, TAMA, Gimel-10-4.

27. Dempsey to MacMillan, March 3, 1947, LHCMA, Pyman, 7/1/3.

28. Dempsey to Montgomery, March 4, 1947, LHCMA, Pyman, 7/1/3.

29. Montgomery to Dempsey, March 4, 1947, LHCMA, Pyman, 7/1/3.

30. From memorandum of the colonial secretary, March 19, 1947, NA PREM8/864.

31. Meeting of the Tel Aviv Municipal Council, March 9, 1947, TAMA, Gimel-10-4; Memorandum of the colonial secretary, March 19, 1947.

32. Dempsey to Montgomery, March 4, 1947, LHCMA, Pyman, 7/1/3; Montgomery to Dempsey, March 22, 1947, LHCMA, Pyman, 7/1/3; Memorandum of colonial secretary, March 19, 1947, NA PREM8/864; "Palestine—Imposition of Martial Law, Report by the Chiefs of Staff to the Prime Minister," March 26, 1947, NA PREM8/864.

33. Memorandum of colonial secretary, March 19, 1947; Memorandum of chiefs of staff, March 26, 1947, NA PREM8/864, see note 32. MacMillan's approach is clear from the very fact of his cooperation with Cunningham, and from his testimony on September 6, 1983, "End of the Empire Transcripts."

34. Warner, *Auchinleck*, p. 212. There was nothing new in the friction between the heads of the branches; it existed during the Second World War as well, but Alanbrooke was able to run the committee efficiently. "Alanbrooke, Notes of My Life, Draft, Vol. V, CIGS: The Beginning 1941–1942," May 19, 1942, LHCMA 5/2/17; Hamilton, *The Field Marshal*, pp. 641–647. Arthur Tedder (1890–1967) was Air Force Commander-in-Chief, Middle East, at the time Cunningham was relieved of command of the Eighth

Army, and from 1946 to 1950 he was chief of the Air Staff and chairman of the Chiefs of Staff Committee (CSC). Admiral Cunningham (1885–1962) succeeded Andrew, Alan's brother, as First Sea Lord and was a member of the CSC in 1946–1948. Frank Simpson (1899–1986) was Montgomery's deputy in 1946–1948.

35. Montgomery to Dempsey, March 4, 1947, March 12, 1947, LHCMA, Pyman 7/1/3; Dempsey to Montgomery, March 4, 1947, March 20, 1947, March 23, 1947, LHCMA, Pyman 7/1/3; Dempsey to MacMillan, March 23, 1947, LHCMA, Pyman 7/1/3.

36. "Palestine: Security Measures, Memorandum by the Secretary of State for the Colonies, Printed for the Cabinet," July 19, 1947, NA PREM8/864.

37. Pinhas Ofer, *Enemy and Rival: The Zionist Movement and the Yishuv between the Arabs and the British, 1929–1948*, Tel Aviv 2001, p. 223 (Hebrew); Cunningham to Creech-Jones, April 4, 1947, NA CO537/2418.

38. High commissioner to colonial secretary, monthly report, July 9, 1947, MECA CP, B2, F1/78. The *History of the Haganah*, in which the data are generally reliable despite the slanted interpretation, struggles to admit to this episode. However, its own information, III, 2, pp. 592–596, reflects this trend. See also p. 956.

39. "Memorandum on the Comparative Treatment of the Arabs during the Disturbances of 1936–39 and of the Jews during the Disturbances of 1945 and Subsequent Years," June 19, 1947, MECA CP, B2, F1/54.

40. Ibid.

41. Cunningham memorandum, June 19, 1947, MECA CP, B2, F1/54.

42. Ibid.

43. Montgomery to MacMillan, June 20, 1947, MECA CP, B6, F1/55.

44. High commissioner to colonial secretary, monthly report for June 1947, July 9, 1947, MECA CP, B2, F1/76.

45. "Notes on the Address Given by the High Commissioner," CZA A366.

46. See, for example, ibid.; High commissioner to colonial secretary, and weekly intelligence assessment, July 13, 1947, MECA CP, B2, F1, no. 93; Daily reports, July 17–30, 1947, MECA CP, B2, F1. Thus, for example, three reports about the Acre Prison break were sent from Jerusalem, all written by Fox-Strangways and all businesslike; not a word from the high commissioner. MECA CP, B2, F1, nos. 5–7.

47. Fox-Strangways for high commissioner to colonial secretary, July 12, 1947, MECA CP, B2, F/1/89; on this affair from the viewpoint of the Yishuv and the breakaways, Slutzky, *History of the Haganah*, III, 2, pp. 925–929; Niv, *Maarachot* 5, pp. 161–163, 277–282.

48. "Palestine: Security Measures," July 19, 1947; Grinwood for high commissioner to colonial secretary, July 17–July 30, 1947, MECA CP, B2, F1.

49. Fox-Strangways for high commissioner to colonial secretary, weekly intelligence assessment, July 25, 1947, MECA CP, B2, F1, no. 164.

50. Weekly intelligence assessment, July 31, 1947, MECA CP, B2, F1, nos. 193, 195; High commissioner to colonial secretary, monthly report for July 1947, MECA CP, B2, F1, no. 33.

51. Weekly intelligence assessment, August 1, 1947, MECA CP, B2, F1, no. 2; Cunningham to Creech-Jones, "secret and personal," August 1, 1947, MECA CP, B2, F1, no. 5; Cunningham to Creech-Jones, "secret and personal," August 2, 1947, MECA CP, B2, F1, no. 7. A preliminary investigation indicated that most of the rioters were policemen; the police inspector-general set up a committee of inquiry. Cunningham to Creech-Jones, July 4, 1947, MECA CP, B2, F1, no. 17; "Notes on the Address Given by the High Commissioner," CZA A366.

52. Cunningham to Creech-Jones, August 1, 2, 1947, MECA CP, B2, F1/5; Weekly intelligence assessment, August 2, 1947, MECA CP, B2, F2/9; Cunningham to Thomas Lloyd (permanent undersecretary of state for the colonies), August 4, 1947, MECA CP, B2, F2, no. 20; Cunningham to Creech-Jones, "secret and personal," August 5, 1947, MECA CP, B2, F2, no. 19.

53. Cunningham to Creech-Jones, July 31, 1947, MECA CP, B2, F2, no. 194.

54. Creech-Jones to Cunningham, August 1, 1947, MECA CP, B2, F1/4. On the street reactions in Britain, see: Michael J. Cohen, *Palestine and the Great Powers, 1945–1948*, Princeton 1982, p. 245; Simon Garfield, *Our Hidden Lives: The Remarkable Diaries of Post-War Britain*, London 2005, pp. 428–432; "Text of Question and Answer in Parliament, Thursday, 31 July 47," July 31, 1947, MECA CP, B2, F1, no. 190.

55. Creech-Jones to Cunningham, August 1, 1947, MECA CP, B2, F1, nos. 3, 4.

56. Cunningham to Creech-Jones, August 4, 1947, MECA CP, B2, F2/17.

57. Cunningham to Creech-Jones, August 1, 1947, MECA B2, F2/5.

58. For more on this topic, see Yaʿakov Shavit, *Open Season: The Confrontation between the "Organized Yishuv" and the Underground Organizations (Etzel and Lehi), 1937–1947*, Tel Aviv 1976 (Hebrew).

59. Cunningham to Creech-Jones, August 1, 1947, MECA B2, F2/5.

60. "Notes on the Address Given by the High Commissioner," CZA A366.

61. Cunningham to Creech-Jones, August 1, 1947.

62. Cunningham to Crocker, August 1, 1947, LHCMA, Pyman, 7/1/8.

63. Cunningham to Creech-Jones, "confidential and personal," July 31, 1947, MECA, B2, F1/194. Crocker (1896–1963) was a veteran of armored warfare. He commanded I Corps in the Normandy landing and until the German surrender in May 1945. Afterward, he was GOC Southern Command in Britain, and from 1947 to 1950 was commander-in-chief, Middle East Land Forces. An unsuccessful candidate to succeed Montgomery as CIGS, he was adjutant general until his retirement in 1953. Crocker was known as "Honest John." High commissioner to colonial secretary, weekly intelligence assessment, August 2, 1947, MECA CP, B2, F2/9.

64. Montgomery to Crocker, July 28, 1947, LHCMA, Pyman 7/1/8. On the eve of Montgomery's visit to Egypt at the beginning of August, Crocker still tried to propose Palestine as an alternative to Egypt: "Operational Factors—Palestine and Egypt," LHCMA, Pyman 7/1/8; Louis, *The British Empire*, p. 446; Phillip Darby, *British Defence Policy East of Suez, 1947–1968*, London 1973, pp. 9–44.

65. Crocker to Simpson, August 3, 1947, NA WO216/221.

66. "Conference No. 2—Location: Commander-in-Chief's Office. Palestine and Discussion with Gen. MacMillan," August 7, 1947, NA WO216/221.

67. Ibid.

68. "The Problems of the Army in the Middle East, Memorandum by the CIGS," NA WO216/670; Crocker to Cunningham, August 13, 1947, LHCMA, Pyman 7/1/8.

69. Cunningham to Creech-Jones, "confidential and personal," August 4, 1947, MECA CP, B2, F2/14.

70. Pyman to Dempsey, September 1, 1947, LHCMA, Pyman, 7/3/6. Pyman (1908–1971) later became deputy chief of the Imperial General Staff (1958–1961) and commander-in-chief of NATO forces in Northern Europe, retiring in 1964.

71. Creech-Jones to Cunningham, "confidential and personal," August 2, 1947, MECA CP, B2, F2/7.

72. Ibid.

73. Cunningham to Creech-Jones, "confidential and personal," August 4, 1947, MECA CP, B2, F2/7.

74. Ibid.

75. On the individual grounds for detention: [First name unavailable] Stewart for high commissioner to colonial secretary, August 10, 1947, MECA CP, B2, F2, no. 52; Weekly intelligence assessment, August 9, 1947, MECA CP, B2, F2, nos. 46–47.

76. Cunningham to Creech-Jones, "confidential and personal," August 2, 1947, MECA CP, B2, F2/7.

77. Ibid.

78. Cunningham to Creech-Jones, August 10, 1947, MECA CP, B2, F2/54.

79. Cunningham to Creech-Jones, August 4, 1947, MECA CP, B2, F2/14.

80. Creech-Jones to Cunningham, "confidential and personal," August 5, 1947, MECA CP, B2, F2/21; Charters, *The British Army*, p. 110.

81. Cunningham to MacGillivray, August 6, 1947, MECA CP, B2, F2/24; MacGillivray to Cunningham, August 22, 1947, MECA CP, B2, F2/80.

82. Stewart for high commissioner to colonial secretary, August 5, 1947, MECA CP, B2, F2/23; Colonial secretary to high commissioner, August 8, 1947, MECA CP, B2, F2/28.

83. High commissioner, weekly intelligence assessment, August 18, 1947, MECA CP, B2, F2/75–76, and also August 23, 1947, MECA CP, B2, F2/82–83; Administration's log of events, e.g., August 16–17, 1947, MECA CP, B2, F2/72, 74.

84. Acting high commissioner (Gurney) to colonial secretary, August 29, 1947, NA C0537/2418; Weekly intelligence assessment, September 14, 1947, MECA CP, B2, F2/104; Cabinet meeting, August 30, 1947, NA CAB128/10; Charteris (Foreign Office) to Mathieson (Colonial Office), September 10, 1947, NA C0537/2299.

85. The Zionist movement's turn to the United States is discussed extensively in Heller, "From Black Sabbath to Partition."

Epilogue

On May 1, 1948, two weeks before he left Palestine, Cunningham turned sixty-one. Having retired from the army in October 1946, he now was about to retire from his brief service in the Colonial Office. The age at which he left the service was not unusual in comparison with the six high commissioners who preceded him in Palestine. With the exception of Herbert Samuel, who was fifty-five when he concluded his term as high commissioner and whose public career lasted many more years, the conclusion of the high commissioners' respective periods in Palestine marked the end of their public service. Five of them, Cunningham included, arrived in Jerusalem when they were between fifty-six and fifty-eight years old. The exception was Herbert Plumer, who was sixty-eight. Two of them, who came from the Colonial Office (John Chancellor, who started out in the army but arrived in Jerusalem after a long career in the colonies, and Harold MacMichael), wanted to go on contributing after their tenure in Palestine but did not receive a meaningful appointment. The military men among the high commissioners—Plumer, Arthur Wauchope, and John Gort—retired immediately. All three, like Cunningham, had joined the Colonial Office for the sole purpose of serving in Palestine. Two of them (Plumer and Gort) retired with the rank of field marshal, which effectively ruled out an additional operational appointment. They died not long after their return from Palestine.

From the point of view of their age and life experience, only Wauchope recalls Cunningham: Scottish, unmarried, a soldier from youth who received the rank of general during his tenure in Palestine in order to retire from the army while still there. Wauchope, too, had to cope with an insurgency—in his case, by the Arabs—which was broader and fiercer than the Jewish uprising during Cunningham's period. He, too, was at loggerheads with the army over control in Palestine, both in principle and in practice. Wauchope's tenure as high commissioner was almost three times as long as Cunningham's (seven years versus two and a half). He was sixty-four when he left Palestine. His death, in September 1947, while Cunningham was on an extended visit to Britain, was a significant loss for the latter. The two had become very close during Cunningham's tenure as high commissioner. Both were ardent proponents of partition. Whereas the support for the Yishuv by Samuel, a Jew and a Zionist, was to be expected (though amid disagreements with the Zionist leadership), this was not the case with Wauchope and Cunningham. Neither man was "prone" to a pro-Zionist stance. In contrast to Wauchope, Cunningham was healthy when he retired; he did not rule out continued involvement in the affairs of the Colonial Office.[1]

However, no one offered General Sir Alan Gordon Cunningham another appointment in the empire. Indeed, such offers were becoming scarcer as the empire itself dwindled. What remained were colonies that wanted to detach themselves from Britain. The traits required for service in them were determination, energy, and a younger age. Cunningham was not appointed high commissioner of Malaya (afterward Malaysia) when that post suddenly became available in summer 1948. The appointment went to Sir Henry Gurney, who was the chief secretary of the Mandatory administration in Palestine from September 1946 until May 14, 1948. Gurney had displayed firmness and sangfroid in Jerusalem, and was more than ten years Cunningham's junior. It is not clear whether Cunningham's name was put forward as a candidate for the Malaya post by anyone else or by himself. What is clear is that the fresh experience of Palestine was very much in demand at the time, particularly in locales of rampant violence, such as Malaya. Accompanying Gurney to Malaya as inspector-general of the police force was William Gray, who had held the same post in Palestine. Gurney was assassinated in Malaya in October 1951 and was succeeded by General Sir Hugh Stockwell, who had been commander-in-chief of the Sixth Airborne Division, Haifa and the North, until May 14, 1948. He served as military governor of Malaya from 1952 until 1954. Cunningham's experience found no takers.[2]

No life story can be neatly schematized. Alan Cunningham had a story of his own. Having spent his whole adult life in the army, even when he was stationed in the British Isles, followed by a brief stint in the colonial service, he was effectively homeless. In part, this was because he did not have a family of his own: he had not yet married. Moreover, even though he came from a Scottish family and viewed himself as a Scotsman, according to his own testimony, the fact that he was born and grew up in Ireland left him without a deep sense of community.

Upon leaving Palestine, Sir Alan was ready to put himself at the disposal of the colonial secretary in regard to the liquidation of Britain's affairs in Israel and to the personal fate of his staff. The aspiration to actualize his newly rehabilitated status, as he saw it, after having emerged unscathed from Palestine—and taking a firm stand against the Jews, the Arabs, and his colleagues or rivals from the army and the Foreign Office—together with the need to find a home occupied him during his final months in Government House. Immediately upon his arrival in Britain, he asked the permanent undersecretary of state for the colonies, Thomas Lloyd, for time off. He wanted to look for a house in a rural region and busy himself in the way so many British generals did after retiring: by puttering in the garden. His fondness for this hobby had been apparent during his residence at Government House. At the beginning of August 1946, at the height of the crisis fomented by the King David Hotel bombing, the harassed high commissioner found time to correspond with a colleague who had retired from the army to his garden. The two discussed saplings and seeds that would be sent for the garden at Government House. Cunningham was very fond of cultivating the garden in Jerusalem, but no garden of his own awaited him in Britain.[3]

Lloyd assured Cunningham that even if he should need him for a few days, he would afterward be able to enjoy an uninterrupted vacation. The tone he adopted with Cunningham showed great appreciation, but also, as can be seen in retrospect, was calculated not to hurt him. Cunningham was also promised a risk increment that would translate into a salary worth two and a half times an annual vacation at full pay, for the two and a half years he had spent in Palestine under conditions recognized as highly adverse. The result was that Cunningham received a onetime vacation grant of £3,000. From his point of view, the principle was no less important than the money. The last time he had been given a long break, in December 1941, he had been forced to take sick leave under circumstances that had hardly been beneficial. As for the financial remuneration, he was very much in need of it. Although he did not realize it upon his retirement, the concrete worth of his pension would continue to haunt him. In 1971, the elderly Sir Alan was compelled to forgo his honor and send a desperate letter to the foreign secretary, Sir Alec Douglas-Home. He complained that he could not subsist on his army pension, despite his long military career, and had not served the minimal time required in the Colonial Office to be entitled to a pension from that quarter. He therefore lived off his relatively small army pension, augmented by an addition of £50 per annum for his first three years of service (1906–1909) and his small savings from his army salary. He requested that the minister arrange for his pension rights to be equalized to those of the early 1970s, which were more generous than for the retirees of the 1940s. Because he had been employed by the Colonial Office for only two and a half years, his pension was not calculated on the basis of his salary as high commissioner. A high commissioner who served a minimum of four years received a government pension equivalent to that of the ranking officers in the armed forces, cabinet ministers, and even the prime minister. Sir Alan never seemed to get what he wanted.[4]

In 1951, the sixty-four-year-old lifelong bachelor married Margery Agnes Slater Snagge, who was twenty years his junior. The widow of Sir Harold Edward Snagge, she was the daughter of Henry Slater, a senior official in the colonial service in India.[5] Alan and Margery set up home in Whitchurch, a small village, quite remote, in Hants (Hampshire) County. Cunningham wanted to live as close as possible to his brother Andrew, the former Admiral of the Fleet, who resided a little to the south of Whitchurch, in a town called Bishop's Waltham, not far from Southampton. As Cunningham could not afford to buy a house, the state rented him the lodge of the guard at Hurstbourne Park. In this Georgian cottage, which was pleasing to the eye but cramped as living quarters, Sir Alan maintained a modest and highly frugal life. An elderly live-in couple looked after the household. Sir Alan was given a few honorific tasks that took up little time, so he was able to devote himself to gardening and fishing. He also spent long hours listening to music. Occasionally, he traveled to London to see and be seen in the club of which he was a member until his last day, the Athenaeum in Pall Mall. In 1969, the state sold the lodge and the former high commissioner had to move again, at the age of eighty-two. The Cunninghams moved to Margery's father's house in Yalding, located in County Kent, south of London. But until this residence could be renovated, Alan and Margery found no other solution than to move into one of the homes of an assistant to the former high commissioner.[6]

Cunningham was not prone to express himself in public, still less about his past. This made sense in connection with the Western Desert episode of 1941, his resounding failure. But why did he not try to capitalize on his period in Palestine? Already in June 1944, Lieutenant General Cunningham wrote to Major General John Kennedy, the director of military operations at the War Office and the officer in charge of the pre-research military history of the Second World War, that when it comes to struggles over the past, silence is golden.[7]

In the late 1970s, General Sir Alan Gordon Cunningham was transferred to a nursing home in Tunbridge Wells, in southern England. He died there on Sunday January 30, 1983, not long before his ninety-sixth birthday. A private funeral was held, attended by family. He remained almost unknown, but not quite. In 2007, there was someone in Whitchurch, now a town, who still remembered Sir Alan. The person, who had bought the lodge in 1969, forcing the Cunninghams to leave, still lived there and recalled him vividly. He was never as salty as his brother Andrew, the man explained, without being asked what he thought about the former tenant.[8]

In fact, the results of Cunningham's activity did not disappear with him. His contribution to the Palestine question from 1945 to 1947 was meaningful in connection with several fraught issues: the political solution, Jewish immigration, the Yishuv/Zionist struggle against British policy, and the terrorism perpetrated by Etzel and Lehi. He was the most outstanding of the senior British officials who dealt with the Palestine question when it came to promoting the partition idea. In 1946, partition was not a popular notion in London, to put it mildly. From late 1947 onward, Britain sought to advance the idea in Palestine, albeit not necessarily according to the United Nations plan. Even if supporters of partition, such as Colonial Secretary George Hall and his successor, Arthur Creech-Jones, and of course Cunningham, lost the battle at the time, the powerful foreign secretary, Ernest Bevin, ultimately made use of the concept in order to promote a division of the country between Jordan and Israel. This effort succeeded and held fast until 1967. (Indeed, de jure the situation has not changed, as long as Israel does not annex the territories it conquered from Jordan in the Six-Day War.) The post-1948 "Green Line" is certainly a possible (some would say a leading) framework for the country's partition, this time between Israel and the Palestinians. In a certain sense, Alan Cunningham was present at the birth of the State of Israel when he grasped, in the winter and spring of 1946, that partition was the only solution to the Jewish-Arab conflict between the Jordan River and the Mediterranean.

On immigration, the last high commissioner thought that a large influx of refugees would engender a bloodbath and most certainly make British rule in the country impossible. At the same time, he was sensitive to the moral aspect, which in this case was bolstered by his basic sympathy for the Zionist cause. Concurrently, he understood that the Arabs could not accept an open-borders policy with regard to Jewish immigration. This was another reason, from his point of view, to persist in promoting the partition idea: partition would resolve the immigration issue, which in his view was second to that of the political solution. It was not only the British who viewed immigration as a political matter, he believed; the Jews, and certainly the Arabs, also considered it so. Cunningham found it highly problematic that on immigration, the Zionist leaders rejected the legality of the Mandate, which they held very dear. For the Arabs, every action concerning immigration done in the spirit of the Balfour Declaration represented a breach of Britain's commitment to them, whereas for the Jews, every action *against* the spirit of Balfour on immigration was considered a breach of Britain's commitment to them. The proponents of Jewish activism were unwilling to talk to the Arabs about this issue and thereby reach what Cunningham believed was a possible compromise to allow measured immigration on a humanitarian basis.

Cunningham's involvement in the "Cyprus episode" made a solid contribution to stabilizing the situation in Palestine in a period that was difficult for both Britain and for the two communities that inhabited the country. His policy in this connection bore a clear implication for his success in withdrawing from the country with at least a semblance of control, a crucial matter for Britain at that time on the world stage. That semblance also reduced significantly the clashes between Jews and Arabs, at least until late in April 1948.

His influence on the handling of the Jewish terrorism of the time is seen mainly in regard to the question of how to combat it. When it came to the practical decision of fighting terrorism in Palestine, Cunningham was more significant than the commanders-in-chief in Palestine during his tenure—D'Arcy, Barker, and MacMillan—as well as the commanders of the Middle East arena and even the chiefs of the Imperial General Staff, Alanbrooke and Montgomery. The civilian administration maintained its supremacy over the army on this issue to the last. Closures, searches, arrests, rampaging through the streets, not to mention an antisemitic remark like the one uttered by Barker in July 1946 (as discussed in chapter 5) may be "flashier," but the fact is that Cunningham, by means of persistent, dogged effort, remained in control of the army and the police under particularly difficult conditions. It was due to Cunningham's firm stand in the face of his opponents—in the government above him, in the army, which operated parallel to him, and among his subordinates in the administration—that restraint was placed on the security forces and martial law was imposed partially for only two weeks, in March 1947. As a result, he was able to maintain the administration's deterrent capability and bring about the eventual moderation of the Yishuv's response to British policy, which did not change quickly enough or take the right direction from the Zionist point of view.

The thrust of Cunningham's policy was that it was pointless to seek a military solution to terrorism. He prevented the army from dealing with the Yishuv in the same way it had dealt with the Arab Revolt of 1936–1939. Of course, two broad external factors came to his aid: the spirit of the time and Britain's grim postwar situation. Still, in the spring of 1946 and again a year later, when conditions were ripe for martial law, Cunningham blocked it. He insisted on a dialogue with the Jewish Agency, and not only about terrorism. He played a major role in thwarting the intention first by the Colonial Office and later by the War Office to liquidate the Jewish Agency. His failure to bring about a replacement of the agency's senior figures—a hopeless idea from the start—was due to his misreading of the organization's democratic dynamics and the basic sympathy for Britain harbored by the strongman of the time, David Ben-Gurion. After grasping the true situation in the final months of the Mandate, he made no more approaches to Weizmann. He turned instead in late 1946 and early 1947 to Ben-Gurion, whom he viewed as his chief interlocutor, notwithstanding his disgust with him. But this was a case of too little and, above all, too late.

Cunningham had a strong appreciation of the Yishuv's organizational, political, and military ability. The Zionist cause benefited from the policy laid down by the last high commissioner. He heightened the administration's cooperation with the Jewish Agency, which had been broken off in 1938, at the conclusion of Wauchope's tenure, and renewed in 1944, under Gort. Cunningham sought cooperation with the Jewish Agency even in the face of its rejection, until summer 1946, of the partition idea and its refusal to work together with his administration against terrorism until summer 1947—and, equally striking, in the light of the agency's view that he was not the right interlocutor.[9] Nevertheless, he never abandoned his attempt to harness the Jewish Agency to the British cause. Nor was this a merely utilitarian approach. As time passed, Cunningham believed, truly and sincerely, that Britain, its administration in Palestine, and he himself had congruent, even common interests with the Zionist movement and the Yishuv. This was not a popular viewpoint at a time when Britain's imperial policy was set by Attlee, Bevin, and Foreign Office officials who considered support for the Zionist cause an obstacle to Britain's postwar policy.

The Palestine Arabs' disappointment in Cunningham had a solid basis. He failed to understand their position at the most basic level. Unlike many veterans of the colonial service, he was not impressed by the Arab society in Palestine and made no effort to familiarize himself with it, for good or for ill. The Yishuv's mode of operation was clearer to him. His lack of interest in the Palestine Arabs was blatant. As a result, he misread the absence of cooperation on their part and was taken aback by their apparently surprising outburst in the autumn of 1947. As far as he was concerned, it would be enough if the Jews were assured a state that would absorb Jewish immigration to keep the Arabs quiescent, even if displeased.

Like his superiors, Cunningham still believed in 1946 that it was possible to decide for another national group who its leaders would be. In the summer of that year, he did not argue with his government, which ruled out David Ben-Gurion and Haj Amin al-Husseini as interlocutors. Cunningham learned the lesson in the Zionist case, but not where the Arabs were concerned. He was not alone. The historic relationship between Britain and King Abdullah and the other Hashemite leaders of Jordan kept the development of the Arab side in Palestine hidden from London. Cunningham was a partner to his government, the Jewish Agency, the Arab League, and the Palestine Arabs—who incessantly undermined their own interests—in excluding the Arabs in Palestine from the political process.

At the end of the day, Cunningham devoted more time and energy to internecine struggles within the British bureaucracy than to the Palestine conflict. In addition to the highly unproductive nature of his contacts with the Jews and with the Arabs, which left him no choice but to take action where he thought he could exert influence—i.e., within the British establishment—this situation was compounded by additional causes: the personal motivation he brought with him to Jerusalem, the methods and character of Montgomery, who headed the army beginning in June 1946, the weakness of the Colonial Office, and the rising power of the Foreign Office.

Over and above these more immediate conditions, Cunningham's tenure as high commissioner, with both its achievements and its difficulties, was saliently a micro-reflection of a macro-historical reality. In short, he was a high commissioner who operated within a collapsing imperial structure. The beginnings of this process antedated 1945, but it was then that the noise of the collapse was first heard loud and clear. What began in the First World War gathered momentum and became a landslide by the second half of the 1940s. From this point of view, we should pay special attention to the year 1947. From the end of the Second World War until the end of 1946, Britain tried to respond to the new international reality of the Cold War using tools of an old empire that was ready to have a young, vigorous, strong, and, especially, rich ally join it in leading the world: the United States of America. In 1947, it became clear that the United States was not a partner but the owner of the firm. On top of this, it became obvious that the new ally's approach differed from that of the previous owner, namely, Britain, and that the new world order required U.S.-Soviet agreement—not Anglo-American agreement, as in the past. The case of Palestine after the war was no exception.

Britain, which had lost control of the empire, was in the process of a turn inward, and a battle raged between the die-hard imperialists and those who insisted that the focus must now be on Britain itself and the severe social and economic crisis it was undergoing. These developments very much hampered the ability of Britain and its "man in Jerusalem" to take the initiative and cope with the deteriorating situation in Palestine. At the same time, and for the same reasons, British public opinion was increasingly less willing to pay the price in human life and material damage that Palestine exacted. It was no different elsewhere in the crumbling empire, whether Crown Colony or Mandatory regime.

Under Cunningham, Mandatory Palestine in its waning days reflected both the general historical situation and the local paralysis caused by Jewish-Arab nonagreement. Nevertheless, the Mandatory regime functioned with impressive efficiency until the end of 1947.

Afterward, from October 1947 on, as an increasingly ferocious civil war raged and the withdrawal process continued, Cunningham's ability to take action was so severely curtailed that he could barely look after his own staff. But despite it all, he was able to preserve a veneer of honorable effort until May 14, 1948.[10]

His success in this regard averted greater bloodshed, kept the administration from having to depart under fire, and actually slowed the West's withdrawal from the Middle East. It is no exaggeration to say that the nonconfrontation between Britain and the Yishuv—which, in contrast to the Arabs, was capable of engaging the British in local warfare—prevented possible deeper Soviet encroachment, allowed Israel's establishment, strengthened Britain's foothold in Jordan, and allowed both Israel and Jordan to lean for support, each in its own way, on the free world and also on each other, in a quiet coalition that bolstered mutual security. Cunningham, in *his* own way, was a partner to the British endeavor with roots in the First World War and discernible afterward as well: the inauguration of the Zionist and Hashemite project in Palestine, both west and east of the Jordan River. From this perspective, his approach was even more traditional than that of the Foreign Office, which underscored the Arab side of the equation and ignored the Jewish side with hostile intent.

Cunningham suffered from a problem that was particularly acute in Palestine but was characteristic of every colonial situation in which two or more national groups competed for the country's future the moment the colonial power departed. He was well aware of this. To his amazement, he noted, in every meeting with representatives of the two parties to the conflict they ignored one another and were unwilling to listen to the other side's problems, not even to further their own cause. He saw no difference between the Jews and the Arabs in this regard. It is very easy to be "black" or "white," he explained, but very difficult to be "gray." We in Palestine, he maintained, stuck closely to the British tradition in this regard. We safeguarded the "gray," no matter the personal opinion of any particular official in the service. He knew that every decision he made or action he took would prompt Jews, Arabs, and others to complain that he was taking one side or the other. In the drama—or tragedy—of Palestine, this was a flagrantly impractical position. Cunningham was compelled to take a stand, a situation that worked clearly in favor of the Yishuv.[11]

The last British high commissioner protected the Jewish community from those in London who wished to do it harm. He held that it was out of the question "to throw the Jews into the sea" and that a solution could be found by which Jews and Arabs could live in Palestine. Britain's departure advanced the partition solution, which Cunningham supported. The Yishuv, which remained intact after Britain blocked the attempt by the Germans and their allies to reach Palestine in the Second World War and treated the Yishuv's struggle against its policy after the war with considerable patience (not least at the behest of the last high commissioner), could now implement the partition principle and establish a state in part of the country.

Let history judge, Cunningham liked to say. His remark, though, was aimed less at history than at memory. That, he knew, was amenable to change.

NOTES

1. On the high commissioners in Palestine, see *DNB*. The volumes are divided by decade and the personalities appear according to year of death: Plumer (1932), Gort (1946), Wauchope (1947), Chancellor (1952), Samuel (1963), MacMichael (1969), and Cunningham (1983). On Samuel's tenure as high commissioner, see Bernard Wasserstein, *Herbert Samuel: A Political Life*, Oxford 1992; on Plumer, see Pinhas Ofer, "The

Emergence of the Mandate Regime and the Laying of the Foundations for a Jewish National Home, 1923–1931," in Moshe Lissak and Gabriel Cohen (eds.), *History of the Yishuv in the Land of Israel since the First Aliya*, Vol. II: *The British Mandate Period*, Jerusalem 1994, Part One, pp. 258–276 (Hebrew); on Chancellor, see the same text, pp. 277–328; on Wauchope, see Eyal, *The First Intifada;* on MacMichael, see Zweig, *Britain and Palestine;* and on Gort, see Colville, *Man of Valour.*

2. Beginning in 1952, the Foreign Office was known as the Ministry for Foreign Affairs and Commonwealth Relations; Golani, *The End of the British Mandate for Palestine.*

3. Cunningham to Lloyd, February 2, 1948, MECA CP, B6, F5/105; Cunningham to John McKenzie, the former moderator of the General Assembly of the Church of Scotland, March 19, 1948, MECA CP, B6, F5/109; Admiral William Tennant to Cunningham, August 1, 1946, MECA CP, B6, F5/47; Cunningham to Tennant, August 6, 1948, MECA CP, B6, F5/48; John Swire to his mother, October 15, 1947, courtesy of Mr. Swire.

4. Lloyd to Cunningham, February 17, 1948, MECA CP, B6, F5/106; Cunningham to Douglas-Home, July 15, 1971, NAM 8303–104/26. The high commissioner earned 5,500 Palestine pounds a year in 1948 (and another 2,500 pounds for essential expenses). *The Colonial Office List: 1948, Comprising Historical and Statistical Information respecting the Colonial Empire. Lists of Officers Serving in the Colonies and Other Information*, London, His Majesty's Stationary Office, 1948, p. 355.

5. Strawson, "Cunningham," p. 104; Slater in the introduction to Winton, *Cunningham*, pp. xiii–xiv; Rosenthal, "The Last High Commissioner Reveals."

6. John Swire, who was his personal assistant in late 1947, kept in touch with Cunningham after the departure from Palestine. Young Swire, who came from an affluent family, rented the Cunninghams one of his homes (at Luton End), where they lived for about a year until the house of Margery's father, who died that year, was ready. Testimony of Swire in a letter to the author, July 10, 2008.

7. Cunningham to Kennedy, June 18, 1944, NAM 8303–104/28.

8. *Times*, February 1, 1983; Strawson, "Cunningham," pp. 103–104; notes by the author on a visit to Whitchurch and surroundings, August 28, 2007.

9. The fact that the Jewish Agency supported partition beginning in the summer of 1937 and also fought against the breakaways' terrorism during the Second World War was no longer relevant when Cunningham arrived in November 1945. At the time, Zionist policy was (as it had been since 1942) to claim all Palestine, while the Anglo-Zionist struggle against the breakaways' terrorism had been curbed some time before.

10. As mentioned, Cunningham's handling of the civil war in Palestine from October 1947 until May 1948 is the subject of my next book, which is now in progress.

11. "Palestine—The Last Days of the Mandate, by General Sir Alan Cunningham, Chatham House, London," July 22, 1948, RIIFA/8/1568. For an adaptation of Cunningham's remarks that evening, see Sir Alan Cunningham, "Palestine—The Last Days of the Mandate," address at Chatham House, July 22, 1948, *International Affairs* 24, no. 4 (October 1948), pp. 481–490.

Bibliography

Archives

BGA	Ben Gurion Archives, Sde Boker, Israel
CZA	Central Zionist Archives, Jerusalem, Israel
LHCMA	Liddell Hart Centre for Military Archives, King's College, London, UK
MECA	The Middle East Centre Archive, St. Antony's College, Oxford (includes Sir Alan Cunningham Papers), UK
NA (PRO)	The National Archives, Kew (formerly the Public Record Office), UK
NAM	National Army Museum, London (includes Sir General Alan Cunningham Papers), UK
RHLO	Rhodes House Library, Oxford, UK
RIIFA	Royal Institute of International Affairs (Chatham House), London, UK
TAMA	Tel Aviv Municipality Archives, Tel Aviv, Israel
WA	Weizmann Archives, Rehovot, Israel

Newspapers

IN PALESTINE	IN BRITAIN
Davar	*Daily Telegraph*
Ha'aretz	*Scotsman*
Hamashkif	*Times*
Hatzofeh	
Hayom	
Ma'ariv	
Mishmar	
Palestine Post	
Yedioth Ahronoth	
Yoman	

Document Collections, Memoirs, and Diaries

Aqavia, Abraham, *With Wingate in Habash* (Ethiopia), Tel Aviv 1944. (Hebrew)

Belchem, David, *All in the Day's March*, London 1978.

Ben-Gurion, David, *Toward the End of the Mandate: Memoirs, June 1946–March 1947*, Tel Aviv 1993. (Hebrew)

———, *Chimes of Independence, March–November 1947*, Tel Aviv 1993. (Hebrew)

Churchill, Winston S., *The Second World War: The Grand Alliance*, Boston 1950.

The Colonial Office List: 1948, Comprising Historical and Statistical Information respecting the Colonial Empire. Lists of Officers Serving in the Colonies and Other Information, London, His Majesty's Stationary Office 1948.

Crossman, Richard, *Palestine Mission: A Personal Record*, New York and London 1947.

Crum, Bartley C., *Behind the Silken Curtain: A Personal Account of Anglo-American Diplomacy in Palestine and the Middle East*, New York 1947.

Cunningham, Sir Alan, "Palestine—The Last Days of the Mandate," *International Affairs*, Vol. 24 (October 1948), pp. 481–490.

Cunningham, Andrew, *A Sailor's Odyssey: The Autobiography of the Admiral of the Fleet, Viscount Cunningham of Hyndhope*, London 1951.

Danchev, A., and D. Todman (eds.), *Field Marshal Lord Alanbrooke: War Diaries, 1939–1945*, London 2002.

Dekel, Efraim, *Shai: The Exploits of Hagana Intelligence*, New York and London 1959.

The Eighth Army, September [19]41 to January 1943, Prepared for the War Office by the Ministry of Information, His Majesty's Stationery Office, London 1944.

Garfield, Simon, *Our Hidden Lives: The Remarkable Diaries of Post-War Britain*, London 2005.

Glubb, John, *A Soldier with the Arabs*, London 1957.

Goldmann, Nahum, *The Autobiography of Nahum Goldmann*, Sixty Years of Jewish Life, New York 1969.

Heller, Joseph (ed.), *The Letters and the Papers of Chaim Weizmann*, Vol. XXII, Series A: May 1945–July 1947, Jerusalem 1979.

Horowitz, David, *State in the Making*, New York 1953.

Kennedy, John, *The Business of War: The War Narrative of Major-General Sir John Kennedy*, New York 1958.

Kimche, Jon, *The Seven Fallen Pillars: The Middle East, 1915–1950*, London 1950.

Klieman, Aaron (ed.), *The Letters and the Papers of Chaim Weizmann*, Vol. XXIII, Series A: August 1947–June 1952, Jerusalem 1980.

Meir, Golda, *My Life*, New York 1976.

Montgomery of Alamein, Bernard Law Montgomery, *The Memoirs of Field Marshal Montgomery*, Barnsley (1958) 2007.

Palestine, Termination of the Mandate, 15 May 1948, Statement Prepared for Public Information by the Colonial Office and Foreign Office, London 1948.

Palestine and Transjordan Administration Reports, 1918–1948, Vol. 6: 1947–1948, Southampton 1995.

Pimlott, Ben (ed.), *The Political Diary of Hugh Dalton, 1918–40, 1945–60*, London 1986.

Report of the Anglo-American Committee of Inquiry into the Problems of European Jewry and of Palestine, Lausanne, April 20, 1946, Parliamentary Document 6808, Jerusalem 1946.

Sharett, Moshe, *Imprisoned with Paper and Pencil: The Letters of Moshe and Zipporah Sharett during the Period of His Detention by the British at Latrun*, June–November 1946, Tel Aviv 2000. (Hebrew)

Sherman, A. J., *Mandate Days: British Lives in Palestine, 1918–1948*, New York 1997.

Tedder, Arthur William, *With Prejudice: The War Memoirs of Marshal of the Royal Air Force*, London 1966.

Zerubavel, Gilad (ed.), *Book of the Palmah*, Vol. 1, Tel Aviv 1955. (Hebrew)

Secondary Sources

Barberis, Peter, *The Elite of the Elite: Permanent Secretaries in the British Higher Civil Service*, Aldershot 1996.

Barnett, Correlli, *The Desert Generals*, London 1960.

——, *Britain and Her Army, 1509–1970: A Military, Political and Social Survey*, New York 1970.

Bar-On, Mordechai, *Of All the Kingdoms: Israel's Relations with the UK during the First Decade after the End of the British Mandate in Palestine, 1948–1958*, Jerusalem 2006. (Hebrew)

Bar-Yosef, Eitan, *The Holy Land in English Culture, 1799–1917: Palestine and the Question of Orientalism*, Oxford 2005.

Ben-Dror, Elad, *UNSCOP: The Beginning of the United Nations' Involvement in the Arab-Israeli Conflict*, PhD thesis, Bar-Ilan University, Ramat-Gan 2002. (Hebrew)

Bethell, Nicholas, *The Palestine Triangle: The Struggle between the British, the Jews and the Arabs, 1935–1948*, London 1979.

Bogner, Nahum, *The Deportation Island: Jewish Illegal Immigrant Camps on Cyprus, 1946–1948*, Tel Aviv 1991. (Hebrew)

Charters, David, *The British Army and Jewish Insurgency in Palestine, 1945–47*, London 1989.

Clarke, Peter, *The Last Thousand Days of the British Empire*, London 2007.

Clarke, Thurston, *By Blood and Fire: Attack on the King David Hotel*, New York 1981.

Cohen, Michael J., *Palestine and the Great Powers, 1945–1948*, Princeton 1982.

Colville, J. R., *Man of Valour: The Life of Field-Marshal The Viscount Gort*, London 1972.

Connell, John, *Auchinleck: A Biography of Field-Marshal Sir Claude Auchinleck*, London 1959.

Corrican, Gordon, *Blood, Sweat and Arrogance*, London 2006.

Darby, Phillip. *British Defence Policy East of Suez, 1947–1968*, London 1973.

Eyal, Yigal, *The First Intifada: The Suppression of the Arab Revolt by the British Army in Palestine, 1936–1939*, Tel Aviv 1988. (Hebrew)

Gelber, Yoav, *The Emergence of a Jewish Army—The Veterans of the British Army in the IDF*, Jerusalem 1986, pp. 11–15. (Hebrew)

———, *The History of Israeli Intelligence, Part I: Growing a Fleur-de-Lis: The Intelligence Services of the Jewish Yishuv in Palestine, 1918–1947*, Tel Aviv 1992. (Hebrew)

Golani, Motti, *Zion in Zionism: The Zionist Policy and the Question of Jerusalem, 1937–1949*, Tel Aviv 1992. (Hebrew)

———, *The End of the British Mandate for Palestine, 1948: The Diary of Sir Henry Gurney*, London 2009.

Goldstein, Amir, *Heroism and Exclusion: The "Gallows Martyrs" and Israeli Collective Memory*, Jerusalem 2011. (Hebrew)

Halamish, Aviva, *Exodus—The Real Story*, Tel Aviv 1990. (Hebrew)

Hamilton, Nigel, *Monty: The Making of a General, 1887–1942*, London 1982.

———, *Monty: The Field Marshal, 1944–1976*, London 1986.

Harris, Kenneth, *Attlee*, London 1995.

Heller, Joseph, "Zionist Policy in the International Arena after the Second World War—The Affair of the Anglo-American Committee, 1945/6," *Shalem*, 3 (5741), pp. 213–294. (Hebrew)

———, "From Black Sabbath to Partition: Summer 1946 as a Turning Point in the History of Zionist Policy," *Zion*, 43 (1978), pp. 314–361. (Hebrew)

Itzhaki-Harel, Rivka, "Toward a State: British Rule, the Yishuv Leadership, the Police Force, and the Supernumerary Police, 1918–1948," PhD dissertation, University of Haifa 2004. (Hebrew)

Jones, Martin, *Failure in Palestine: British and United States Policy after the Second World War*, London and New York 1986.

Kedourie, Elie, *The Chatham House and Other Middle-Eastern Studies*, Hanover and London 1984.

Keegan, John (ed.), *Churchill's Generals*, London 1991.

Kendall, Henry, *Jerusalem, The City Plan: Reservation and Development during the British Mandate, 1918–48*, with a foreword by General Sir Alan Gordon Cunningham, High Commissioner of Palestine, London 1948.

Keynan, Irit, *The Hunger Has Not Abated: Holocaust Survivors and the Emissaries from Eretz-Yisrael: Germany 1945–1948*, Tel Aviv 1996. (Hebrew)

Kochavi, Aryeh, *Displaced Persons and International Politics: Britain and the Jewish DPs after the Second World War*, Tel Aviv 1992. (Hebrew)

Krik, Hagit, *Palestine versus the Holy Land*, master's thesis, University of Haifa 2008. (Hebrew)

Kroyanker, David, *Jerusalem Architecture*, New York 1994.

Lazar, Hadara, *In and out of Palestine*, Jerusalem 2003. (Hebrew)

Lissak, Moshe (chief ed.), *The History of the Jewish Community in Eretz-Yisrael since 1882: The Period of the British Mandate, Jerusalem*, vol. 1 (1993), vol. 2 (2001). (Hebrew)

Louis, William Roger, *The British Empire in the Middle East, 1945–1951*, London 1984.

——, "British Imperialism and the End of the Palestine Mandate," R. Louis and W. Stookey (eds.), *The End of the Palestine Mandate*, London 1986, pp. 1–31.

Louis, William Roger, and Robert W. Stookey (eds.), *The End of the Palestine Mandate*, London 1986.

Medzini, Meron, *The Proud Jewess: Golda Meir and the Vision of Israel*, Jerusalem 1990. (Hebrew)

Michel, Henri, *The Second World War*, London 1975.

Monroe, Elizabeth, *Britain's Moment in the Middle East, 1914–1956*, London 1965.

Morris, Benny, *The Road to Jerusalem: Glubb Pasha, Palestine and the Jews*, London, New York 2002.

Nachmani, Amikam, *Great Power Discord in Palestine: The Anglo-American Committee of Inquiry into the Problems of European Jewry and Palestine, 1945–1946*, London 1987.

Niv, David, *Campaigns of the Irgun Zvai Leumi [Etzel]*, Part IV: "The Revolt (1944–1946)," Part V: "The Revolt (1946–1947)," Tel Aviv 1973, 1976. (Hebrew)

Ofer, Pinhas, *Enemy and Rival: The Zionist Movement and the Yishuv between the Arabs and the British, 1929–1948*, Tel Aviv 2001. (Hebrew)

Osborne, Richard E., *The World War II in Colonial Africa*, Indianapolis 2001.

Pappé, Ilan, *Britain and the Arab-Israeli Conflict, 1948–51*, London 1988.

——, *The Making of the Arab-Israeli Conflict, 1947–1951*, London 1992.

——, *The Rise and Fall of a Palestinian Dynasty: The Husaynis, 1700–1948*, Berkeley 2011.

Playfair, I. S. O., *The History of the Second World War, United Kingdom Military Series, The Mediterranean and Middle East*, Vol. I: *The Early Successes against Italy: 1939 to May 1941*, London 1954.

——, *The History of the Second World War, United Kingdom Military Series, The Mediterranean and Middle East*, Vol. II: *The Germans Come to the Help of Their Allies: June to August 1941*, London 1956.

——, *The History of the Second World War, United Kingdom Military Series, The Mediterranean and Middle East*, Vol. III: *British Fortunes Reach Their Lowest Ebb, September 1941 to September 1942*, London 1960.

Reinharz, Jehuda, *Chaim Weizmann: The Making of a Statesman*, Oxford 1993.

Reuveny, Jacob, *The Administration of Palestine under the British Mandate, 1920–1948: An Institutional Analysis*, Ramat Gan 1993. (Hebrew)

Reynolds, David, *In Command of History: Churchill Fighting and Writing the Second World War*, London 2005.

Rose, Norman, *Chaim Weizmann: A Biography*, New York 1986.

Schaary, David, *The Cyprus Detention Camps for Jewish "Illegal" Immigrants to Palestine, 1946–1949*, Jerusalem 1981. (Hebrew)

Segev, Tom, *One Complete, Palestine: Jews and Arabs under the British Mandate*, New York 2001.

Shavit, Yaʿakov, *Open Season: The Confrontation between the "Organized Yishuv" and the Underground Organizations (Etzel and Lehi), 1937–1947*, Tel Aviv 1976. (Hebrew)

———, (ed.), *Struggle, Revolt, Resistance: British and Zionist Policy and the Struggle against Britain, 1941–1948*, Tel Aviv 1987. (Hebrew)

Shealtiel, Eli, *Always a Rebel: A Biography of Moshe Sneh, 1909–1948*, Tel Aviv 2000. (Hebrew)

Shepherd, Naomi, *Ploughing Sand: British Rule in Palestine, 1917–1948*, London 1999.

Slutzky, Yehuda, *History of the Haganah*, Vol. 3, Parts I and II: "From Struggle to War," Tel Aviv 1972. (Hebrew)

Smart, Nicholas, *Biographical Dictionary of British Generals of the Second World War*, Barnsley 2005.

Strawson, John, "General Sir Alan Gordon Cunningham," Lord Black and C. S. Nichols (eds.), *The Dictionary of National Biography (DNB)* (1981–1985), New York 1990.

Teveth, Shabtai, "Puzzling Exercise (Dr. Moshe Sneh's Slipping Away, Flight, or Invitation to Paris, July–August 1946)," *Zmanim* 76 (fall 2001), pp. 71–89. (Hebrew)

———, *Kinat David* (David's Jealousy): *The Life of David Ben-Gurion*, vol. 4, Jerusalem and Tel Aviv 2004. (Hebrew)

Tiratsoo, Nick (ed.), *The Attlee Years*, London and New York 1991.

Tuchman, Barbara W., *Bible and Sword: England and Palestine from the Bronze Age to Balfour*, New York 1956.

Warner, Philip, *Auchinleck: The Lonely Soldier*, Barnsley 2006.

Wasserstein, Bernard, *Britain and the Jews of Europe, 1939–1945*, London and Oxford 1979.

———, *Herbert Samuel: A Political Life*, Oxford 1992.

Winton, John, *Cunningham: The Biography of Admiral A. B. Cunningham*, London 1998.

Zweig, Ronald W., *Britain and Palestine during the Second World War*, London 1986.

Index

defense, 87; Operation Agatha and, 85–86, 90, 95, 113; and political solution, 61. *See also* Palmah

Hall, George: on Anglo-American Committee report, 48; Cunningham's appointment and, 18–19; Cunningham's correspondence with, 60, 62, 78, 88, 94, 100–101, 112, 114, 116; declining influence of, 110; and Jewish terrorism, 147; and King David Hotel bombing, 148, 151–54; and Operation Agatha, 85–86, 88–89, 96, 100; on Palestine question, 41–43, 53, 108, 110–11, 124, 232

Herzog, Isaac, Rabbi, 101, 115, 189

high commissioner of Palestine and Transjordan: Cunningham's predecessors as, ix–x, 55n12, 228; Jewish views on, 31, 55n12. *See also* Cunningham, as high commissioner; *specific commissioners*

Husseini, Haj Amin al-, 38, 46, 87, 117–18, 235

Husseini, Jamal al-, 117–18, 134n27

Irgun. *See* Etzel (Irgun)

Jacobs, Julius, 60, 143

Jewish Agency: and Anglo-American Committee, 48; British influence over, 58–59; British views on, viii, 45; conflicting pressures on, 112; Cunningham on, viii, 45–46, 53, 234; debate on cooperation, 62; and Jewish Resistance Movement, 32, 64; and negotiation of political solution, 45–46, 66, 80, 108, 115–16, 120, 132; Operation Agatha and, 85, 87, 90–91, 94–95, 97, 113; and partition plan,

53, 62, 238n9; relations with Cunningham, 28, 30–31, 53–54, 62–63, 174–75; as source of anti-British sentiment, 44; support for Jewish state, 38, 48

Jewish Agency, British action against: army and, 64–69, 73–74; Cunningham's delay in implementing, 77; Cunningham's preparations for, 72–73; Cunningham's views on, 58, 63–64, 68–69, 72–74, 76–80; government position on, 58, 63–64, 77, 79–80; "Night of the Bridges" as catalyst for, 76–78; and political solution, 80; SIME report on, 69–71. *See also* Operation Agatha

Jewish Agency and Jewish terrorism: British efforts to gain cooperation, 49–50, 58–63, 65, 72, 77–80, 90, 96, 98–101, 122, 149, 154, 171, 186, 188–89, 192, 196, 200, 207–8, 218–19, 233–34; lack of cooperation, 186, 190–91, 196, 204, 210; Operation Agatha and, 85, 87, 90, 94, 97, 149, 157; partial cooperation, 112, 200–201, 210, 213–14; support of terrorism, 20, 39, 66, 71, 75, 141–42, 144, 149, 157–58

Jewish Agency Council, Paris meeting (1946), 112

Jewish-Arab violence: dismantling of Mandatory government and, 221; before UNSCOP decision, 220–21

Jewish community. *See* Yishuv

Jewish immigration: as act of resistance, 204; American views on, 46, 109, 122, 124; Anglo-American Committee report on, 46; Arab views on, 122–23, 125–26, 128–29, 233; British policy on, 110, 152; Cunningham on, 122–27, 131–32, 135n42, 232–33; Cunningham's influence on, 232–33; Cyprus as transit site in, 126–33, 233; efforts to control, 32, 36, 122–24, 126–30; impact on British rule, 46, 48; and influx of partisan fighters, 129; Jewish views on, 119, 121–25, 130–32; negotiations on, 85–86; and political solution, 109, 126; U.S. support of, 43, 45, 109. *See also* Anglo-American Committee of Inquiry

Labour government, British, 16, 40

Lavon, Pinhas, 195

Lehi (Stern gang), xii; arrests of members, 207; assassination threats by, 147–48; attacks by, 37, 65, 75, 131, 135n36, 160, 174, 186, 204, 220; attacks on, 82n25; Cunningham's familiarity with, 65; executed members, 203; Haganah and, 71; leaders of, 155; rise in influence of, 44; as target of British Operations, 113, 217; undermining of political solution by, 61, 74

London, Cunningham in (July, 1946), 108–9, 141

London conference (1946), 114–18, 121, 135n39

MacMichael, Sir Harold, ix, 33, 50, 55n12, 88, 228

MacMillan, Gordon, xiv, 194, 198–99, 203, 212–13, 218

martial law: army's views on, 215; as bargaining tool, 211, 216–18; brief imposition of, 192–96, 233; casualties under, 194–96; CSC views on, 197–99; Cunningham on, 39–40, 187–88, 191, 195, 203–4, 233–34; decision to forgo, 205, 214–19; goals of, 192; impact on civilians, 193–94; insufficient British forces for, 198, 210–14; powers of army under, 193–94; pressure to impose, 191–92, 200, 207, 210, 220; success of, 196. *See also* Montgomery-Cunningham policy struggle

Meyerson, Golda, 115, 208, 210

military career of Cunningham, 1–16; retirement, vii, 29–30, 230–31. *See also entries under* Eighth Army

Montgomery, Bernard: and chain of command, 89, 154; on Cunningham, 86, 164–67, 170, 172, 183, 213; and downsizing of British forces, 212; and Jewish terrorism, 64–65, 67–68, 86, 154; on martial law, 195–96, 198, 213–14; and Operation Agatha, 89; on Palestine security, 213–14; simplistic strategy of, 166–67; in World War II, 14–15, 17, 21n11

Montgomery-Cunningham policy struggle, 164–83; cabinet decision on, 164, 175–76, 182–83; CSC on, 197–99; Cunningham's advantages in, 175–76; Cunningham's position in, 167–69, 171–72, 175, 178–79, 181–82; figures involved in, 164–67, 170; and Jewish terrorism, 190; meeting at Colonial Office (Jan. 1947), 177–82; meeting in Jerusalem (Nov. 1946), 170–71; Montgomery's apology, 170–71; Montgomery's position in, 167, 171–73, 175, 177–79; and political solution, 174–75; restraints on army as issue in, 171–73, 178; time wasted in, 235; vindication of Cunningham's position, 197, 199

Morrison-Grady Committee, 69, 85–86, 107, 110, 116–17, 151–52, 158

Moyne, Lord, 93, 135n36, 203

"Night of the Bridges," 75–78

"Night of the Trains," 20, 23n44

O'Connor, Richard, 4, 6

Operation Agatha (Black Sabbath): approval of, 84–85; Arab response to, 101, 103; arrests under, 87, 90–92, 94–97, 103, 113, 115; behavior of British soldiers in, 98; casualties,

108, 115–16, 120, 132; Jewish immigration and, 109, 126; Montgomery-Cunningham policy struggle and, 172, 180; Operation Agatha and, 109; supporters of, 42; terrorism's undermining of, 49–50, 61–62; U.S.-British relations and, 110; Yishuv and, 44; Zionist extremists and, 113. *See also* binational state plan; partition; provincial autonomy plan

provincial autonomy plan, 42, 107, 110–12, 128, 133n13, 152

Pyman, Harold, 183, 215

Remez, David, 91, 100, 115

Rokach, Israel, 35–36, 115, 131, 194, 217

Saison ("hunting season"), 72, 82n25, 93, 210

Samuel, Edwin, 28

Samuel, Lord Herbert, ix, 50, 55n12, 228–29

Security Intelligence, Middle East (SIME), 69–72

Shamir, Yitzhak (Yitzhak Yzernitzky), 155

Shaw, John: career of, 160; Cunningham's appointment and, 18; Cunningham's correspondence with, 72; Gort and, 17–18; on Jewish immigration, 45; and King David Hotel bombing, 141, 146–48; and Operation Agatha, 93, 101; and partition, 110; relations with Jewish community, 60; terrorists' targeting of, 147–48

Shertok, Moshe: arrest, 130; Cunningham and, 45–46, 182; as fugitive, 63; and Operation Agatha, 96, 100, 115; political views, 54, 62, 75, 119–20, 122

Silver, Abba Hillel, 99, 113

SIME. *See* Security Intelligence, Middle East (SIME)

Simpson, Frank, 198, 212–13

Smuts, Jan, 3, 14–15, 50–51

Sneh, Moshe, 58, 62, 95–96, 112–13, 115

Sprinzak, Joseph (Yosef), 62, 115

Stern gang. *See* Lehi (Stern gang)

Tedder, Arthur, 198, 223–24n34

Teveth, Shabtai, 59, 95–96

Transjordan: Cunningham as high commissioner of, 29; independence talks with, 120

Truman, Harry, 46, 109, 121, 124, 159

United Nations, and partition, 41

United Nations Special Committee on Palestine (UNSCOP), 204, 206–8, 215, 219–20

United States: Anglo-American Committee report and, 46; and British Palestine policy, 64, 85–86, 110–11, 129–30, 151, 182, 236; Cunningham's desire for support from, 74; Jewish influence in, 48, 79, 116; support for Jewish immigration, 43, 45–46, 109, 124

Von Wiesel, Ze'ev (Wolfgang), 114, 217

War Office: and Palestine policy, xi, 68, 165; poor intelligence assessments of, 157–58; postwar decline in influence, 165

Wauchope, Sir Arthur, ix, x, 34, 49–50, 55n12, 88, 193, 228–29, 234

Wavell, Archibald, 2–4

Weizmann, Chaim, 50–51; anglophile inclinations of, 59; and British Mandate, acceptance of, 59; and Jewish Agency, efforts to moderate, 59, 61, 63, 77–79, 99–101, 114; loss of influence, 61, 113, 158, 234; and Operation Agatha, 99–102, 104n11; on partition, 119–20; and political solution, 116, 135n39; relationship with Cunningham, 59–61, 96

White Paper of 1939, 31–32, 43, 52, 103, 124

Wickham, Sir Charles, 148–49, 178

Wilson, Henry, 6

Windham, Ralph, 186

Wingate, Orde Charles, 30, 82n28

Wingate Night, 73, 82n28

Wise, Stephen, 99, 114

World War II: Cunningham in, 2–16; end of, and return of turmoil to Palestine, 17, 36–37. *See also entries under Eighth Army*

World Zionist Organization, 50

Yishuv: community support of, xii; control of agenda by, 37; Cunningham's contacts in, 34–36, 72–73; early evaluations of Cunningham, 30–33; expectation for Jewish state, 32, 38, 48; moderate elements, loss of influence, 157–58; motivations of, 159; and "Night of the Trains," 20; and political solution, 44; relations with Cunningham, 30–31, 33, 36–37; as term, xii; threats against moderates in, 158; views on British rule, viii, 31, 44; views on Jewish terrorism, 17, 142, 158, 197

Yishuv press, 31–33, 156, 159

Yzernitzky, Yitzhak (Yitzhak Shamir), 155

Zionist movement: agenda, revision of, 119–22; Arab views on, 38–39; Biltmore Program and, 38, 119; on British policy, 31, 48, 59, 63–64, 78; British views on, viii, 121; Cunningham and, 53, 80, 113, 234; goals of, 112; on Jewish immigration, 123–26; leadership of, 30, 58–60, 112; policies of, 37, 52, 119; U.S. and U.N. support for, 221

Zionists, American, support for extremists, 75, 113